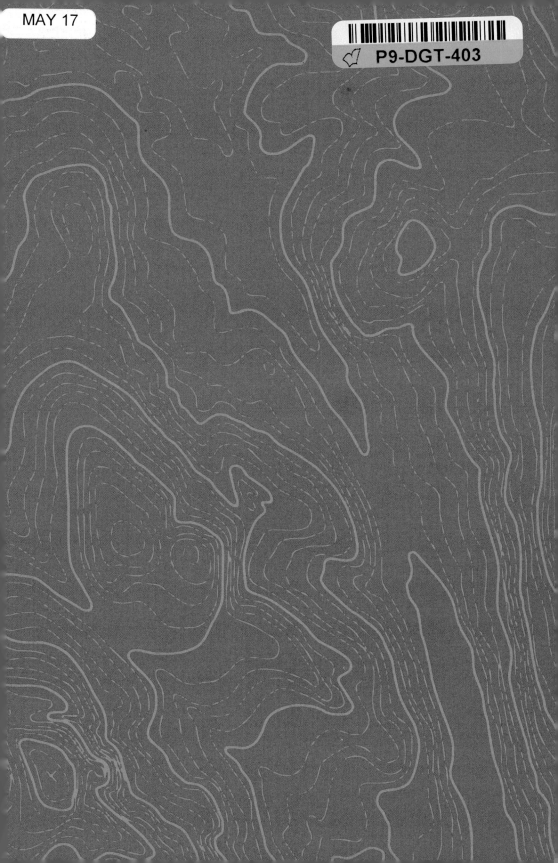

THE GREAT OUTDOORS
A USER'S GUIDE

THE GREAT OUTDOORS

A USER'S GUIDE

EVERYTHING YOU NEED TO KNOW BEFORE
HEADING INTO THE WILD (AND HOW TO
GET BACK IN ONE PIECE)

BRENDAN LEONARD

ILLUSTRATIONS BY SETH NEILSON

ARTISAN

NEW YORK

Library of Congress Cataloging-in-Publication Data

Names: Leonard, Brendan, author.
Title: The great outdoors : a user's guide / by Brendan Leonard ;
    illustrations by Seth Neilson.
Description: New York : Artisan, [2017] | Includes index.
Identifiers: LCCN 2016038071 | ISBN 9781579657079 (hardback, paper over board)
Subjects: LCSH: Outdoor recreation.
Classification: LCC GV191.6 .L46 2017 | DDC 796.5—dc23 LC record available at https://lccn.loc
    .gov/2016038071

Design by Seth Neilson

Artisan books are available at special discounts when purchased in bulk for premiums and sales promotions as well as for fund-raising or educational use. Special editions or book excerpts also can be created to specification. For details, contact the Special Sales Director at the address below, or send an e-mail to specialmarkets@workman.com.

Published by Artisan
A division of Workman Publishing Co., Inc.
225 Varick Street
New York, NY 10014-4381
artisanbooks.com

Artisan is a registered trademark of Workman Publishing Co., Inc.

Published simultaneously in Canada by Thomas Allen & Son, Limited.

Printed in China

First printing, April 2017

1 2 3 4 5 6 7 8 9 10

CONTENTS

INTRODUCTION

Not too many generations ago, our ancestors hardly distinguished between "indoors" and "outdoors." What we now think of as roughing it and camping were just a part of everyday life. People cooked over open fires, pooped on the ground, ran from animals bigger than they were, killed and ate animals smaller than they were, and walked around in the woods while doing what we would now call "hiking."

Nowadays, most of us (okay, pretty much all of us) are disconnected from the outdoors, spending most of our days looking at glowing screens and not having to worry about staying clean and dry or fed. We only occasionally visit wild places, and some of us never see them at all. But do we, as a species, have some sort of submerged memory about those days of life in the outdoors and somehow miss them? There's a sort of inherent, ineffable satisfaction we get from staring at the red-hot embers of a campfire, sleeping under the stars, or living for three or four days while carrying everything we need on our backs—even though we know we don't need to do these things anymore given that we have gas furnaces, comfortable beds, and fully stocked pantries and nearby grocery stores at home.

So we're lucky in that we get to choose to go on adventures in the outdoors as a respite from our comfortable lives, and to push ourselves to climb mountains, ride waves, and ski deep snow on steep slopes. But it can be tough to know where to start—what kinds of activities you might be good at, what will challenge you most, mountains versus ocean, what kind of gear you need, and where you should go. It can be daunting, scary, and sometimes awkward as we fumble our way through a new endeavor (carving a turn on a snowboard is in no one's DNA, for example).

This book represents more than a dozen years of my personal fumbling through all the activities in it, learning the hard way so you don't have to. I've spent my vacations and weekends climbing sheer rock faces, getting altitude sickness, paddling down rivers, pedaling across the United States, shivering in a sleeping bag, getting rained on, snowed on, and sunburned, swinging ice tools into frozen waterfalls, warming frozen fingers and toes, gaining experience but not necessarily skill, and wondering what the point of it all was more than once. The point of it is, of course, the accomplishment you feel from the doing rather than the watching, and the experience and joy you gain once you leave the comfy confines of your home.

The point of it is also this book, which I hope will help you dream up some adventures of your own, have some basic but essential knowledge that will help you be a little more confident and comfortable when you venture out—and keep you healthy, alive, and thriving through all of it.

1

MAN
VERSUS
WILD

So you've got an idea that getting outside more might be fun—not outside your office or your apartment but outside your city. There are so many activities to choose from, so many places to go, and so many different pieces of gear and equipment to buy and/or rent for those activities that it can all seem a little complicated and confusing.

So where do you start? This chapter. It'll give you some basic knowledge about what activities might be right for you, in what season each is best, gear items that would work well for your pursuits, how to get into nature, guidelines of where you can and can't go, and a few ideas for adventures to put on your wish list, as well as some straightforward principles for surviving in nature—and not ruining it for everyone else. You don't go from neophyte to the summit of Everest in a couple of weeks, but a little knowledge and some basic gear are all it takes to get you off the couch and into the wild.

Why should I go outside?

There are plenty of studies showing that time outdoors is good for your physical health and mental well-being, that being in places that inspire awe makes you a more generous and happy person, and that camping for a week and avoiding non-natural light is enough to reset the body's clock to natural sleep patterns. But one of the best reasons is that the outdoors can be like a gym, only better: if you find something you like to do that makes you work hard (like hiking, skiing, surfing, biking, or climbing), you begin to have fun first and gain fitness as a side effect. You can lose weight, build muscle and cardiovascular fitness, and have a good time (maybe getting a little dirty in the process, which is a different kind of fun). Not that riding a stationary bicycle while watching CNN on a gym television for an hour isn't a good use of your time, but most people would say mountain biking for an hour (or hiking, or trail running, or cross-country skiing) is a more rewarding experience.

I live in the city. How can I spend more time outside?

"The Outdoors" isn't only big things like national parks and sprawling wilderness areas, or weeklong backpacking trips and ski vacations. If you live in a major city, you can find plenty of what are now called "microadventures" within a few minutes of downtown—after-work mountain bike rides, short hikes and trail runs, and kayak routes. If you want to find people to get outside with, check out your local bike shop, climbing gym, outdoors club, and outdoor gear shop for event postings, bulletin boards for people looking for climbing or hiking partners, or announcements of group bike rides.

If you're efficient about your planning and time management, you can take advantage of the sixty-four hours between the end of the workweek (5 p.m. Friday) and the beginning of the next workweek (9 a.m. Monday). Plan your weekend adventure throughout the week, pack and shop for food on Thursday, and have the car loaded and ready to go the minute you get home from work on Friday.

Do I need to be fit?

A good base level of fitness helps, but Olympic-athlete-level stamina isn't required to start your outdoor adventures. A sense of humility is probably more important at the beginning of anything. If you haven't tried to do a pull-up since you were a teenager, rock climbing will probably be a little challenging when you first try it. No matter how many hills you bicycle up on a regular basis, the steep climbs on a mountain bike ride will probably test your lungs and heart on your first ride. If you don't do a lot of squats or lunges, skiing will probably tire your quads out at the beginning of the season. The outdoors will challenge your body in ways that you can't replicate in a gym—carrying a thirty-five-pound backpack, sitting on a bicycle seat for miles and miles, hiking up steep trails of dirt and rocks. It all takes a little getting used to, and it might make you feel as if you're out of shape at first. You're really just out of shape for that specific sport, but if you stick with it, your stamina will improve. Climbers develop finger and grip strength with practice; hikers develop strong stabilization muscles from moving on uneven terrain; back-packers' hips and shoulders learn to deal with the weight of a backpack waist belt and shoulder straps; and cyclists build up tough skin in the right places from clutching handlebars and sitting on seats for hours.

The Best Seasons for Each Sport

- **Cross-country skiing:** Winter, early spring

- **Downhill skiing:** Winter, early spring

- **Snowboarding:** Winter, early spring

- **Sledding:** Winter, early spring

- **Snowshoeing:** Winter, early spring

- **Ice climbing:** Winter

- **Mountaineering:** Late spring, summer, early fall

- **Hiking:** Late spring, summer, early fall

- **Backpacking:** Late spring, summer, early fall

- **Canoeing:** Late spring, summer, early fall

- **Sea kayaking:** Late spring, summer, early fall

- **Whitewater kayaking:** Late spring, summer

- **Whitewater rafting:** Late spring, summer

- **Surfing:** Spring, summer, fall

The Different Types of Public Land

For most people, outdoor sports take place almost exclusively on some type of publicly accessible land. That public land is managed by a variety of agencies, and there are a few differences between what you can and can't do on each type of land.

- **State parks** and what they have to offer vary widely from state to state, but generally they have infrastructure like campgrounds with designated sites (and often running water) and well-marked and well-signed trails. State parks are also generally smaller than national parks. You'll almost always pay an entry fee to visit a state park and usually an additional fee to camp there.

- **National parks/national monuments** are generally large tracts of wild land with lots of infrastructure built in—paved roads, campgrounds with designated sites, visitor centers, sometimes bus shuttle systems, and even hotels. Many national parks and monuments can be very popular and even feel crowded, but solitude is usually easy to find if you hike a mile or more into the backcountry. National parks almost always have an entry fee and always have an additional fee for camping. Backpacking in national parks is usually regulated and requires a permit and a fee; usually it is allowed only in designated backcountry campsites.

- **National forest** is land managed by the US Forest Service and is regulated but has much less infrastructure than a national park—visitor centers are more sparse and usually located in the nearest town, and trailheads are often accessed by dirt roads. Campgrounds tend to be less cushy than in national parks, and trails have less signage. National forest land usually gives users more freedom to roam—backcountry camping is less regulated, and dispersed car camping is allowed in many areas, meaning if you find a nice spot you can camp there, usually for free.

- **Wilderness** is roadless land, often inside national forest land but sometimes inside national parks. Wilderness is managed and regulated by US government agencies: the US Forest Service, the Bureau of Land Management, the National Park Service, and the US Fish and

Wildlife Service. Motorized, or mechanized, vehicles are not allowed on wilderness land, including motorcycles on trails; somewhat more controversially, mountain bikes are not allowed either. Camping is allowed on wilderness land.

- **Bureau of Land Management (BLM) land** is primarily located in the western United States and has few restrictions. This often means you can drive a van or truck along a dirt road in the desert, pull off to the side, and camp wherever you want—which makes it a favorite for itinerant climbers and travelers. But it also means that commercial mining and drilling are allowed on the same land, as well as livestock grazing. BLM campgrounds are common and are usually fairly bare-bones, with vault toilets and self-issued camping permits.

Gear: How much do I need?

Here's the thing about gear: you can always have better gear. But top-of-the-line equipment doesn't mean you'll have a top-of-the-line experience. Even the most expensive, best-designed, most technologically advanced backpack on the market will be heavy when you fill it with your stuff. Your legs and feet will still be tired at the end of a long hike no matter how much money you spend on boots. That said, proper gear is nice to have, but you don't need all of it to get started. If you want to try mountain biking before you drop $1,500 on a mountain bike, you can try one out at most bike shops for $100/day or less. If you want to go hiking, all you need is a sturdy pair of shoes, a waterproof jacket, and something to carry your snacks and water—if you like it, you can buy hiking boots and a backpack later. Most popular recreational areas near rivers and lakes have nearby outfitters that rent canoes and kayaks. You can rent camping gear at many outdoor stores, and you can rent skis and snowboards at or near any ski resort. So don't worry about how much a particular activity is going to cost up front—you don't need to own all the gear before you try the sport.

Ten Best American Towns for Outdoor Adventures

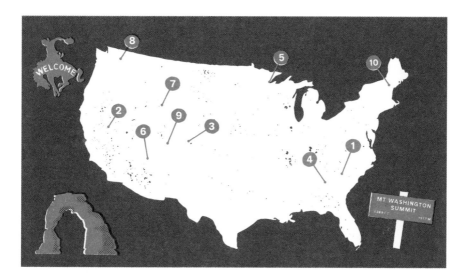

1. **Asheville, North Carolina:** Its proximity to world-class rock climbing, whitewater, and mountain biking makes it a destination for many outdoor adventurers.

2. **Bishop, California:** Located at the foot of the Sierras, Bishop features nearby bouldering, rock climbing, hiking, and hot springs.

3. **Boulder, Colorado:** Boulder has thousands of rock-climbing routes within a 1-hour drive, plus close access to Rocky Mountain National Park and Colorado skiing.

4. **Chattanooga, Tennessee:** This southern part of the state has whitewater rafting and kayaking, mountain bike trails, and some of the Southeast's best rock climbing.

5. **Duluth, Minnesota:** Head to Duluth for great mountain biking, hiking, skiing, and paddling on the shore of Lake Superior.

6. **Flagstaff, Arizona:** You'll find Arizona's best rock climbs here. You can also mountain bike in nearby Sedona, and the Grand Canyon is about a 90-minute drive away.

7. **Jackson, Wyoming:** Skiing at Jackson Hole is not to be missed, plus the hiking and climbing in Grand Teton National Park are unforgettable.

8. **Leavenworth, Washington:** Some of the best rock climbing in Washington is near this gateway to the Cascades.

9. **Moab, Utah:** Located between two national parks, Moab offers opportunities for nearby desert mountain biking, rock climbing, hiking, and off roading.

10. **North Conway, New Hampshire:** Surrounded by national forest land, North Conway is close to prime skiing and rock- and ice-climbing locations.

The Top Eight Adventures Worldwide

1. **Climb Mont Blanc, France:** Take a three-day guided snow climb of Europe's 15,781-foot crown jewel.

2. **Ski the Haute Route in Switzerland:** The classic seven-day hut-to-hut ski route travels from Chamonix to Zermatt.

3. **Trek Torres del Paine, Chile:** A four-day backpacking trip winds in and out of Patagonia's sculpted granite peaks and glaciers.

4. **Hike the Inca Trail/Machu Picchu, Peru:** A four-day, 20-mile hike leads to the ruins of the famous fifteenth-century Incan city.

5. **Climb Mount Fuji, Japan:** Popular, but not easy, the trek to the summit of Japan's most famous mountain goes up 4,500 feet.

6. **Annapurna Circuit trek, Nepal:** See Nepal with a 128-mile backpacking trip around the giant peaks of the Himalayas.

7. **Ski Portillo, Chile:** South America's oldest and most famous ski resort is 100 percent above treeline.

8. **Trek Routeburn Track, New Zealand:** New Zealand's most famous trail features 20 miles of hut-to-hut trekking.

What should I carry in my vehicle in case of emergency?

If you're headed into the backcountry, you don't need as many items in the emergency kit in your vehicle, since you're likely carrying many of them in your fully packed backpack already: sleeping bag, food, water, headlamp, multitool, and some duct tape. In addition to those items, though, you should have tow straps, a set of jumper cables, and in winter some kitty litter (for traction if you get stuck in the snow or ice) and a small shovel. When buying a shovel, consider purchasing the type of avalanche shovel that backcountry skiers use—although a little more expensive, it collapses or breaks down to stow away without taking up as much space as a regular shovel, and for car-related emergencies it works just as well (if not better). For travel on bumpy or sandy roads, a small piece of wood can be great to shove under a wheel if it's spinning above a hole—or to place under your jack if you get a flat tire in sandy or muddy soil.

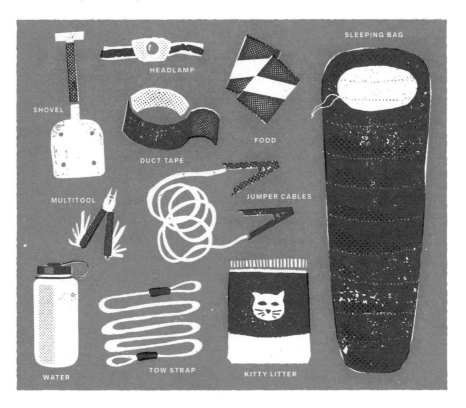

SLEEPING BAG

HEADLAMP

SHOVEL

FOOD

DUCT TAPE

JUMPER CABLES

MULTITOOL

WATER

TOW STRAP

KITTY LITTER

Do I need a Jeep/four-wheel-drive truck to get into the mountains?

If your primary objective is hiking, climbing, or mountain biking, not necessarily —as a quick survey of all the Honda Civics and other passenger cars in Colorado trailhead parking lots will tell you. A regular-clearance, two-wheel-drive car can get you to where you want to go most of the time, especially if you're willing to push what you think are its limits. Plenty of off-road experts will tell you that the line you pick on a rough road is way more important than having a lifted vehicle or four-wheel drive (although those things obviously help). Drive slowly, examine angles before committing to a line, roll over rocks with your tires (as opposed to your oil pan), and if you're really in doubt about a section, park your car wherever you can and walk the rest of the way to the trailhead if it's only a mile or two extra—the goal of your excursion is to exercise anyway, right?

How do I keep my vehicle from getting stuck in sand?

If you're on a sandy road, deflate your tires to 20 PSI before driving on it— the lower pressure will widen your tire and give you better flotation. This of course leaves you with the issue of putting air back in the tires when you're done with the sandy portion of the drive. Off-road enthusiasts carry an air compressor in their car to deal with this, but if you don't want to buy/carry one, a standard bicycle tire pump will work (just be warned that it will take much longer and burn a lot more calories than the compressor). If you're driving a road and spot a sandy patch, don't slow down through the sand; keep your foot on the gas until you're out of the sandy spot—you don't have to floor it or drive dangerously, but keep power going to the drive wheels. If you get stuck, don't spin the wheels trying to get out—your wheels will just dig holes for your heavy vehicle to sink into. Get out a shovel and scoop out the sand from in front of your tires, and then rally your friends to push the car to help you get out. If you're still stuck, you'll probably need a pull from a friend in another vehicle.

Top 10 Towns for Adventure around the World

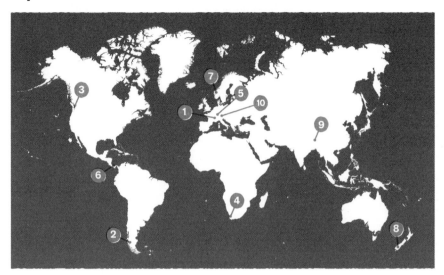

1. **Chamonix, France:** Located at the foot of Mont Blanc, Chamonix has long been the adventure capital of Europe, with limitless climbing, skiing, mountaineering, and hiking opportunities.

2. **El Chalten, Argentina:** El Chalten is near Patagonia's famous granite towers. It is known as the trekking capital of Argentina and is considered one of the best alpine climbing destinations in the world.

3. **Squamish, British Columbia, Canada:** The granite at Squamish is as famous in rock-climbing circles as Yosemite, and the mountain biking, windsurfing, and kayaking combined give it the title of Canada's outdoor recreation capital.

4. **Cape Town, South Africa:** Close proximity to the ocean and the backdrop of Table Mountain make Cape Town a well-known destination for surfing, hiking, rock climbing, windsurfing, caving, and mountain biking.

5. **Interlaken, Switzerland:** Just down the valley from the north face of the Eiger, Interlaken is a quick drive to some of the best mountaineering, skiing, rock climbing, BASE jumping, and hiking in the Alps.

6. **Turrialba, Costa Rica:** Turrialba is known for two whitewater rivers, but it's also got world-class mountain biking, hiking, and surfing, not to mention year-round warm weather.

7. **Voss, Norway:** Tucked into the fjord lands in western Norway, Voss is most famous for whitewater rafting and kayaking, as well as BASE jumping. It's also got great hiking and is the largest ski destination in western Norway.

8. **Queenstown, New Zealand:** At Queenstown, New Zealand's unique Alps drop almost right into the ocean. Whitewater, heli-skiing, climbing, jet boating, and mountain biking are available—and the town has the unique distinction of being the birthplace of bungee jumping.

9. **Kathmandu, Nepal:** Kathmandu is the gateway to the Himalayas, including famous long treks through the world's highest mountain range, not to mention Mount Everest.

10. **Cortina d'Ampezzo, Italy:** In the winter, Cortina is known as one of the best ski towns in Europe and as a chic gateway to skiing in the Dolomites. In the summer, it's just as appealing: hiking, rock-climbing, and protected-climbing routes (called *via ferrata*) abound.

Do I need to carry a big knife for camping, hiking, and cooking outdoors?

Probably not. Think about what you would need a knife for before you buy the knife: as macho as you'd like to think outdoor pursuits are, your knife is likely to be used for small repairs and for cutting cheese or food wrappers. Big knives are bulky, and if they're heavy they're likely to get packed away where you can't access them. A small knife that fits in your pocket will prove to be more useful in the long run.

How do I get my vehicle out of mud?

The best way to get unstuck from mud is to avoid it in the first place. If you're driving on a muddy road, be cautious of ruts left by taller vehicles—your Subaru Outback might not make it through the same path as someone with a lifted Jeep. When driving through mud, keep your speed up and keep the power going to the drive wheels as much as possible (i.e., keep the gas pedal depressed). If you do get stuck in mud, you may be able to get unstuck by turning the steering wheel back and forth while pressing the gas pedal—but don't spin your tires, as this will only dig you deeper. If that doesn't work, your passengers will have to push you out, and if that fails, it's time to get out your tow straps (see page 17) and hook your car up to another car that's not stuck in the mud.

What's the difference between all-wheel drive and four-wheel drive?

Despite their similarities—both all-wheel drive (AWD) and four-wheel drive (4WD) propel your vehicle using both the front and rear axles (or front and rear wheels, if that makes more sense)—they're not the same. As opposed to your standard two-wheel-drive car, in which all the propulsion goes to the front wheels and the rear wheels just roll along obediently behind, an AWD or 4WD vehicle will be more responsive on icy or snowy roads or on extremely bumpy roads because all four wheels can grip the driving surface. If you live in a mountain town, choose AWD or 4WD: you'll get stuck less often. A vehicle with 4WD is generally a two-wheel-drive vehicle with the option to switch into 4WD when necessary. An AWD vehicle essentially has 4WD all the time, with no ability to switch out of it. Although they sound the same, 4WD is generally better than AWD if you're doing a lot of off-roading, and AWD is generally better than 4WD for on-road mountain driving, since it's always on. So if you're driving an AWD vehicle to go skiing and you hit a patch of ice or snow, you don't have to turn on the 4WD (but you would if you were driving a 4WD vehicle).

EXPERT WITNESS

ELEVEN TIPS FOR DRIVING BUMPY (NONSNOWY) ROADS

Sinuhe Xavier, professional commercial filmmaker for off-road clients like Land Rover and Toyota

Xavier has driven thousands of miles of gnarly roads throughout the world in his film work and as creative director for *Overland Journal*. He shares his tips for navigating bumpy, rutted, rocky roads in the backcountry:

1. Go as slow as possible and as fast as necessary when navigating difficult terrain. Don't be afraid to take your time getting over an obstacle, because doing it right once slowly will take less time than hurrying through it and getting stuck.

2. Lower the pressure in your tires to 20 PSI for a smoother ride and better traction on washboard roads.

3. Use your floor mats as traction devices when nothing else can be found.

4. Travel with another vehicle when possible, in case you become stuck and need a tow out of a situation or just a small pull or push.

5. Never cross a body of water without knowing how deep the water is all the way across.

6. If you are unsure of what lies above the horizon or around the bend, get out of the car and walk it first.

7. Turning around is not failure.

8. Put your tires on the highest point of an obstacle. This will lift everything up, giving you more clearance.

9. Know the following numbers about your vehicle: approach angle (the maximum angle from the ground of an incline or obstacle that the front of your vehicle can clear), departure angle (the maximum angle from the ground of an incline or obstacle that the rear of your vehicle can clear), and break-over angle (the angle between the bottom of your tires and the midpoint of your vehicle's underside).

10. Four-wheel drive does not give you superpowers.

11. Four-wheel drive only gives you the skills to get stuck farther away from help.

EXPERT WITNESS

HOW TO TAKE A GREAT PHOTO OUTDOORS

Forest Woodward, photographer

Adventure photographer Forest Woodward has shot adventure photos all around the world for publications like *National Geographic Adventure*, *Outside Magazine*, *Esquire*, *Climbing*, *Alpinist*, *Rock and Ice*, *Surfer Mag*, *Afar*, and *Forbes*, and he understands what it takes to make a quality image when you're up against Mother Nature.

1. **Get tough.** The best outdoor photographs don't come from having the most expensive equipment or even going to the most beautiful places. They come from being tough, from sucking it up, and from pulling out the camera in those moments when the human experience of wild places is most raw and exposed to the elements—battling mosquitoes, fording a river, or taking shelter in a rainstorm. If you are exhausted, uncomfortable, and at odds with the elements, chances are there's a good adventure photo in the making.

2. **Invest in good lenses.** The camera is important, but just as important is the lens you choose. A 24mm to 70mm zoom is a great lens to start with, but the next lens to get is a 50mm with a large aperture (f1.8 or lower). With one of these you can begin experimenting with depth of field and low-light shooting. The 50mm most closely replicates what our eyes see and thus is a good challenge—eliminating the trickery of a wide angle or telephoto and forcing you to move your feet to get the shot.

3. **Shoot during the "golden hour."** The golden hour is the first hour after the sun rises and the last hour before it sets. The vast majority of landscape photographs are taken during this time. It's called the golden hour because of the golden

warmth to the light—it is the most dramatic and descriptive light. If you want to create beautiful landscape photographs, get a tripod and be ready to hunt during the golden hour.

4. **F8 and be there.** The street photographer Weegee has been oft quoted as saying, "F8 and be there." This applies not just to street photography but to outdoor adventure photography as well. Set your camera at F8, be in the right place at the right time, and let the camera do the rest. The F8 setting will allow a wide range to be in focus, so when you find your shot, your camera will be ready to capture it.

What's the best camera for shooting in the outdoors?

The best camera to take with you in the outdoors is the one you know how to use, whether it's the one on your smartphone or a $5,000 digital camera. When deciding what number of megapixels (literally the number of pixels that make up the photos your camera takes, or the size of the digital file produced by the camera) is appropriate for your needs, consider what you're going to do with your outdoor photos—if your mountain bike photo is destined for a billboard, yes, you might need that 42MP camera, but if you're just sharing the shots on Facebook and Instagram, your smartphone probably has an ample number of megapixels for your needs. A DSLR camera (generally a larger, heavier camera with interchangeable lenses) is a good investment if you're interested in learning photography, especially about what's possible with different manual settings and lenses. But if you just want snapshots of your adventures, a small camera or smartphone is great. The most expensive camera you can buy won't do much for you (besides take huge photos) unless you know how to use it. Learn how to frame a good shot first, and then, when you're feeling limited by your camera's capabilities, start shopping for a better one.

Ten Adventure Books Everyone Should Read

1. *Kon-Tiki*, by Thor Heyerdahl (1950)

2. *Touching the Void*, by Joe Simpson (1988)

3. *Into the Wild*, by Jon Krakauer (1996)

4. *Endurance: Shackleton's Incredible Voyage*, by Alfred Lansing (1959)

5. *Annapurna: First Conquest of an 8,000-Meter Peak*, by Maurice Herzog (1951)

6. *Desert Solitaire: A Season in the Wilderness*, by Edward Abbey (1968)

7. *Moby-Dick*, by Herman Melville (1851)

8. *The Emerald Mile: The Epic Story of the Fastest Ride in History through the Heart of the Grand Canyon*, by Kevin Fedarko (2013)

9. *A Walk in the Woods: Rediscovering America on the Appalachian Trail*, by Bill Bryson (1998)

10. *The Worst Journey in the World*, by Apsley Cherry-Garrard (1922)

Should I buy a GPS?

Handheld GPS units (or GPS watches) can be great for specific applications—plotting routes, measuring statistics during a climb, run, or mountain bike ride, or sending text messages to let friends or family know you'll be late for dinner. But plenty of adventurers would say that your smartphone works just as well. Smartphone GPS apps have similar functionality to handheld GPS units, and if you just want the ability to see where you are on a map or navigate, they'll do just fine. If you take your phone on a trip, keep it on airplane mode and keep the screen brightness turned down; it can last days on a single battery charge. You can download US Geological Survey (USGS) topography maps before your trip and use the GPS app while the phone is on airplane mode.

If you're concerned about needing a GPS more durable and water resistant than a phone, or would like more functionality (like the ability to text-message via satellite when you're out in the wilderness), GPS units are the way to go.

Nine Outdoor Adventure Heroes

1. **Thor Heyerdahl:** This Norwegian explorer captained a 5,000-mile ocean expedition on a traditional balsa wood raft from Peru to French Polynesia in 1947 to prove his theory that the islands were originally settled from South America.

2/3. **Sir Edmund Hillary and Tenzing Norgay:** The first people to summit Mount Everest, in 1953.

4. **Ernest Shackleton:** The leader of the Imperial Trans-Antarctic Expedition, an epic journey from 1914 to 1917 in which the expedition's ship became stuck and then was crushed in sea ice. Shackleton's incredible leadership enabled the entire crew to survive.

5. **Lynn Hill:** The first person to free-climb the Nose on El Capitan, in 1993, and to free-climb the Nose in a single day, in 1994. Both feats remained unrepeated for more than a decade after her ascents.

6. **Duke Kahanamoku:** "The Duke," a native Hawaiian and Olympic swimming medalist, is credited with popularizing the sport of surfing in his travels around the world in the early 1900s.

7. **Reinhold Messner:** The first person to climb Everest without supplemental oxygen; he's also the first person to climb all fourteen 8,000-meter peaks.

8. **Kenton Grua:** Grua masterminded the fastest speed run of the Colorado River through the Grand Canyon in a rowboat in 1983. He led a team that rowed 280 river miles in under thirty-seven hours.

9. **Emma "Grandma" Gatewood:** At age sixty-seven in 1955, Gatewood became the first woman to thru-hike the Appalachian Trail; she was also the first person to hike the Appalachian Trail three times.

What's the protocol when a date knows more than I do about an outdoor sport?

Humility is the best policy. We're not living in the days of Jeremiah Johnson and Jim Bridger, when men knew how to build a log cabin from scratch, skin a grizzly bear, and track an elk, and women were supposed to keep the home fires burning. No one has an innate knowledge of outdoor sports, and most people don't expect us to. If a prospective love interest invites you out for a day of sailing, hiking, or climbing for your first date, be honest up front and admit your lack of experience or knowledge. Giving him or her the chance to help you right away will save you awkward situations in the long run. Being "bad" at something, or being a slow learner, is way better than faking it and looking like a jackass.

Is hiking/skiing/climbing/mountain biking a good first date?

If your prospective girlfriend or boyfriend is already a hiker or skier or climber, it can be a great experience enjoying a common interest. If she or he is not, it's probably a better fifth date. Teaching someone to ski is probably the worst first-date idea ever, because the success of the date will be largely dependent on the success of that person's first time skiing, which could go really badly. Taking someone climbing for the first time could have terrible implications as well, especially if she or he just happens to discover a paralyzing fear of heights halfway up the first route (and fairly or unfairly blames everything on you). Mountain biking also has lots of potential to end catastrophically with a crash. Kayaking or canoeing on a calm lake or river can be fun and is fairly low-risk, although there is a slight possibility that one of you might fall into the water. Hiking is of course a much easier theater for a date, since it's really just a step up from walking and any fit person can do it without having to learn additional skills. The important thing to remember, if you do choose an outdoor activity for your first date, is that an easy day of climbing or skiing or mountain biking for you might be a completely terrifying or frustrating day for someone who has never done it before, so adjust your objective accordingly.

The Seven Principles of Leave No Trace/Don't Pollute

The Leave No Trace Center for Outdoor Ethics has, since 1994, educated people about their recreational impacts on nature. Use their seven guiding principles to enjoy the outdoors responsibly.

1. **Plan Ahead and Prepare:** Give yourself enough time to hike in and reach proper campsites. If you don't plan ahead and give yourself plenty of time to find a good spot, you can run out of daylight and have to set up a camp in a spot that's less sustainable (and less comfortable).

2. **Travel and Camp on Durable Surfaces:** In high-use areas, use already existing sites; in remote areas, spread out to minimize impact. If everyone who visited an alpine lake, for example, used a brand-new campsite, the lake would eventually be surrounded in barren spots with fire rings next to them. Use a spot that's already been camped in.

3. **Dispose of Waste Properly (Pack It In, Pack It Out):** Pack out all trash, scatter dishwater far from water sources, and bury human waste (see page 229).

4. **Leave What You Find:** Leave the things you find for others to enjoy— don't pocket rocks, wildflowers, or archaeological artifacts. Stealing a potsherd from an ancient site alters the site, making it less enjoyable for future visitors.

5. **Minimize Campfire Impacts:** Minimize campfires, and when you do build one make it no bigger than necessary; use existing fire rings when possible.

6. **Respect Wildlife:** Give animals proper space; don't leave food where animals can get into it. If animals become accustomed to finding food that campers leave out, they'll continue to revisit certain areas, becoming a danger to humans and to themselves.

7. **Be Considerate of Other Visitors:** Travel and camp quietly; give other users enough space when camping. Yelling and shouting may seem natural in the outdoors, but you're infringing on other hikers' experiences when you create unnecessary noise.

Eight Classic Outdoor Trips of a Lifetime

All you need for this diverse list of outdoor adventures is some enthusiasm, a little fitness, and some spare time (and some spare cash)—none of them requires specialized skills or training, outside of hiking boots and backpacking gear.

1. **Raft the Grand Canyon (Arizona):** One of the biggest rivers in America, it has 280 miles of rafting.

2. **Hike Half Dome (Yosemite National Park, California):** A climb to the top of Yosemite's iconic granite monolith doesn't require specialized skills or equipment.

3. **Climb Katahdin (Baxter State Park, Maine):** A thrilling hike to the top of one of the Northeast's most famous mountains, the northern terminus of the Appalachian Trail.

4. **Climb Mount Hood with a guide (Oregon):** A great introduction to snow climbing and mountaineering, this can be done in a single day and is one of the most famous mountains in America.

5. **Ski Tuckerman's Ravine in the spring (New Hampshire):** Use your own power to climb and then ski down the Northeast's most well-known backcountry run.

6. **Mountain bike the White Rim Trail (Utah):** A three-day beginner-friendly mountain bike adventure takes you through southern Utah's famous desert canyon country.

7. **Backpack to Havasu Falls (Arizona):** Hike into turquoise-blue waterfall-fed pools in a side canyon of the Grand Canyon.

8. **Climb a 14,000-foot mountain (Colorado):** Experience high altitude at the top of the Rocky Mountains; no specialized equipment is needed other than a sturdy pair of hiking boots.

How do I ask out a woman or man I meet on a trail?

There are all sorts of ways asking someone out on a trail can go wrong—keep in mind that depending on how remote said trail is, asking someone out can come off as quite creepy. A trail is somewhere on the spectrum between a bar (where lots of people are open to meeting people to potentially date) and a gym (where lots of people are just there to work out, and potential dates are the last thing on their mind). That said, it's possible—it just takes more of an opening conversation than buying someone a drink. Start with the scenery or something about the environment ("Beautiful view up here" or "Hope those rain clouds stay where they are") and test the waters, and if the conversation flows from there, that's positive. If you end up talking for a few minutes and feel that you might have enough in common to suggest getting together sometime, go for it—"I was going to head down into town and get a beer (or a burrito) after this, would you like to join me?" or "I hike this trail every Tuesday after work—maybe we should meet up and hike together sometime."

Thirteen Pieces of Must-Have Gear for All-Around Adventures

If you want to get started in the outdoors but have no idea what you should buy first, this list is a good start for hiking, camping, and backpacking activities.

1. **Thirty-liter backpack:** Perfect size for day-long hikes, climbs, or summit hiking missions.

2. **Sixty-liter backpack:** The right size for two- to seven-day backpacking trips.

3. **Headlamp:** Illumination for car camping, backpacking, and keeping in your pack just in case you're still outdoors after sunset.

4. **Two-person backpacking tent:** A solid tent will last for a decade of backpacking and car-camping adventures.

5. **15°F sleeping bag:** For camping in the mountains or desert, a 15°F-rated sleeping bag is perfect for every season except winter, or summer in the desert (see page 216).

6. **Sleeping pad:** No matter what kind you buy, it will make your nights sleeping outside better.

7. **Isobutane (canister fuel) stove:** Simple, reliable, and easy to maintain, this little stove should last for years.

8. **Backpacking pot or pot set:** You're not cooking complicated meals in the backcountry, so a pot or two is usually all you need.

9. **Water bottles:** Two 1-liter bottles will get you through most day-long adventures.

10. **Lightweight soft-shell jacket:** It's a great all-around layer for hiking, climbing, and cold-weather trail running.

11. **Trail-running shoes:** Not just for trail running—wear for day hiking and peak bagging, as well as road running.

12. **Rain shell:** A good rain jacket is indispensable—if you spend enough time outdoors, you're eventually going to need it.

13. **Puffy jacket:** A down or synthetic insulated jacket is the lightest, warmest insulation you can carry on a backpacking trip. It makes a great pillow too.

Should I buy a multitool for camping, hiking, and cooking outdoors?

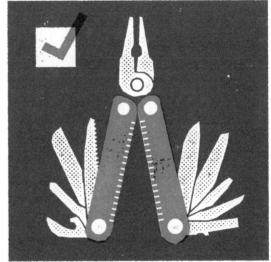

Yes. There are dozens of multitools on the market, and you can decide what tools you want yours to come with. A basic multi-tool often includes a knife blade, a can opener, both Phillips head and regular screwdrivers, and pliers with wire-cutting capability; these tools will cover most of your camping and backpacking needs. You can spend lots of money if you want, but just because you can imagine a hypothetical use for a specific tool (think about what it would be like to saw a branch with that 3-inch serrated blade) doesn't mean you're actually going to use it. Plenty of multitools under forty dollars will do exactly what you need them to do in the wilderness—don't forget that climber Aron Ralston amputated his arm with a dull, non-name-brand multitool when he got trapped behind that boulder in a canyon in Utah.

How do I know if a hike/climb is beyond my skill level?

Before you set out on a new adventure, if you're wondering, "Can I do it?" you should consider two things:

1. **The type of terrain.** An 8-mile hike on a manageable, flat trail is a lot different from an 8-mile hike to the top of a rocky peak, especially if the last 2 miles are a continuous field of boulders that you have to scramble over using your hands and feet. You can learn to move fast over rock debris (called talus), but it takes some practice. If you're terrified of steep drop-offs and your research of the hike indicates that there's a very exposed section of trail or scrambling, it might be beyond your skill level.

2. **The elevation gain.** A flat trail is easy to hike quickly, but a steep trail gaining 1,000 feet per mile might slow you down to 1 mile per hour or slower, not to mention what it will do to your legs and lungs. If you haven't been doing a lot of hiking (or Stairmaster workouts), it might be a good idea to pick a route less steep.

Of course, there's no harm in trying a new trail to test your abilities—if you get out there and realize you've bitten off more than you can chew, you can turn around and head back to the car in almost all cases (except in the case of the Grand Canyon, where people often get themselves in trouble by hiking downhill for a few hours without realizing how hard it will be to climb out again).

The Ten Best Day Hikes in America

1. **Angels Landing, Zion National Park, Utah, 5 miles:** This hike has a jaw-dropping exposure looking down 1,500 feet to the floor of Zion Canyon.

2. **Tall Trees Grove Trail, Redwood National Park, California, 3.7 miles:** The tallest redwood tree in the world—and several close contenders—call this grove home.

3. **Presidential Traverse, Presidential Range, New Hampshire, 20 miles:** One of the most coveted backpacking trips on the East Coast, the majority of it is spent along the spine of the Presidential Range.

4. **Chesler Park Loop, Canyonlands National Park, Utah, 11 miles:** Towering striped needles and other Dr. Seuss-ish sandstone sculpture make this hike feel like a trip to the moon.

5. **Harding Icefield Trail, Kenai Fjords National Park, Alaska, 8.2 miles:** A short but steep hike leads to a view of the largest ice field in North America.

6. **Half Dome Cables Route, Yosemite National Park, California, 16.5 miles:** The only hiking route to the top of Half Dome features a trail so steep you have to hang on to the namesake cables for the last 300 feet to the summit.

7. **Longs Peak, Rocky Mountain National Park, Colorado, 15 miles:** This challenging high-altitude hike and scramble over varied terrain takes you to the top of the most famous 14,000-foot mountain in Colorado.

8. **Knife Edge, Katahdin, Baxter State Park, Maine, 6.4 miles:** The most famous mountain ridge in the eastern United States, the narrow and exposed Knife Edge ends at the summit of Katahdin, which is also the end of the Appalachian Trail.

9. **Grandview Trail to Horseshoe Mesa, Grand Canyon National Park, Arizona, 6 miles:** This trail is the best way to get down into the Grand Canyon without committing to a backpacking trip.

10. **Camp Muir, Mount Rainier National Park, Washington, 9 miles:** A stout day hike up the Muir Snowfield (which is present year-round) to Camp Muir, the starting point for summit climbs of Mount Rainier.

How close should I get to wildlife?

Although you'll likely see tourists in Yellowstone National Park doing something different, you should never get close enough to a wild animal that it
can kill you. Moose, bison, and bears may look slow, but adult grizzlies can
run 30 mph—faster than world record–holding Olympic gold medalist Usain
Bolt, who has the fastest human foot speed ever recorded: 27.74 mph. So
before you try to sneak in a little closer to get a better photo, imagine a really
angry 400- to 700 pound Usain Bolt coming at you. With claws. A moose's
top speed is 30 mph, and many people say they'd rather spook a grizzly than
a moose (maybe because moose weigh 1,000 pounds). And bison? Their top
speed is 35 mph. These numbers are something to think about when you
wonder how close is too close: if you do get too close and the animal charges
you, your chances of outrunning it are zero. But if you do outrun it, you might
consider trying out for the Olympic 100-meter dash. So staying 300 feet
away is safe; more than 300 feet is safer.

How do I keep insects away?

For years, DEET, or diethyltoluamide, has been the standby for those venturing into mosquito territory, and stores now sell sprays and lotions with
concentrations of DEET up to 100 percent. Concerns have been raised about
DEET causing health issues in humans, specifically cancer, but research isn't
definitive. Sprays containing more than 30 percent DEET are not significantly more effective than those with lower percentages, and they expose
you to higher levels of the chemical (if you're concerned about that). The
EPA has found DEET to be slightly toxic to birds, fish, and aquatic inverte-
brates, but since it's applied directly to skin, those species' exposure is very
light. Still, don't jump into a creek and rinse off your skin after you've been
wearing DEET repellent.

DEET will damage clothing if you spray it directly onto the fabric, so keep it
away from your Gore-Tex, and keep it out of your eyes. A good way to apply it

to your face without risking getting it in your eyes or mouth is to spray it on the back of your hand, then wipe your hand across your forehead and cheeks.

If you're not willing to use sprays containing DEET, there are plenty of other options, including picardin, permethrin, bug nets, and hiking shirts, pants, and jackets that have been treated with permethrin to repel insects.

How do I know if clouds mean a storm is coming?

You know the saying "Don't like the weather? Wait a minute—it'll change." In the mountains this is definitely the case, and you'll have fewer places to take cover if a storm rolls in. Fortunately, you don't have to be a meteorologist to stay safe up high—you just have to keep an eye on things and show some good judgment of when to turn back and go down. Storms tend to build throughout the day in the mountains, so even if you start hiking under bluebird skies, it's important to watch clouds forming. If cumulus clouds (tall puffy clouds that resemble cotton balls) start to gather, they can turn into cumulonimbus clouds, which often produce thunderstorms. Keep your eye on them—even when they seem far away—and if you notice them getting taller, darker, and looking more threatening, it's a good time to call it a day and come back for the summit another time. Over the ocean, you have a much better vantage point to watch a storm coming in since you're not blocked by mountains—but the signs are generally the same: watch for building clouds and dark skies over the water.

Top Five Smartphone Apps for Adventure

It wasn't so long ago that people thought having cell phones in the backcountry was an abomination—and some purists still swear by leaving theirs at home so they can enjoy the solitude. But these five apps help make the argument that smartphones are a tool to enhance adventure, not to distract from it.

1. **Offline Topo:** Downloads USGS topography maps to your phone.

2. **Gaia GPS:** Sets GPS tracks and waypoints and downloads USGS topography maps to your phone.

3. **Weather Underground:** Provides hyperlocal, detailed, by-the-hour weather forecasts.

4. **My Altitude:** Uses your phone's GPS signal to determine your altitude (even when you're out of cell phone service range).

5. **SkyView Free:** Identifies constellations when you point your phone up at the sky.

STAYING ALIVE

You should have some goals for your time in the outdoors: maybe you want to reconnect with nature, find something that will help you get in shape, learn to take better photos, or totally disconnect from our fast-paced world for a few hours. Here are the two goals that should be at the top of your list, and all your other goals can fill in the spots after them:

1. DON'T DIE.
2. HAVE FUN.

This chapter will help you with goal number one, which will ensure that you have plenty more opportunities to achieve goal number two. Learning some survival techniques before you head outdoors will make you better prepared for your adventures and will help you avoid anything that could mess up your experience in the wild. This chapter will teach you how to deal with cold temperatures, hot weather, running out of food and water, getting lost, bears, snakes, mountain lions, bees, scorpions, equipment failure, crossing rivers, and avoiding avalanches. And if all else fails, you'll learn how to arrange for a rescue. But obviously getting rescued is a huge bummer, so read up on the other stuff before you head out and you'll have a safe and enjoyable adventure.

How long can I make it without food and water?

Remember the "rule of threes" when it comes to survival: you can survive about three hours in bad weather without shelter, three days without drinking water, and three weeks without eating food. These are fairly general estimates, and there's a lot of variance depending on the situation and a person's physical condition—for instance, you can last a lot longer without water if you're lying in a hospital bed than if you're trudging through the desert under the hot sun. And a person who has a high percentage of muscle and fat can make it a lot longer before starving to death than a skinny person with 5 percent body fat (when your body starts to eat itself, it will eventually run out of "food"—fat and muscle). The point of the rule of threes, though, is that you'll die of dehydration a lot faster than you'll starve to death, so prioritize water first and then food. In extreme cases, mountaineers pinned down in a storm have survived almost a week in a snow cave with almost no water, and others have survived up to six days in arid environments without any water. Suffice it to say that if you've gone a day and a half without water somewhere in the wilderness, you should start looking for it in earnest. And if you find water, then maybe start looking for some food.

How long can I survive in the cold?

Many factors need to be considered when it comes to surviving in the cold: How cold is it and are you wet or dry? Are you physically fit? Hypothermia, when the body's core temperature drops below 95°F, happens much faster when your body is wet and even faster if you're submerged. If you should fall into water that's just half a degree above freezing, you probably won't survive more than a half hour. If you're in cold rain or your clothes are soaked, your body won't be able to warm itself, and if you can't get out of your wet clothes or find shelter, you'll eventually go hypothermic. If you're just cold and you stay dry, you can survive a lot longer. And if you have a good fitness level, your body will be able to shiver and/or keep moving longer, potentially postponing the amount of time you have before your body temperature becomes hypothermic.

If your body is approaching hypothermic temperatures, stop moving and find a place to give yourself some shelter. Remove any wet clothing that's next to your skin and add as many warm layers as you can. If you have the ability to make warm drinks, do it, and drink and eat immediately. If you have a sleeping bag with you, get in it. If you are with another person, spooning them is a great way to use their body heat to rewarm yourself (whether you want to spoon them romantically or not).

Your body has several mechanisms that work before hypothermia sets in: first you start shivering in an attempt to get warm, and if that doesn't work, your body will start shutting off blood flow to your extremities in order to keep your core warm. After that, the body's metabolism will begin slowing down in an attempt to decrease the need for blood and oxygen. At 95°F, the body is clinically hypothermic, but the heart won't stop beating until your core temperature drops just below 65°F. Between those two temperatures, you'll experience difficulty with everyday tasks (like putting on a pair of gloves to keep your hands warm) and confusion will set in (some hypothermia victims have removed all their clothes before dying, for unknown reasons). It's impossible to say exactly how long you can stay alive in the cold, but the longer you keep your core warm, the better off you will be until help arrives.

How do I protect myself from a swarm of bees?

If you find a beehive, stay away from it—at least 300 feet away from it. Count on one hand all the reasons it would be cool to get up close to a beehive (zero), and count on the other hand all the reasons it would not be cool to get stung by about five hundred bees (one). If it's just not your day, and the bees swarm you, here's one thing you should do:

- **Run.** Run in a straight line as fast as you can. Do not, as you may have seen on a TV show, run in a zigzag pattern. Run in a straight line away from the bees, into a building or a car where you can shut the door, and if that's not an option, just keep running away—most bees won't go more than a quarter mile from their hive. Does that sound like too far a distance to run? How about 1,300 feet? That's safe. If you have a jacket handy, cover as much of your face and head as possible with the jacket while running. But your first priority is to run away, and fast.

Here are a couple of things you shouldn't do if you encounter a bee swarm:

- **Do not run and jump into a body of water.** The bees will wait for you to come up for air, and then they will sting all the parts of you that are sticking out of the water (like your head).

- **Don't swat at the bees or flap your arms or wave wildly.** The bees will just get mad and sting you.

How do I get out of a forest fire?

If you find yourself in the middle of a forest fire, it's not exactly your lucky day: fire can move at up to 14 mph without getting tired, and unless you're an Olympic marathoner, you probably can't run that fast for very long. Your best bet is to find a natural firebreak—a place where the fire will not have any fuel to burn, such as a wide creek, a river, a lake, a road, or even a rocky canyon.

If you see a fire, figure out where you are on a map and locate a firebreak to put between you and the fire (keep in mind you also don't know how the fire will spread or in which direction or directions). But if you can very quickly put a nearby road or creek between you and the fire, your bad luck might change to good. If your nearest best bet for a firebreak is a pond or lake, get to it, and if the fire gets close, swim out into the water, away from the shore.

How do I navigate by the stars?

Although humans have navigated by stars for thousands of years, it's a bit of a lost art nowadays since we've developed so many other ways to navigate (thanks, science!). But should all those other methods fail, and you find yourself walking around at night, you might need to figure out where you are. You

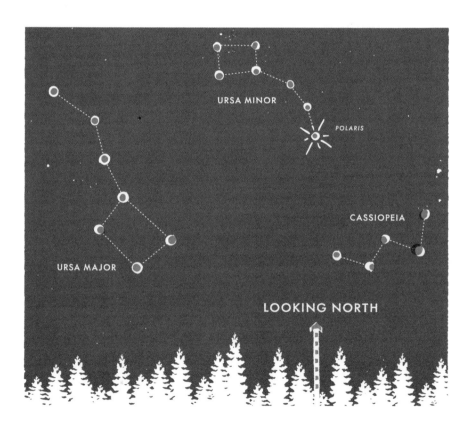

may not be able to do extensive navigation by stars, but if you know a few constellations you can at least get a bearing and find north, and using north, find east, west, and south. Identify Cassiopeia (see page 250) and the Big Dipper. Between them should be the Little Dipper/Ursa Minor. The very tip of the handle of Ursa Major is Polaris, the North Star, which is always over the North Pole, and if you face Polaris, you're facing north. And if you're facing north, east is to your right, and west is to your left.

What should I carry in a survival kit?

There's no magic ingredient list for a survival kit—although on the Internet you can choose from hundreds of different survival kits that might make you believe you can live through anything. If you're on a wilderness trip, your survival kit is whatever you have in your backpack, in your head, and as your means of communicating with the outside world. You should be carrying the Ten Essentials (see page 82) and a small first aid kit (see page 92) and should have (1) a way of communicating with someone who can initiate a rescue (such as a personal locator beacon, satellite phone, or cell phone—which will work only if you have reception), or (2) a plan worked out with someone who knows where you are and will call the authorities if you do not report back within a certain time frame (see page 47). But for long-term survival, your primary concerns are staying warm at night and finding drinking water, so two things you should always carry, even if you're just going on a day hike, are water purification tables and an emergency blanket. One small jar of iodine tablets weighs 3 ounces and contains enough iodine to purify 6 gallons of water, which is enough for up to six days. An emergency blanket weighs another 3 ounces and will give you an emergency shelter to keep you alive for several nights. Note that we're talking here about keeping you alive, not sleeping comfortably. The total cost of both those items is about eleven dollars, so for 6 ounces and eleven dollars you've got a pretty good insurance policy. Yes, you might get hungry, but unless you're a very, very thin person, you will be able to survive a couple of weeks without eating while you're waiting for a rescue.

What should I carry for emergency gear repairs?

You don't need to carry an entire hardware store of repair supplies in your backpack—have a little faith in your innate ability to MacGyver yourself a solution out of whatever materials you have and can find out there. But these few basic items can get you through a jam.

- **A travel sewing kit:** Or a needle and a small spool of thread. You're not going to hem a pair of pants or take in a shirt out on the trail, but if you rip a hole in a backpack or jacket, a few yards of thread and a needle will be a lifesaver, even if your patch job reflects that you haven't sewn anything since your tenth-grade home economics class.

- **Multitool:** Your tool should at the very least contain a knife blade and pliers (see page 33).

- **Krazy Glue:** It's light, small, and surprisingly strong. Krazy Glue can fix all kinds of things, including lacerations in your skin. Just make sure the tube you keep in your repair kit doesn't dry out over time.

- **Duct tape:** Obviously you need to carry duct tape, but not an entire roll. Tear off several 3-foot sections and roll them into small spools, and that should be enough to fix almost anything, including small tears in your sleeping bag or your down jacket.

- **Baling wire:** A 12-foot roll of baling wire (again, don't take a whole spool of it, but cut some off and make a small roll of it for your repair kit) can be used to repair or jury-rig broken snowshoes, backpacks, crampons, and all kinds of other things.

- **Seam Grip and tent patches:** If you rip your tent fly or floor, a tube of Seam Grip and a few patches are the best fix you can get in the field. They also work well if you happen to punch a hole in your rain jacket.

- **Sleeping pad repair kit:** Carry the kit made by the manufacturer of your sleeping pad (see page 223).

- **Safety pins and nylon cord:** These will fix almost anything that duct tape can't fix (yes, duct tape is the wrong tool for certain situations).

What is the one thing you should always do before hiking by yourself?

Aron Ralston famously amputated his own arm after it became pinned beneath a boulder in a Utah canyon in 2003. Plenty of people have opinions on what he did wrong, but most everyone can agree that his situation could have been quite different if he had just done one thing: let someone know where he was going. Ralston's biggest mistake was that no one knew where he was, and only after some very skilled and determined detective work by his mother and law enforcement agencies was he found—after he had already cut off his arm and started to walk out. If you leave on a hike or backcountry trip, always let at least one person know where you'll be— including the trailhead location, your license plate number, your plan, and when you expect to come home. If you're supposed to return home by 5 p.m. on a Tuesday and you don't, your friend can alert the authorities and organize a search. That way, instead of spending five days and cold nights outside by yourself with a broken ankle, hopefully you can limit it to only one or two days before someone finds you.

What should I do if I see a bear?

Seeing a bear in the wild is a lucky thing—provided you're far away from it (300 feet or more is ideal). If you're nearby and the bear has not seen you, or isn't paying attention to you, calmly and quietly move away. Scan the area— you do not want to place yourself between a grizzly sow and her cubs. Don't run, and keep your eyes on the bear, watching to see if it notices you and/or starts to charge you, but don't make eye contact with the bear. Do you have bear spray in your backpack? Bear spray is a form of pepper spray. It comes in a small container that you can attach to your pack so that when you need it, you can have it ready to fire. If the bear notices you, stand your ground. Don't make any sudden moves, don't run, and don't climb a tree (the bear is a better climber than you). Avoid making eye contact with the bear, and speak to it in a submissive tone, saying, "Whoa, bear. Whoa, bear." Back away slowly while saying this. The bear can do several things at this point: ignore you (great!), stand up and get a better look at you, make any number of signs that it might charge you—or just charge you with no warning. A bear that's making eye contact with you with its ears back, or a bear that is popping its jaw, may charge you. Sometimes bears will "bluff charge," getting close and then peeling off course at the last second—but don't count on this, because a bear can move up to 35 mph and that doesn't give you much time

to escape. If the bear gets close, fire your bear spray at it, aiming at its face, or creating a cloud it has to run through. That should repel and occupy the bear long enough for you to walk away. If the spray doesn't work, fall to the ground and get into a ball, protecting your head and neck with your arms. If the bear starts to swat at you and you can't protect your head and neck, it's time to fight.

How do I fight off a bear?

It pretty much goes without saying that you should never try to fight a bear (because the odds you'll win are very slim). But if a bear starts getting physical with you, you really don't have a choice except to put up a fight. Well, you have a choice between giving up and fighting, but let's assume you want to put up a fight. Hit, kick, punch, gouge at its eyeballs, and generally concentrate your efforts around the bear's face, nose, and eyes. You have about zero chance of knocking the bear out à la Muhammad Ali or Mike Tyson, so instead try to be enough of a hassle that the bear will just leave you alone because you're not worth its time. A few people have survived bear attacks by throwing themselves off cliffs or into deep ravines where the bear couldn't climb down and reach them (obviously, a last resort), and it's been documented that at least one person has shoved his arm down a bear's throat and made the bear gag. If you are unlucky enough to have a bear pick a fight with you, fighting back might work and it might not, but it's really your only chance for survival.

Should I carry a gun in the backcountry?

The subject of guns in the backcountry is, of course, a hot debate topic. If you're hunting, obviously you're probably carrying a gun or guns. If you're not hunting, however, it's your call. If you feel you need a gun to protect yourself from bears, consider that it takes a pretty large-caliber bullet to penetrate a bear's muscle and fat and actually reach a vital organ—so your 9mm pistol won't be much protection from bears. Studies have shown that bear spray is more effective than a gun in a situation where a bear charges. In the heat of the moment, you might not be able to hit a target moving at 30 mph with a rifle shot, but you can probably spray a cloud of bear spray that will deter the bear. If you are wondering about carrying a gun for something other than wildlife (i.e., to protect yourself from other humans), it's up to you, but crime in the back-country is rare and the majority of hikers and backpackers don't carry firearms.

Are moose dangerous?

Author Bill Bryson wrote in his famous book *A Walk in the Woods*, "Hunters will tell you that a moose is a wily and ferocious forest creature. Nonsense. A moose is a cow drawn by a three-year-old." Yes, moose are goofy-looking animals, but unfortunately they're also dangerous. They kill more people annually in the United States than bears do. Moose are not aggressive animals, but they will attack if they're threatened, surprised, or disturbed—so if you see one in the wild, don't try to walk over to it and take a selfie. Mothers will protect their young calves from threats, so if you see a cute little moose (which will still be a large animal), be wary of your position relative to it and its mother. If you make one mad, it will charge, and it's not a good thing to have one intent on running you over—they weigh 1,500 pounds and can run up to 35 mph. If you see a moose while you're on the trail, give it a wide berth. If it's standing in the middle of the trail, definitely go out of your way to go around it.

Should I worry about mountain lions?

Human encounters with mountain lions are very rare, and human sightings of mountain lions are rare too—but that doesn't mean a mountain lion hasn't seen *you* (even though they do have fairly bad vision). It's a good idea to know if the area you're venturing into is mountain lion country, and if it is, hike with a friend and wear bright colors. Mountain lions' prey are earth-toned animals like deer, and if you're wearing a bright shirt or jacket, this will clue the lion in to the fact you're not a deer. If you're hiking with a dog, keep it on a leash and close to you. If you do see a mountain lion, do not make one feel cornered. Look as big as you can and back away. If the lion charges you, it will be very fast—lions can accelerate up to 45 mph very quickly. If the lion attacks, fight back—claw, punch, kick, whatever you can do. Again, human–mountain lion encounters are rare, so in general don't worry about them, but be aware that you're on their turf.

3 INCHES

How do I avoid scorpion bites?

Here's the good news about scorpions: they aren't out to get you. Unlike mosquitoes, which love to land on your skin and bite it (and usually hang out with dozens of friends intent on doing the same thing), scorpions are content minding their own business. But if you mess with a scorpion, it will sting you, and it will be one of the most painful stings you ever experience. Yes, bee stings hurt, but they're nothing compared to scorpion stings, which can cause tingling and/or burning, numbness, difficulty swallowing, difficulty breathing, blurry vision, seizures, and, in rare cases, pancreatitis, which has its own set of very uncomfortable symptoms.

If you're camping or hiking in the desert, don't walk around with bare feet, because a scorpion chilling under the sand will not hesitate to whip its tail around and sting you if you step on it. Zip your tent closed every time you go in and out of it, and if you keep your shoes outside your tent, take a good look inside before putting your feet in them (yes, even in the middle of the night when you get up to go pee)—a curious scorpion may have crawled into the toe of your shoe, and surprising it with your toes will lead to, again, a painful sting. If you get stung by a scorpion, it will hurt, but it will not kill you. Clean the wound, and do not take ibuprofen or aspirin for the pain, as they can make the venom spread more quickly; instead take acetaminophen. Apply a cold compress (but not ice) at the area of the bite.

How do I avoid rattlesnake bites?

Here's a fun fact for you: 40 percent of rattlesnake bites happen to people who are playing with or handling snakes, and 40 percent of people bitten by rattlesnakes have a blood alcohol content of .10 or higher. Rattlesnake bites are rare, and in the United States they somehow happen almost exclusively to males. One study divided rattlesnake bites into categories of "legitimate" and "illegitimate," the latter being bites that happened to people who did not attempt to move away from the rattlesnake after they recognized it was a rattlesnake. Only 43.4 percent of the rattlesnake bites in the study were deemed "legitimate." So for the most part, leave rattlesnakes alone and you'll be fine. However, you can obviously accidentally encounter a rattlesnake on the trail. To protect yourself, remember that spring and summer are the prime seasons for rattlesnake activity. Wear ankle-height boots, and know if the area you're hiking in has seen rattlesnake activity lately. Avoid brushy trails or trails where foliage covers the trail in spots and you can't see your feet, and if you do hike brushy trails, carry trekking poles to help you push aside plants to see the trail. If you encounter a rattlesnake, walk away from it or give it a wide berth as you pass. If you're already too close, freeze and move back slowly. If the snake feels threatened, it may coil up, then shake its rattle, and as a last defensive move to strike you. If you're carrying trekking poles, hold a pole between you and the snake, and the snake may go for the pole instead of you. If you don't see a snake but hear a rattle, make sure you know where the rattling sound is coming from before you dart away—or you may step right on the snake.

How do I deal with a snakebite?

If you are bitten by a snake, the first thing you will want to do is decide if there's a chance the snake could be venomous. Actually, the first thing you will want to do is yell something like "ouch," possibly in addition to a string of curse words. That's natural. So then, the second thing you'll want to do is try to determine if the snake is venomous. If you have no idea or aren't sure, err on the side of caution and call 911 or initiate a rescue. Lie down with the snakebite area below your heart, and move as little as possible to keep the venom localized. Do not (as you may have seen on TV) try to suck the venom out of the wound or tie off the bitten appendage with a tourniquet. If a snake is venomous, you will need to get antivenom at a hospital—there is no other effective treatment (including those snakebite kits you can buy, which have been proven to do more harm than good).

If you are absolutely sure the snake is not venomous, then you just have a puncture wound—which is still painful and needs to be dealt with, but is much less terrifying. Clean and bandage the wound, and monitor it for bleeding and pain.

How do I know if a snake is dangerous?

There are four types of venomous snakes in North America, and many more throughout the world, each with different characteristics separating them from nonvenomous snakes. If you aren't that interested in herpetology or memorizing the characteristics of venomous snakes, here's a good rule of thumb to protect you from getting bitten by one: treat all snakes as if they're venomous. If you're tempted to pick up a snake and play with it, ask yourself a couple of questions first.

1. Why am I messing with this snake that's minding its own business and not messing with me?

2. What is the worst-case scenario possible if I pick up this snake?

The answer to Question #2 is the snake bites you and it turns out to be venomous, and you're in a heap of trouble. So it's not worth it; leave the snake alone.

How do I know if I'm getting frostbite?

The first sign of trouble is the first stage of frostbite, called frostnip: a part of your body (usually extremities like fingers, toes, or the end of your nose) gets cold and tingly and/or numb and turns red. If you feel these symptoms, you may have frostnip, which is serious but won't leave permanent damage. Frostnip can turn into frostbite if you don't rewarm the skin.

Depending on where the skin is, you can rewarm it using other body parts—if your fingers have frostnip, you can put them in your armpits inside your clothing. If your feet have frostnip, a common rewarming method is to put them on your tentmate's stomach inside their clothes. If you don't/ can't rewarm the skin, it will next turn white or very pale and possibly begin to feel warm again. This is bad news. When deep frostbite, the next stage, sets in, it means the frostbite has gone past the epidermis into the deeper layers of your skin—you will stop feeling pain and cold in the frostbitten area as underlying tissues freeze. If this happens, you should not try to rewarm the skin if you're outside in the backcountry—instead get yourself to a hospital, where there's no chance of the skin refreezing after it thaws. If you experience deep frostbite, expect to lose lots of dead tissue and possibly even appendages.

How do I know if I'm becoming hypothermic?

We think of hypothermia as something expected in very cold temperatures, but it's actually more common at milder air temperatures combined with wet weather. Hypothermia starts when your body's core temperature drops to 95°F, and the first thing you'll probably notice is shivering—not like the kind of shivering you have when you sit down on cold bleachers at a football game and decide you could use a cup of hot chocolate, but intense, wow-I-can't-stop-shivering shivering. You might have a difficult time doing tasks with your hands (like putting on gloves or clipping a buckle), or you'll stumble when you're walking. This is mild hypothermia. If you don't warm up after mild hypothermia and it progresses into moderate hypothermia (a core body temperature of 89 to 82°F) or severe hypothermia (below 82°F), you'll stop shivering and basically start acting very similarly to someone who is drunk: you are confused, slur your speech, have a hard time remembering things, and may pass out. Your breathing may become shallow and your pulse may become faint.

To treat hypothermia, as soon as possible (obviously preferably before it escalates to moderate or severe hypothermia), remove wet clothing; get out of the wind; cover up with any available warm clothing, sleeping bags, and other layers; and drink fluids—warm liquids are preferred, but the priority is on drinking any liquids to help rehydrate the body.

What should I do if I'm caught in a thunderstorm?

If you're caught outside in a thunderstorm, your main objective is to find natural shelter from lightning: if you're on a ridge or exposed summit, make your way to lower ground as fast as you can (but carefully). Find a low spot in a valley, or find a cluster of trees to take shelter under (but don't ever take shelter under a single tree standing by itself). Get away from water sources like lakes, ponds, and creeks—and if you're swimming in water, get out of the water immediately. Don't try to set up a tent—although it will give you shelter from the rain, the poles can conduct electricity and make you a target for lightning. If you're carrying any metal objects that might attract lightning, take them off; this includes trekking poles, ice axes, tent poles, and crampons. Minimize your contact with the ground: squat on a foam pad or sit on your backpack with your knees pulled up to your chest and your feet resting on the pack. This will insulate you from ground currents caused by lightning hitting the surface or a nearby tree. Wait out the storm before moving on.

How do I know if a snow slope might avalanche?

Avalanches, like weather, are the subject of books, classes, studies, and frequent monitoring in mountainous regions. There are no simple rules that can tell you which slope might slide and which slope won't slide, but a few things can help you understand avalanches and mitigate your risk.

- Most avalanches occur on slopes steeper than 30 degrees—and of course, slopes steeper than 30 degrees are what we like to ski and snowboard.

- If you're traveling on a slope measuring 30 degrees or less, a steeper slope above can still avalanche and hit you.

- Avalanche risk is greatest within the twenty-four hours after a storm drops twelve or more inches of snow.

- In nine out of ten avalanche accidents involving humans, the victim or someone in the victim's party unintentionally set off the slide.

- Just because one person, or twenty people, walked or skied across a slope and it didn't avalanche doesn't mean it won't avalanche when you walk or ski across it. Generally, staying on marked ski runs and on popular snowshoe trails will keep you out of harm's way.

How do I ford a river safely?

If you're on a hike and there's a spot where you have to cross a river or creek without a bridge, it might be the most dangerous part of your trip. A river that looks calm from the bank can surprise you with the amount of force it pushes against your legs once you're in the middle of it, so don't underestimate the power of rushing water. Here are a few tips for safe passage.

- If you're wearing a backpack, unbuckle the waist belt and sternum strap. If you fall in while crossing, ditch your pack and worry about it later. Dozens of hikers have drowned when a backpack took on water and dragged them under the current.

- Don't try to cross water more than knee-deep.

- Cross at the widest part of the river—the current is stronger where the river has to funnel through narrow passages.

- Look upstream but cross at an angle that points slightly downstream.

- Use trekking poles for balance, pushing their tips under the water down into the riverbed.

- Move slowly. Don't be in a hurry, and move your legs with purpose—stay in balance first and make progress second.

How do I avoid being caught in a flash flood?

In the desert, especially in the American Southwest, flash floods occur when rain falls and funnels into the tributaries of a canyon, growing and building until it pulses through a narrow passage in a 5-, 6- or even 20-foot-tall wave of water, dirt, and debris with massive force, obliterating anything in its way (except the canyon walls, usually). If you're standing in a narrow canyon or slot canyon and it's raining 15 miles away, a wall of water can build in a matter of minutes, pushing rocks, trees, and logs with it—you might see a 3-inch-deep stream of water come from up canyon and two minutes later it could be a wave 6 feet high that rips you off your feet and drags you down the canyon. Flash floods are serious and scary and can kill you. To stay safe, know the weather forecast where you're going, especially during the desert monsoon season of May through October. If there's a chance of rain in the forecast, don't venture into narrow canyons. If you're camping in a canyon, camp on high ground so you're not surprised in the night by a flash flood. If you can see thunderhead clouds in your area when you start the hike, change your plans—once you're in a canyon, it may be hard to see weather forming, and as previously stated, you may not even see the storm 15 miles away that causes the flash flood in your canyon.

How do I know if I'm dehydrated?

If you're dizzy or lightheaded when on a trail, it might be because you're get-ting seriously dehydrated. Try to remember the last time you stopped for a bathroom break, and if it's been hours and you're feeling slightly lightheaded, you're probably dehydrated, so drink some fluids. As you hike, when you stop to pee, always check the color of your urine—if it's yellow, you're starting to get dehydrated. If you're drinking enough fluids your urine should be clear or the color of lemonade. If it's not, drink more water. Remember that your body can process only a maximum of 32 ounces of water per hour, so don't chug a liter and a half of water if you notice your urine is yellow—sip it gradually for a few minutes.

If you know you're going to be hiking or spending all day being active, it might be a good idea to skip that second cup of coffee in the morning—coffee is a diuretic and dehydrates you, so if you drink a lot of coffee, you're setting yourself back a step before you've even left the house. The same is the case if you decide to drink five or six beers the night before and you go to bed dehydrated, then wake up thirsty and peeing dark yellow. You'll have a tough time hydrating yourself, especially if you drink a couple cups of coffee to get things going in the morning too.

What do I do if I run out of water in the backcountry?

Always keep an eye on the amount of water you have in your bottles and how much water you're drinking compared to how much terrain you have to cover until your next water source (or, if you're day-hiking, until you get back to the car). If you're starting to run low on water and you still have a few miles to hike until you get back to the trailhead, don't panic—remember, you don't need to be sipping water right up until the moment you step off the trail and into the parking lot. Your body will be just fine walking a couple of miles without water (especially if you have some extra water in the car or can drive a few minutes to a place where you can get some water). It's also a good idea to keep a small supply of iodine tablets in your backpack, just in case you do run out of water—you can refill your bottles in a stream or lake and purify them with your iodine tabs so you'll have drinkable water in half an hour.
If you do run out of water far in the backcountry and have no purification options available, it's better to keep hydrated by drinking untreated water than it is to go without water because you're worried about catching something from untreated water. Giardia, for example, one of the more common parasites people pick up from drinking untreated water in the backcountry, usually takes weeks to form in your gut—whereas dehydration can kill you in a matter of days. You need to keep moving to get home, so to stay hydrated, drink the untreated water, and worry about the side effects later.

Can I get water by cutting open a cactus or digging in sand?

Survivalist Bear Grylls famously has squeezed elephant dung to get water out of it, which is a neat trick but may not be that sustainable if you're really thirsty.

Plus, the water tastes like crap, or so we've heard. The techniques of digging in sand for water and cutting open a cactus are fairly dubious in emergency situations. If you're already running low on fluids, digging in sand is unlikely to yield enough water to make it worth your effort, and cutting open a cactus is the same—also, if you cut open a cactus for its water, it's likely to be in an acidic or bitter state that might not agree with your stomach, causing further dehydration. Plus, cutting open a cactus isn't the easiest thing in the world, and you're pretty likely to get some spines stuck in your hands—talk about more trouble than it's worth. For better options, see page 239.

Can I drink my own urine in an emergency situation?

This is a free country. You can drink your own urine in any situation, emergency or not. But for survival purposes? It's not very effective. If you run out of water, you can drink your urine once, maybe twice, but remember, your body peed that urine out the first time because it is a waste product, and now you're forcing your body to deal with those waste products again, and it has to work harder each time as your urine becomes darker and darker—and more disgusting to drink. That said, if you're stumbling back to the trailhead, haven't had water in hours, and can't find a nearby creek or pond, a little dose of urine might get you those last few miles back to your car—if you can actually pee enough to drink. Bon appétit.

Should I eat snow if I'm thirsty?

You already know not to eat yellow snow. But it's also true that you shouldn't eat snow of any color—white or otherwise—to try to rehydrate yourself. Although eating snow doesn't directly dehydrate you, your body has to use a lot of energy to melt it and warm it to a temperature where it can use it. If you're hiking or camping in cold temperatures, eating snow can make your body hypothermic, which will dehydrate you further. So eating snow, while something you might have done as a little kid and fondly remember as a sort of flavorless sno-cone, isn't a good policy in the wintertime for survival pur-poses. In an emergency, you can melt snow in a pot on a backpacking stove, heat it until boiling (to purify it), and then drink it.

Should I carry a personal locator beacon?

If you are going somewhere where cell phones don't work, and you're unlikely to encounter other people, and you'll be far from the nearest road or town, a personal locator beacon is a good idea—especially if you're venturing into the wilderness by yourself. Even if you're going on a trip with another person, consider how far you or your partner would have to go to get help in case of a broken bone or other injury or medical emergency. If you're hiking 20 miles into the wilderness from a trailhead that's a two-hour drive from the nearest town or cell phone service, and you break your ankle on a rock, your friend will have to hike, at best, six or seven hours and drive two hours just to get help—and then the help has to come find and rescue you. With a personal locator beacon, you can push a button and start the rescue process as soon as you break your ankle. Obviously personal locator beacons should be used only for real emergencies and you should never call for a rescue if you're tired, or if you run out of the snack mix you like so much, or if you're not really having fun anymore. But a beacon can save your life in an emergency.
Note: A personal locator beacon is not the same thing as an avalanche beacon. If you're spending time in avalanche terrain, you'll need an avalanche beacon. A personal locator beacon enables emergency rescue crews to find you using a locator signal. An avalanche beacon sends a signal that can be picked up only by someone nearby who has an avalanche beacon too—that is, the friends you're skiing or snowshoeing with.

How do I get rescued?

Before you leave the trailhead, riverbank, or lakeshore, know your options. If you'll have cell phone reception where you're going, that's your best bet.

If you won't have cell phone coverage, carry a personal locator beacon (see opposite) or satellite phone and know how to use it. If you're going some-place where a cell phone won't work and you won't be carrying a personal locator beacon or satellite phone, let someone know what your plans are before you leave (see page 47).

When something happens that requires a rescue, consider alternatives before you take action (because even if you have a cell phone in your hand, a rescue will take a long time and will mobilize ten or more people, most of whom are volunteering for the job out of the goodness of their hearts). For example, can you walk out on that sprained ankle, even if it's painful? Are you really starving to death or dying of thirst? (see page 64).

If rescue is your only option, figure out your location as accurately as you can. GPS coordinates are great, but if you don't have a GPS, knowing how far you are along a trail (in miles or in hours of hiking) or how close you are to a certain lake can help a rescue go much more quickly. Call 911 using your cell phone or satellite phone, or activate your emergency locator beacon. If you can't make a phone call, send a text message with as many details as possible to an emergency contact and ask them to call 911.

Once you've called or signaled for a rescue, try to get to an open area and spread out bright clothing or your tent, and if it's safe to do so, build a fire. These things can all help a rescue helicopter or passing aircraft spot you. If you do see a helicopter and can stand up, hold both arms over your head so your body forms a Y—this means "Yes, I need a rescue"; one arm over your head means "No, I don't need a rescue."

How do I survive an unplanned night outside?

For one reason or another—you're lost, the climb or hike took way longer than you thought, you forgot to bring your headlamp, you took a wrong turn—it's getting dark and you have the sinking feeling you're going to have to stay out in the backcountry for the night. It's not the end of the world, and it's happened to many people who came out of the situation with no more than a good story to tell. There's one thing that can make your unplanned night out much more comfortable, and that's an emergency blanket—a four-dollar, 3-ounce sheet that takes up almost no space in your backpack but will take up a huge space in your heart if you ever have to use it.

So if it's getting dark and there's no way you're making it back home tonight, first thing, stay calm. Second thing: stay put. If you got lost in the dimming light of dusk, you're not going to do yourself any favors by wandering around in the dark. Then get out of the wind, find a comfortable spot, and figure out how you're going to spend the hours before the sun comes back up. If it's raining or going to rain, try to find some shelter a rock outcropping doesn't have to be deep to help shield you from the rain, and if you can't find one, look for a partially downed tree you can lean some branches against and hide under. Is there a spot where you can build a small fire? If so, do it. If you don't have an emergency blanket with you, a fire is your best hope to stay warm through the night. If it's winter, you'll want to dig a snow cave (see page 307). Once you're set up for the night, have some food and water—your body has more of a need for the calories in your remaining food during a cold night than it will in the morning.

Should I carry my wallet in the backcountry?

You're probably not going to need to carry a credit card if you're going into the backcountry, but if you're worried about your car being broken into at the trailhead, it's not a bad idea to keep your wallet in your backpack. If you're the type of person who has a 2-inch-thick George Costanza wallet, thin it out before you leave the house and bring just your driver's license, credit card, and some cash, so you're not hauling an extra 6 ounces the entire time you're on the trail. Or just clean out your wallet, for heaven's sake.

Even if you're not worried about your car being broken into at the trailhead, it's good to keep your driver's license or ID and your health insurance card in your pocket or in your backpack as you hike. If you for some reason become unconscious (from a fall, heart attack, etc.) and passing hikers find you, they'll be able to identify you when emergency personnel arrive to take you to a hospital.

What does poison ivy look like?

The old saying "Leaves of three, let it be" has helped many hikers avoid the itchy burning of a poison ivy skin reaction, and it's still a good rule to remember: poison ivy plants are green and have leaves that grow in clusters of three (not a three-tipped leaf). Poison ivy leaves are pointed at their tips. Poison oak grows on the Pacific and Atlantic coasts in North America, and also can be identified by its three-leaved leaflets,  which, unlike poison ivy, have scalloped edges. Poison sumac grows in very wet soils, and can be identified by its compound leaves that have seven to thirteen leaflets, each of which grow from red veins.

If you are exposed to poison ivy or think you might have been, wash the areas of your skin with liquid dishwashing detergent; apply it directly to your skin to remove the oils from the poison ivy plant and then rinse it off. Wash your hands first before rubbing them onto other areas of your body, because you can easily spread the poison ivy oil from your hands to other skin areas. If your clothes brushed poison ivy plants, wash them as soon as you can, and if you are in a situation where you can't wash them, put them in a plastic bag before storing them with other clothes.

If needed, apply poison ivy treatments such as hydrocortisone creams or calamine lotion to your skin. If the itching is persistent, over-the-counter antihistamines like Benadryl can help ease your discomfort.

How do I remove cactus spines?

Finding cactus spines in your skin is about as fun as finding a wood splinter in your skin— they're painful and seem to snag on everything. You'll want to remove cactus spines as soon as possible. If you have a piece of cactus, like a bulb of cholla, stuck to your skin, don't grab it with your hand to pull it away—have a friend grab two sticks to pull it off for you. And then it's time to remove the

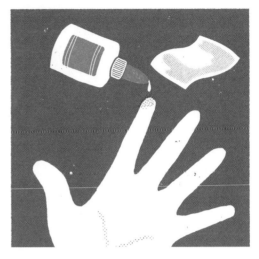

spines. Removal depends on the size of the cactus spine (or spines) embedded in your skin. You'll want to pull out very large spines with pliers; for thinner spines, tweezers are more effective. For glochids, the tiny spines that look like small fine hairs, you'll need a piece of gauze and a tube of white glue (the kind you used in elementary school). Spread a layer of the glue all over the affected area, and gently smooth the sheet of gauze over it. Wait for the glue to dry (ten to fifteen minutes), and peel the sheet of gauze and the glue off slowly. The glochids should come out with the glue/gauze. If there are still some remaining, pull them out with tweezers, or do a second glue/gauze application.

If I get lost for several days, what's more important, finding food or water?

The conventional wisdom is that you can live for three weeks without food but only three days without water (and of course every situation will be different and may not be exactly three weeks/three days; see page 40). Unless you have spectacularly low body fat (i.e., you can see your oblique muscles), your body will be able to work off its fat stores (and in extreme conditions your muscles) for a long time—but it won't be able to do so without water. Food, in the places most people go backpacking and climbing, will probably take more effort to find than it's worth, calorie-wise—unless you're an expert at hunting and skinning animals with a pocketknife or have a gift for foraging and mushroom hunting. Find water first, and if you can purify it, do so. If you can't purify it, worry about potential parasites later, and get hydrated now.

What is snow blindness?

Snow blindness is temporary blindness caused by overexposure to UV rays from the sun. It's actually—as painful as this sounds—a sunburned cornea. High-altitude mountaineers and skiers are at risk for snow blindness, especially when they spend long periods of time crossing snowfields or glaciers. The sunlight coming from above reflects off the snow and bounces upward, doubly exposing the eyes to the UV rays. Judicious use of glacier glasses, specially darkened sunglasses with full eye coverage, is the best defense against snow blindness. If you're spending a lot of time on snow or glaciers, it's best to use a pair of glacier glasses and carry a pair of regular sunglasses or ski goggles as a backup just in case you lose your glacier glasses.

What's windburn?

In most cases, windburn will feel just like sunburn, and it can even look like it. You'll have red dry skin that hurts when you wrinkle or scratch it. Windburn can happen anytime your skin is exposed to cold, dry winds for a long period of time. The good news is, windburn doesn't usually last as long as a sunburn—your skin will recover faster. To prevent it, wear sunscreen on exposed skin (even if it isn't sunny), and use lip balm to protect your lips and around your nostrils. If you're out all day in the wind, reapply sunscreen often, just as you would if you were outside in the sun for several hours. If you do get windburn, apply lotion to the affected area when you get home. In extreme cases, lotion or gel containing aloe can help soothe painful areas.

How do I avoid ticks?

Ticks are about as fun to find as parking tickets, and like parking tickets they will often show up even after you think you've done everything right. Ticks can drop off tree branches onto you or hop onto your clothes or skin as you pass through tall brush or grasses on a slightly overgrown trail. If you're venturing into an area that has ticks, wear a hat (a brimmed hat is best), pants, and a long-sleeve shirt. Spray your skin with an insect repellent with DEET, and spray your clothing and shoes with a repellent containing permethrin. After your time outdoors, do a thorough tick check of your entire body—yes, everywhere, including your groin and armpits. Ticks can imperceptibly creep around under your clothes for minutes or hours before burrowing into (or more ideally, falling off) your skin. A mirror or cell phone camera can help with your post-hike inspection. Have a friend thoroughly check your hair and scalp.

What do I do if I find an embedded tick in my skin?

You may have heard of tick removal strategies such as using a match or a lighter to get a tick to back out of your skin, or painting a tick with Vaseline or nail polish to suffocate it, or any number of things that just annoy the tick and force it to dig itself deeper in. If you find a tick that's burrowed its way into your skin, get tweezers and grab the tick as close to your skin as possible, and pull with  even pressure straight out (lengthwise along the tick's body, or from the mouth toward its rear end). Don't pull with jerky motions—it shouldn't be that hard to remove, and if you yank it you could break off its mouth parts in your skin. If you do accidentally leave its mouth parts in your skin, do your best to get them out with tweezers. Swab the area with rubbing alcohol or soap and water, and place the tick in a plastic bag or other sealed container in the trash (don't crush it with your bare fingers).

Is it possible to drink too much water?

It is possible to drink too much water and cause hyponatremia—a condition in which the level of sodium in the blood is too low, causing cells to swell. It can be dangerous and has even been fatal in some cases. Exercise-associated hyponatremia happens when athletes drink too much water over a long period of time—for example, a long day of hiking in the Grand Canyon—and the body can't keep up and is unable to get rid of the excess water through sweating and urination. Symptoms include headaches, nausea, vomiting, and confusion. Hyponatremia is rare, but it can happen. To prevent it, drink if you're thirsty, drink more at high altitudes, and if you're sweating a lot (on a hot day in the desert, for example), consider adding electrolyte drink mix to one of your water bottles—this will supply your body with enough electrolytes to stay in balance as opposed to flushing them out by drinking too much plain water.

How do I know when to bail?

Although it's disappointing to abort a backpacking or climbing trip and retreat to civilization to sulk over a cheeseburger and a beer, it's far better than pushing your luck and never getting to eat a cheeseburger or drink a beer again. All kinds of things happen when you're experiencing the outdoors— bad weather moves in, partners get injured, equipment fails (and sometimes you say it "failed," but the truth is you actually broke it), and people get sick. Sometimes a combination of a bunch of factors adds up to you realizing that continuing the trip won't actually be fun and you have to call it quits. Bailing is okay—it happens to everyone, and the more adventures you go on, the more often you'll have to bail because something wasn't quite right. In all situations, trust your gut, talk to your partners, and make a decision. The trip can always be rescheduled next week or next year; you can come back and try again.

Ten Classic Survival Books Everyone Should Read

1. *Touching the Void*, by Joe Simpson (1988)

2. *Endurance: Shackleton's Incredible Voyage*, by Alfred Lansing (1959)

3. *Adrift: Seventy-Six Days Lost at Sea*, by Steven Callahan (1986)

4. *Alive: The Story of the Andes Survivors*, by Piers Paul Read (1974)

5. *Between a Rock and a Hard Place*, by Aron Ralston (2004)

6. *The Long Walk: The True Story of a Trek to Freedom*, by Slavomir Rawicz (1956)

7. *Minus 148 Degrees: First Winter Ascent of Mount McKinley*, by Art Davidson (1969)

8. *The Worst Journey in the World*, by Apsley Cherry-Garrard (1922)

9. *The Journals of Lewis and Clark*, by Meriwether Lewis (1814)

10. *K2: The Savage Mountain*, by Charley Houston and Robert Bates (1954)

3

IN THE MOUNTAINS

There are myriad reasons to head into the mountains: fresh air, beautiful views, challenging trails, the chance to see wildlife, and the perspective you gain from going to a place that reminds you how small you are in the grand scheme of things. Mountains are awe-inspiring and seemingly endless, they look great in your vacation photos, and they are a lot more accessible than most people think. Sure, you might think a day in the mountains means hanging off a cliff by one hand, skiing down a slope while barely outrunning an avalanche, or spending days hunkered down in a snow cave at 18,000 feet, but the mountains are much friendlier and more accessible than lots of the images we often see of them in the media.

If you have a basic level of fitness—meaning you can walk or jog 3 to 5 miles without stopping (or feeling like you're going to cough up a lung)—exploring mountain terrain may be right for you. This chapter will introduce you to where to go, how to stay safe and mostly comfortable, what to wear, what equipment to take with you, and how to avoid getting lost in the mountains.

How do I read a topographic map?

Map reading is a skill that's often lamented as being a thing of the past. But even with all the new technology we have, you should still have a basic knowledge of how to read topographic maps. A GPS only tells you where you are on a topo map, and sadly, unlike your smartphone, it can't give you directions to the summit or the next alpine lake. Topographic

maps use contour lines to show where terrain goes uphill and downhill, and navigating in the outdoors requires the ability to look at a map and match the formation of contour lines to a geographic feature—for example, mountains don't often display signs telling you which one is which, but with a topographic map you should be able to tell them apart.

Here are a few basic features of topographic maps.

- The path of a contour line shows land of equal elevation—if you were to walk the exact path of a contour line, you would never gain or lose elevation.

- Contour lines that are closer together represent steep grades (if contour lines are very close together, that's a cliff), and contour lines that are farther apart represent flat areas.

- When contour lines form Vs or Us signifying a gully, creek, or couloir, the tip of the V (or U) is pointing uphill, and the V or U opens downhill. When contour lines form Vs or Us signifying a mountain ridge, the V or U points downhill and opens uphill.

- When contour lines form a circle, oval, or ring, this signifies a summit of a mountain. An hourglass-shaped formation of contour lines is a pass or a col, which is a low point between two peaks.

Do I need to carry a map, or can I use a smartphone app?

There are plenty of great apps that will enable you to download topographic maps to your smartphone, as well as navigational apps that use the GPS in your phone. While you may not need a map of a short day-hiking trail just outside the city, a longer trip in unfamiliar terrain is a different story, and it's good to have a paper map along, or a paper map plus your smartphone-based map or navigation program. If you're on a five-day backpacking trip and your phone battery dies, or your phone gets too cold and shuts itself down, or it gets soaked in a rainstorm, or you drop it and crack the screen . . . you get the picture. A paper map is good to have, at the very least to serve as a backup. It can also be nice to look at a map that shows your entire trip in one place, as opposed to scrolling around the digital map on your 2-inch screen.

Can I bring my dog on a hike?

There is no national law or rule that covers dogs on all public lands—there are different rules for different types of land. National parks allow dogs in campgrounds and in parking lots but not on trails. National forests generally allow dogs, state parks usually allow dogs on leashes, and dogs are allowed on most Bureau of Land Management lands. To find out if your dog is welcome on your hike, call the agency that oversees the area you're visiting before you leave home. When you're there, keep in mind that if you do bring your dog and let him or her roam off leash, there are a lot of other animals in the wilderness, and their interactions with Fido might be bad for one or both of them (think: porcupines). And make sure to pick up your dog's poop—it's as unpleasant for people to step in it in the backcountry as it is on a city street.

Why should I try hiking?

Hiking has the lowest barrier to entry of all outdoor sports—all you need to start are a pair of decent walking shoes and a water bottle. Hiking includes trails in length from a few hundred feet to thousands of miles, depending what your objective is. If your objective is to see amazing natural features—mountains, waterfalls, desert towers, deep canyons, alpine lakes—then you should try it. If you can walk a few miles without stopping, and taking the stairs instead of the elevator doesn't make you gasp, you have a good baseline fitness level for hiking. Hikes are generally rated easy, moderate, or difficult, and if you're not sure what level is right for you, start with an easy hike and work your way up—there's no sense in having your first experience feel like an endless death march.

Should I go hiking by myself?

As long as you let someone know your plans (see page 47) and have some common sense, there's no reason you can't go hiking by yourself. Know where you're headed and how to navigate there, be prepared to take care of yourself during inclement weather or in case of a minor injury, take a cell phone and/or emergency locator beacon along with you in case of emergency (depending on how remote your hike is) and bear spray (if applicable), and be aware of the environment—some urban parks are not as safe as others, and if your destination has had recent incidents in which lone hikers have been targeted, take a friend with you. For the most part, there's no reason to be nervous or hesitant to head out by yourself, as long as you give it some thought and planning beforehand.

How do I drive in the mountains?

If you've ever driven up or down a steep mountain road, you might have asked your passenger, "What's that smell?" It's brakes—yours or someone else's. The best thing you can do for your car when driving in mountainous terrain is to know how to use its transmission: on long, steep downhill grades, shift down to a lower gear until you feel the transmission slowing the car down. Then use your brakes appropriately until the grade lessens, and as you come out of the downhill onto flatter terrain, shift back into drive (or the appropriate gear if you have a manual transmission). When you're going uphill, if your engine is losing power while climbing, shift down into a lower gear and make sure your air conditioning is turned off because the A/C sucks power from the engine. When driving on curvy two-lane mountain roads, be mindful if other cars start to line up behind you, and pull off onto the shoulder to let them pass. At high altitudes, keep your eyes out for moisture, black ice, and snow, which will stay on high-altitude roads much longer into the spring and summer and will form much earlier in the fall than at lower elevations. Give yourself plenty of time to get to your destination—25 miles of curvy, switchbacking mountainous roads will take much longer to drive than 25 miles on a wide, straight freeway.

Ten Mountain Terms Defined

1. **Couloir:** A steep gully on a mountain; the term is French in origin but used internationally and is pronounced "*cool-whar.*"

2. **Crag:** An outcrop of rock; commonly used to refer to a rock-climbing area with several climbing routes.

3. **Crevasse:** A fissure splitting a glacier; it can be a few feet deep or hundreds of feet deep and can be hidden by snowfall.

4. **Cornice:** A formation of snow overhanging a ridge or cliff and built up by wind.

5. **Glacier:** A slow-moving but permanent field of ice and snow on a mountain.

6. **Pass:** A low point between two peaks that allows passage.

7. **Saddle:** A flat, broad area between two high points.

8. **Scree:** A loose surface of small rocks on the side of a mountain.

9. **Talus:** An area of large boulders on the side of a mountain or at the base of a cliff.

10. **Treeline:** The elevation above which trees do not grow; it varies widely according to local climate, soil, and latitude.

Should I take my phone when I go hiking?

Opinions on phones in the outdoors vary widely, but there's a big difference between incessantly talking and texting on your phone when you're in a beautiful place and turning that phone to airplane mode and still using it as a camera, navigational device, or music source (preferably with headphones). The point of hiking to many people is to get away from daily connected life, so if your phone gets in the way of your getting away, leave it in the car or just turn it off and throw it in your backpack, because it's still good to have the ability to contact someone in case of emergency. If your hike takes way longer than anticipated, you can potentially call a spouse or friend and prevent him or her from worrying and/or calling the local search-and-rescue outfit to come out and look for you. And of course, in the unfortunate event that you have an accident out on the trail, you can call for help—if you have cell phone reception.

How do I orient myself with a compass?

Finding north with a compass seems fairly straightforward: hold the compass flat in the palm of your hand, parallel to the ground, and turn until the compass needle points north. Navigating, or getting somewhere, is a little more complicated.

- To take a compass bearing with a topographic map, place the compass on the map surface with the compass's orienting arrow (not the needle) lined up with the north-south lines on the map, and turn the baseplate of the compass so the index line is aimed at your objective (for example, a lake or peak). The number on the rotating housing is your compass bearing.

- Navigating with a topographic map is complicated slightly by something called magnetic declination, or the difference between magnetic north and true north—which, believe it or not, are not the same thing in many places. Your compass finds magnetic north, and true north is often a few degrees to the east or west of that. In the western United States, for example, magnetic declination is several degrees: in Denver, Colorado, a compass needle pointing at magnetic north is actually 8 degrees east of true north, so you would adjust your compass bearing accordingly. Don't worry about

memorizing or researching magnetic declination—if you're using a paper map, it will be printed on the map, and if you're using a GPS or GPS app, it will have an option to use true north instead of magnetic north. Be aware, though, that the compass app in most smartphones does not adjust for declination.

What are the rules of hiking etiquette?

Hiking trails, unlike many cities' freeways, lines outside nightclubs, and your last flight when it was time to deplane, tend to draw a fairly courteous crowd. Except on the few extremely crowded trails, hiking traffic generally flows in a civilized manner with two rules.

1. **Always yield the trail to hikers moving uphill**—they're working harder, and momentum is more important to their morale than to the morale of downhill hikers. Of course, if you are the uphill hiker and you'd like to step off for a rest and let some downhill hikers pass, just let them know.

2. **Always let faster hikers pass you.** Just step off to the side for a second and they'll walk by. If you happen to come up on a slower hiker from behind who doesn't hear you and step aside, a simple "excuse me" will alert him or her to your need to pass.

Who has the right of way, hikers, mountain bikers, or horses?

Right-of-way between hikers is pretty simple (see above), but the addition of non-foot-propelled traffic makes it a little confusing: you might see signs that say mountain bikers have to yield to everyone else (hikers and horseback riders), but local practices often differ. Many times hikers will yield the trail to mountain bikers because it's easier for hikers to stop and step to the side than it is for a mountain biker to pull off. It's your call—if a group of five hikers encounters only one mountain biker, for instance, then it makes sense for the single biker to yield the trail. In the case of horseback riders, always step off the trail and give the horse a wide berth to pass—horses generally spook much more easily than mountain bikers. In all cases, use common sense and be nice—there seems to be no hard-and-fast rule about mountain bikers and hikers, so courtesy is the best policy.

Should I say hi to other hikers on the trail?

Most people are in a pretty good mood when they're hiking—even the most strenuous day in the mountains is better than a great day in the office, and people's attitudes generally seem to reflect that. If hiking isn't making you happy, you usually stop doing it. But by and large, people feel good when they're hiking. So it never hurts to be friendly to the other hikers you see on the trail, within reason. Some trails are so busy that saying hi to every single person can feel like trying to say hello to everyone coming in or out of the men's restroom during the seventh-inning stretch at a Major League baseball game—way too many people. If it's not that busy, though, greet people coming the other way with a friendly hello, and if it's a group of two or three people, something like "How are you guys doing today?" works. Smiling and being friendly to other people forces you to adopt a sort of positivity and keeps your own mood light—even if you're suffering on a long, steep trail.

If I'm hiking up a mountain, should I bother asking people coming down how far it is to the top?

If you spend any time hiking on popular mountains, you'll notice no shortage of people asking you, "How much farther is it?" as you're descending and they're climbing up. Most people descending from a summit can't really give a good answer to that question. You can make a somewhat educated guess, but keep in mind you have no idea how fit the uphill hiker is—what takes you twenty minutes might take them forty. In addition, you're descending, which is much faster than going uphill in most situations. So the 300 vertical feet you just skipped down in four minutes might take someone twenty minutes to climb. Any answer you get will be very inexact—it's better to just keep hiking.

How fast should I hike?

The great thing about hiking is that unless you're being chased by a bear or a thunderstorm (which is hopefully never), you can choose your own pace. It's easy to blaze out of the parking lot at a fast pace (and you probably will do just that whether you're consciously trying to or not), but once you realize you'll be hiking for several hours, you'll want to set a more sustainable pace. It's okay to walk at a clip where you're breathing a little harder, but you don't want to be so out of breath that you can't have a conversation with someone. Plus, if you can't sustain that fast pace, you'll have to stop a lot to catch your breath. Imagine you're driving on a street and can choose either to drive 35 mph and come to a complete stop every block or to drive 25 mph and not stop every block. The latter strategy will be much less frustrating and less strenuous in the long run—and of course if you're not rushing you have more time to enjoy the views too.

How often should I take breaks?

Hikes can sometimes feel like taking a long car trip with the family—every five minutes someone has to pee, or someone else is hungry, or another person needs to stop the car for some other reason, and then it takes eight hours to get to Grandma's house instead of five. Obviously hiking is not a race, and you're free to take your time as much or as little as you want to, but ten- or fifteen-minute breaks start to add up if you take enough of them (and you start to run out of snacks, which is a bigger emergency). A good goal is to stop once every hour to take a break, get off your feet, use the bathroom, take in a few calories, and rehydrate before moving on. If you're climbing a peak, you might need to take more frequent breaks as you get into higher elevations, or even just a few minibreaks every fifteen minutes or so.

How do I cross a creek?

Unless you're tackling an off-trail route worthy of a National Geographic Society grant, or a flood has washed out a trail bridge somewhere, you won't actually be "fording" too many rivers on your hikes and backpacking trips (see page 56). You will, however, likely have to cross a few creeks, and of course you'd prefer to not fall in them on your way to the other side, and maybe even to keep your shoes dry. Both of these goals are attainable. The best piece of gear you can have with you during a creek crossing is a trekking pole (better yet, two) or a hiking stick to aid your balance as you step across the creek on rocks. If you don't have one, take a second before you cross to look around the trail for a stick that might help. Trails with any significant traffic have usually been built to cross creeks at sensible points: where the creek narrows, and/or where a handful of rocks forms a decent path across. When you're crossing the creek, try to suss out your path before committing—look for rocks that are close together so you're not taking big, lunging steps between them, and try to step on dry rocks if at all possible. Go slowly, testing each rock just a little bit before committing all your weight, and if you have poles or a walking stick, plunge them into the water next to your path and use them to ease your way across.

If you do slip and your foot goes in the water, it's not the end of the world—get to the other side, take off your shoe or boot, empty out the water, wring out your sock, and move on with your day. The shoes will dry eventually, and unless it's really cold outside you should be fine, albeit with one wet foot.

How do I know where the trail goes?

Quotes about the road less traveled are great for motivational purposes but are not much help for wilderness navigation. You are generally looking for the trail *most* traveled, at least until you have a few hundred hiking miles under your belt. Trails in national parks and state parks are well marked and well signed, but in other areas like national forests they can be less clear, especially if you're on a less popular trail. Above treeline, trails can disappear when going through talus fields. In some areas of the country, blazes painted on trees or rocks are used to show the way, and in others, cairns, or piles of rocks, signify a route where there isn't a trail. If you see a cairn but aren't sure where the next one might be, stand next to the cairn—from that vantage point, you can often just see the next one. Sometimes trails in the woods fork, with no indication of which trail is the correct one. Usually one is more worn than the other one, and the more popular one is the one you want. Sometimes a false trail can be "blocked" with a row of rocks or a few tree branches, signifying that it's not the correct path. This technique can be very subtle and can look like nothing at all until you realize what it is. As you hike more, you'll learn to spot signs of use, faint trails, broken rocks, worn tree roots, and other indications of where a trail goes.

Can I go off trail?

In general, if there's a trail, you should stay on it. Cutting switchbacks to save a little distance isn't good for the scenery (it kills vegetation and makes new unnecessary "social" trails), the plants (in high-altitude areas, five footfalls in a day can kill fragile plants), the trail (it causes erosion, which can wash out existing trails), other hikers (on steep terrain you can dislodge rocks and boulders and accidentally send them crashing down onto people hiking on the trail), or you, in that it typically wastes your energy. That said, you can obviously step off the trail to use the restroom (most people would probably prefer it if you did) or to sit on a log for lunch. Also, above treeline in the mountains and across slickrock in the desert, trails sometimes disappear completely because it's hard to build a trail across a boulder field or cut one into a slab of sandstone. The trail is generally going to be the easiest path to your desired hiking destination, and usually the safest, but use your judgment in your particular situation. If you see a puddle in the middle of the trail, walk through it, not around it—the more people step off to the side, the wider the trail becomes and the puddle will grow.

Do my hiking shoes need to be waterproof?

Waterproof shoes are a wonderful thing for rainy climates, creek crossings, and trails with puddles from rain or snowmelt. Even if it's not actually raining, a trail that's a bit overgrown with brush or grass that has morning dew on it can soak your shoes (and your feet) in a matter of minutes. Shoes that have a breathable waterproof layer can keep your feet dry through almost anything—unless you step in water or snow that goes higher than the shoe goes on your foot or ankle, at which point it will pour into the top of the shoe. For general hiking, waterproof shoes are helpful but not mandatory. For snow climbs or treks that cross a significant amount of snowy terrain, you'll definitely want waterproof shoes: even if you stay mostly on top of the snow when you walk, enough of it will hit the sides and tops of your shoes that it will eventually start to seep in, leaving you with wet feet.

How do I keep hiking boots waterproof?

Your boots are waterproof because of two things: a breathable waterproof membrane inside the boot and a durable water-resistant (DWR) finish on the outside of the upper. Through use the DWR finish may start to wear off, but you can apply a waterproofing product, such as Nikwax, to refresh or reinforce it. To do so, clean the boot's upper as much as you can (if you apply Nikwax to dirt, you'll have waterproof dirt, not waterproof leather), and then get the boot's upper damp with a wet towel—the moisture inside the leather will actually draw the waterproofing product into the material. Use the wet towel and do your best to "push" water into the upper, and then, while the boot upper is still wet, apply the product per the manufacturer's directions. If you decide to do a second application, you should get the boot upper wet again for that application. Let the boots dry naturally (i.e., don't use a hair dryer on them) before you wear your boots hiking again.

What should I take in my backpack?

You can take whatever you want on a hike: portable coffee grinder, paperback books, beer, a hammock, your entire collection of stuffed animals. . . . Your pack might get heavy, but that's up to you. But there's a difference between what you can take and what you should take, and this widely accepted list of the ten essentials is a good base of items to take on most hiking and backpacking trips.

1. **Navigation:** Map, compass, and/or GPS. You don't necessarily need a paper map—a photo of a good map on your phone can work as long as you don't drop or lose your phone or run out of batteries—but obviously a paper map is more fail-safe. Many smartphones also have a compass, but just as with maps, a real compass is a safer bet.

2. **Sun protection:** Sunglasses and sunscreen.

3. **Extra clothing:** Rain jacket plus appropriate insulating layers.

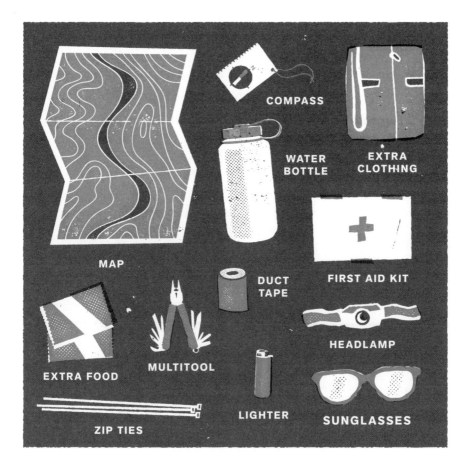

COMPASS

WATER
BOTTLE

EXTRA
CLOTHING

MAP

DUCT
TAPE

FIRST AID KIT

HEADLAMP

EXTRA FOOD

MULTITOOL

LIGHTER

SUNGLASSES

ZIP TIES

4. **Headlamp:** A flashlight works too. Remember to check the batteries before you leave. This might seem like overkill, but carrying a 6-ounce headlamp on every outing is way better than spending an unplanned night outside because you underestimated your time and ran out of daylight.

5. **First aid supplies:** A few basic items can save the day. You don't need to pack a huge first aid kit; after all, you can only use the things you know how to use, so keep that in mind.

6. **Fire:** A lighter or matches.

7. **Repair kit:** A multitool, a small amount of duct tape, baling wire, and a few zip ties.

8. **Food:** Bring enough food for one day, and a little extra in case you end up accidentally spending more time on the trail than you planned.

9. **Water:** Carry enough water for your hike. Consider bringing a small vial of iodine tablets to purify water, just in case you need more.

10. **Emergency shelter:** A space blanket, a sheet of thin plastic designed to reflect heat, can be a lifesaver for unplanned nights out, and it weighs as little as 3 ounces.

How much extra clothing do I need for an overnight backpacking trip?

When you're carrying everything you need in a backpack, the weight adds up—so don't overpack with extra clothes. The fewer redundancies you pack (e.g., try toughing it out with one T-shirt on a three-day trip instead of three T-shirts), the lighter your pack will be. A basic wardrobe for a spring, summer, or fall trip might include this list.

- **Pants**

- **T-shirt or short-sleeved shirt**

- **Socks (wear one pair and pack one extra pair)**

- **Underwear**

- **Light soft-shell jacket**

- **Rain jacket**

- **Beanie (for evenings in camp)**

- **Puffy jacket (for cool evenings and mornings in camp; also acts as a pillow)**

- **Light gloves**

- **Camp shoes (optional; consider lightweight flip-flops, Crocs, or Sanuks)**

Do I really need to wear sunscreen?

Sunburns on spring break are understandable. Sunburns in the mountains are for amateurs and can ruin a trip. If you're hiking, backpacking, or climbing, you're often in locations that can be light on shade (above the treeline or in the desert), exposed to the sun, and at higher altitudes than where you live. Moab, Utah, for instance, isn't known as "the Mile High City," but it's a little under a mile high in elevation, and most of the popular terrain surrounding the town is a mile high. At higher elevations, your risk of sunburn increases 4 percent for every thousand feet, so if you live near sea level and you're visiting Yellowstone (roughly eight thousand feet), your risk of sunburn is 32 percent higher—or in Moab, 16 to 20 percent higher. No one's going to make you wear sunscreen (except your mother), but there are plenty of reasons to, including increased risk of skin cancer, wrinkles, and other sun damage to your skin.

Should I try mountaineering?

If you think you might like hard work, incredible views, and clear, easily defined goals (i.e., getting to the top of a mountain), mountaineering might be the perfect activity for you. It starts with the basic knowledge of hiking and adds in other skills and elements like snow climbing, backpacking, roped rock climbing, and potentially travel across crevassed glaciers. Mountaineering tends to be high on suffering, with long ascents up mountainsides that can feel like endless stadium stairs, cold temperatures, and camping in uncomfortable places. But it's also high on great photos set against unforgettable backdrops, summit euphoria, and bonding with other team members/partners. Mountaineering is also fairly easy to try. With a good base level of fitness, a guided snow climb of a peak like Mount Hood or Mount Shasta is within reach for many people; it costs less than $700 and takes one to three days. If you like hiking, you can ease your way into nontechnical mountaineering. One way is to try the summer climbs of most of Colorado's "fourteeners" (14,000-foot peaks).

How do I climb a mountain?

The biggest obstacle in climbing a nontechnical mountain—one that doesn't require specialized equipment or skills other than knowing how to hike—is often getting out of bed early enough to do it safely. After that, if you've done some hiking and have a good level of fitness, it's fairly straight-forward. Research the route (and carry a map of it), carry food, water, and extra layers, and stick with the hike until you get to the top. There are three important things to remember.

1. **Pick a pace you can sustain all day.** It's easy to start out strong, but it's tough to keep up that pace when you get to a higher elevation, or once the terrain starts to get steeper. Remember that it's better to walk at a medium pace for an hour straight than it is to walk fast and have to stop and catch your breath every five or ten minutes.

2. **Summit early.** Give yourself more time than you think you need to get to the top of the mountain by noon. Thunderstorms often arrive in the afternoon, especially in the high elevations of the western United States, and mountaintops are usually exposed and leave you no shelter from lightning strikes.

3. **Know when to turn around.** Don't be afraid to admit that the weather doesn't look good, or that you don't have the fitness to summit—that mountain will be there next week or next year, and you can try again.

How do I acclimate to high altitude?

The best way to acclimate to high altitude is to give yourself time to do so. If, for example, you fly from Chicago to Denver in the morning, then drive to Breckenridge and take the Imperial Express chairlift to 12,840 feet on the same day, there's a good chance you won't feel too good when you start exerting yourself (several people have had heart attacks doing similar things). If you're climbing a mountain, your body will acclimate as you slowly ascend, but altitude sickness can still zap you if you try to do it too fast—and everyone's "too fast" is different. The best strategy to getting acclimated is to stay hydrated and well fed, to move up in elevation at a slow pace, and to be conservative with big chunks of altitude. For example, if you live at sea level and want to climb a Colorado fourteener (that's a peak of 14,000 feet or higher), a good progression to 14,000 feet might include spending a night in Denver (5,280 feet), then camping near the trailhead of a fourteener (around 10,000 feet), and then climbing to 14,000 feet the next day. That way you're giving your body a chance to deal with the lower pressure gradually (not to mention the drier air if you're coming from a humid place like New York), instead of shocking it all at once.

How do I know if I have altitude sickness?

If you're climbing a mountain, you're not exactly going "into thin air"—more like "into lower atmospheric pressure," which doesn't exactly roll off the tongue (and is a little harder to understand). At higher altitudes, the pressure is lower, so there are fewer oxygen molecules in the air—for example, there's only 40 percent as much oxygen at 12,000 feet as there is at sea level, so essentially you have to take two and a half breaths to get the same amount of oxygen in your lungs. Altitude sickness, or acute mountain sickness (AMS), afflicts plenty of people who venture into the mountains. Symptoms are actually quite similar to a hangover—headache, lack of appetite, nausea, vomiting, dizziness—and if you don't deal with it, AMS can get worse and turn into something very serious. To avoid altitude sickness, eat plenty of food (even when you don't feel hungry, your body needs 250 to 400 calories per hour to keep climbing), drink plenty of water, and remember that your body acclimates to altitude if you give it the chance. If you can "sleep high" the night before you head out on the trail (for example, camping near the trailhead), do it—it gives your body a head start on acclimating for the next day.

What are crampons?

It's difficult to get traction when walking on ice (maybe you've noticed), so on climbs that involve a significant amount of travel on snow and ice, mountaineers wear crampons, essentially plates with long, sharp metal teeth that are

strapped to the bottom of boots. They're like football cleats, but way more dangerous and way more functional on snow and ice—the teeth literally sink into hard snow or ice patches and give the wearer traction on almost any angle. Crampons made for vertical ice climbing have sharp, serrated front points near the toes, so when the climber kicks the toe of the boot into the ice, the crampon points grip and don't come out.

What kind of shoes should I wear mountain climbing?

If you're just starting to climb nontechnical mountains (ones that require just hiking and scrambling), you don't need $500 mountaineering boots—unless you really want to go out and buy $500 mountaineering boots, of course, because you're obviously free to do that. Above all else, your shoes should be comfortable and not give you blisters. After that consideration, think about ankle support—do you roll your ankles easily? If so, a pair of sturdy boots might be best. If not, you might be able to get away with a pair of solid trail-running shoes. Are you going to spend a lot of time scrambling on rock slabs and boulder fields? A hiking boot or approach shoe with a sticky rubber outsole will help that. Do you plan to go on overnight trips (backpacking) in those shoes? A stiffer, more supportive midsole will help your feet carry that extra 25 to 40 pounds in your backpack. When you're just getting started, a pair of general hiking shoes or boots will be just fine for most things—but if/when you graduate to multiday ascents, technical rock climbing, and/or snow travel, you'll need to upgrade to more specialized footwear.

When should I wear gaiters?

Traditional mountaineering gaiters, the durable water-resistant fabric coverings that go from the tops of your boots all the way up to your midcalf, do three things: make you feel a little bit like a superhero, protect your pants from rips and tears caused by wearing crampons, and keep snow and water out of your boots and pants by covering the places where snow can sneak in. You should wear them if you expect a significant amount of

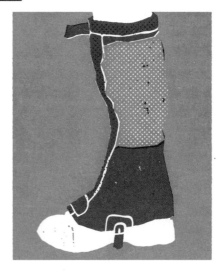

snow travel on your hike or climb—if your feet punch through the snow and your leg sinks in up to your knee, snow can go right into the top of your boot, and gaiters will prevent that.

Trail gaiters, a newer type of gaiter, are lightweight short gaiters that cover hiking boots or trail-running shoes and are popular with long-distance hikers and trail runners who want to keep trail debris and small rocks out of their shoes while they are hiking quickly or running.

What kind of socks should I wear?

Cotton takes a long time to dry, doesn't wick away moisture, doesn't help you retain heat after it gets wet, and can cause blisters—so don't wear cotton socks. When blended with other materials, cotton can be okay, but a sock made of 100 percent cotton is not usually an experienced hiker's first choice. Wool is the most popular type of sock for most contemporary outdoorspeople, for good reason: it does everything cotton doesn't (wicks sweat away, keeps you warm when wet or damp, and generally works better at preventing blisters). If you remember wool only as something itchy sweaters are made out of, merino wool (or merino wool blend) hiking socks will impress you. They can be expensive, but you're not often buying half a dozen pairs of hiking socks for everyday use. One or two pairs are enough, and a worthwhile investment, as they're padded in the right places to complement your hiking boots. Thinner socks are good for most hiking applications, unless you plan on doing a trip during the cooler "shoulder season" between winter and spring or between fall and winter, or you have naturally colder feet or circulation issues.

How do I treat blisters?

The best way to treat blisters is to prevent them. Blisters are caused by friction between your shoes, your socks, and the skin on your feet. Friction builds up with the presence of moisture from sweat or other water that gets into your boots or shoes. If you don't absolutely have to have leather hiking boots, think about something more breathable and

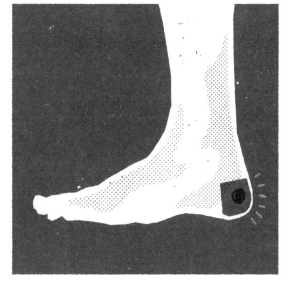

flexible, like trail-running shoes. If you do wear boots, make sure you break them in before you hike in them—wear them around your house or on a few walks around town before you test them on the trail. When hiking, make sure your boots or shoes are tied snugly so your feet aren't sliding around in them.

If you start to feel rubbing or friction anywhere on your feet when you're on a hike, you might have a "hot spot," which could be the start of a blister if you don't deal with it. You can use any variety of medical products to cover a hot spot, but standard duct tape usually does the job best because it stays in place while you hike better than anything else.

If you do develop a blister, there are several methods of treatment. If it is a small blister and it hasn't popped, cover it with a bandage and/or duct tape. If it's a large, painful blister, you can pop it with a sterile needle and then cover it with a bandage and duct tape. If by the time you see the blister it's popped already, clean it with treated drinking water from your water bottle and/or apply some hand sanitizer to it, and bandage it. In all cases, if you carry moleskin, you can use it to take some of the pressure off the blister by cutting a piece just larger than the blister, with a hole in the middle of the moleskin to accommodate the blister itself, and apply it to the skin under the bandage. When you're finished hiking for the day, remove the bandages and let the blister dry as much as you can.

How much water should I take with me?

Your water consumption on a hike will depend on a few factors: how hot it is where you are hiking, altitude, how hydrated you were when you started hiking, how much you're sweating, how long and steep the hike is, how many beers you had at happy hour the night before, and how many beers you had after happy hour the night before, among others. A general rule for a full day of hiking is 2 to 3 liters of water per person. Keep track of how much water you drink while hiking and try to gauge your own personal needs. Carrying more than 3 liters is bulky and heavy (3 liters of water equals 6 pounds of weight in your backpack), and if you need more than that, you might consider refilling your bottles at a water source along your route (check maps to find out if your trail will cross creeks or pass by lakes, and obviously purify the water before drinking; see page 240). Of course it's always better to have too much than not enough when it comes to water, but if you're carrying three 1-liter water bottles every time you go out on a 10-mile day hike and you notice you still have a full one every time you return to the trailhead, you can probably get away with taking just 2 liters next time.

What kind of first aid kit is right for me?

You can buy the most tricked-out and expensive first aid kit you can find at your nearest outdoor gear store, but that doesn't mean you're going to know what to do with any of the supplies inside it when the time comes. Check out the contents of all the available kit options and ask yourself what you really, truly need to take with you. For example, do you need to take tablets for upset stomach and heartburn, or would a few antidiarrheal pills cover you in case of emergency? Do you need both aspirin and ibuprofen, or just one of the two? Do you really need eight 4-by-4-inch sterile pads for a day hike? You can build your own basic first aid kit, but an advantage of buying one from an outdoor gear store is that the items are already in single-use sizes—you get one pair of latex gloves instead of having to buy an entire box, and the pills are already in two-pill envelopes, for example.

Here are a few basic items you should have in a first aid kit for single-day adventures as well as for longer backpacking trips.

- Four to six ibuprofen or aspirin pills

- Four to six antidiarrheal pills

- One pair of latex gloves

- A small assortment of bandages

- A couple of ¼-inch-by-4-inch Steri-Strip skin closures

- A few wound dressing pads

- A small roll of gauze

- A small roll of adhesive tape

- Tweezers

- Five or six Q-tips

- An ACE bandage

- Sanitary wipes

- Antibiotic ointment or gel

- Moleskin for blisters or hot spots

Should I carry water bottles or a hydration reservoir?

When it comes to carrying water, lots of hikers and mountain bikers prefer hydration reservoirs, flexible water bladders carried in a backpack with a drinking hose running over the shoulder. The best system is actually to carry neither bottles nor a reservoir and to make your hiking partner carry all your water instead. But if that doesn't work, you have to make a choice. Both bottles and reservoirs have pros and cons: it's best to sip water often throughout the day when exercising, and it's difficult to do that if you're carrying water bottles that are stowed away in your pack. Reservoirs are made to sip from all day and don't always develop leaks, but they do leak more often than water bottles. Reservoirs can also freeze in low temperatures, cutting off your access to your water, and a frozen drinking hose or mouthpiece can be very difficult to thaw—although if you're mountain biking or skiing, a reservoir is much safer to crash on because it's not a hard-sided object in your pack that can break bones.

Both bottles and reservoirs have their pros and cons, and if you don't want to buy both right away, just get two decent-quality water bottles and use them. One system that somewhat splits the difference is to carry a 40-ounce hard-sided bottle in your pack and a 20-ounce bicycle-style squeeze bottle in your hand to sip from as you hike. Obviously you'll be carrying a bottle in your hand the whole time, which is a compromise.

What kind of water bottles should I buy?

There's no perfect water bottle for everyone—although for a long time you might have assumed that the hard-sided plastic Nalgene 1-liter bottles were the only thing true hikers carried. These bottles are popular for good reasons: they're virtually unbreakable, can hold scalding hot liquids without melting, and have wide mouths that are easy to fill from any source, and for quite a while Nalgene was the only company that made anything like them. Of course, now there are plenty of options on the rack at your local gear shop, including bottles made of stainless steel, soft plastic, and even glass.

Stainless steel bottles are wonderful but can dent easily if you're not careful, and if you pour boiling water into them they're impossible to hold with a bare hand. Soft plastic bottles with bite valves (like bicycle water bottles) are great for trail running, mountain biking, and fast hiking, but not as good for sealing and then tossing in the bottom of your pack (even the tightest-sealing ones seem to leak a tiny bit of water in certain situations, like changes in altitude). And bottled-water bottles or recycled sports drink bottles work just fine (and are actually ultralight) but don't have the long-term durability of other bottles designed for the outdoors. Whatever bottle you choose, be sure to get enough capacity for your activity—2 to 3 liters is a good average.

Where should I pee when I'm on the trail?

Your first instinct when you have to pee during a hike is to find a place to obscure yourself, which is great for your privacy (and probably for the emotional well-being of other hikers). In an alpine environment, you should always try to pee directly on rocks—animals are attracted to the salt in your urine, and if you pee on plants they'll eat the plants (as gross as that sounds). On popular trails and mountain routes that means plants can start to disappear. So pee on rocks, because no mountain critters will eat a rock. They'll just lick it and move on. In fragile environments like the desert, it's more important to find a spot where you won't damage plants and cryptobiotic soil (or step on a cactus), so look for a wash or a slab of slickrock, or, if you haven't seen too many other hikers that day, pee right in the middle of the trail—it'll dry quickly in the desert environment.

How do I keep my hands clean on a hike?

Let's just be honest: the word *clean* is a very relative term in the outdoors. There are no restrooms with soap and running water—when you get away from the rest of society, you get away from the restrooms too. There are a few ways to keep your hands "clean" while hiking. If you're just on a day hike, keep a travel-size bottle of hand sanitizer in your backpack and use it before eating. And offer some to your hiking partner before he digs his hand into your bag of trail mix.

If you're crossing a stream or hiking past a lake, you can also dip your hands in for a quick rinse—obviously this won't be hospital-grade sanitary, but you'll get a little more of a clean feeling than you would from using hand sanitizer alone.

If you're on a multiday trip, carry a small bottle of biodegradable soap (such as Dr. Bronner's). Fill your cooking pot with some creek or lake water, carry the pot at least 100 feet from the water source (to avoid contaminating it), and wash up using the pot and your soap. When you're done, scatter the wash water as far across as broad an area as you can. Rinse away any soap residue with water from your water bottle.

What should I eat on a hike?

Eating can be one of the best things about hiking. As the saying goes, "Hunger is the best sauce," and nothing drums up hunger like some calorie-burning time on the trail. Learning the best method of replacing those calories takes some trial and error, and each person packs different foods for different reasons: some people prefer "real food" like sandwiches, crackers, and candy bars because they're foods that always taste good. Other people prefer energy bars and gels because they're easy to carry and designed not to spoil in almost any temperature.

There are no hard-and-fast rules for what you should eat when you're hiking, but keep in mind your body will burn a lot of calories on a hike—especially longer hikes that cover a lot of miles and/or take all day. When you're looking at the type of calories you're eating on your hike, aim for a ratio of approximately 60 percent carbohydrates, 15 percent protein, and 25 percent fat. Simple carbohydrates, such as those found in energy gels and blocks, are easy for your body to digest (as opposed to high-fiber carbs). Always try to start with a "full tank," or several hundred calories for breakfast—this gives your body a good base of calories to work with and will prevent crashing later in the day. Stop and eat every hour or so throughout your hike so you can take in a couple hundred calories. Don't think you have to buy energy bars just because you're hiking—foods like burritos, peanut butter and jelly sandwiches, and leftover pizza have been fueling outdoor pursuits for a long time. Obviously the convenience of a prepackaged energy bar is great, but if you don't like the flavor, you're not going to eat it—especially when your appetite wanes at higher altitudes. Nuts, dried fruit, crackers, and candy bars all make for great hiking foods.

Sample Food Packing List for a Multiday Trip

Breakfast:

- Oatmeal, cooked and mixed with peanut butter, dried fruit, and walnuts
- Instant coffee

Lunch and snacks:

- Energy bar
- Salami
- Cheese
- Flour tortilla
- Candy bar

Dinner:

- Pasta or dehydrated backpacking meal (see page 246)
- Powdered soup mix
- Dark chocolate bar
- Herbal tea or hot chocolate

Do I need to hike with trekking poles?

It's a fact that five out of five trekking pole manufacturers recommend trekking poles. Can you live without them? Yes. Are they nice to have? Yes. Trekking poles help your hiking posture and take a small amount of compressive force (up to 25 percent) off your knees as you walk, as well as help you balance through sections of tricky terrain. Twenty-five percent might not sound like much, but over three days of hiking 8 miles a day with a 35-pound pack on your back, 25 percent off every step adds up. If you buy a pair of poles, you don't necessarily have to use them every time you go hiking. But they're nice to have when you're carrying a heavy pack on a multiday trip, and even nicer on trails that have a few creek crossings—having three points of contact (pole, pole, foot) instead of one as you step from rock to rock across a moving stream of water helps balance, boosts confidence, and significantly reduces the chance that you'll fall into the water, soaking your clothes and your pack—and possibly getting injured. Newer, more expensive poles are made of lightweight carbon fiber and collapse down to a little over 12 inches (which is great for air travel), but if you don't want to spend a ton of money, an old pair of ski poles is a fine substitute.

What should I do if I get lost?

Get comfortable with the idea that if you spend any significant amount of time in the outdoors, you're going to get lost a couple times. You probably won't stay lost long enough to resort to killing and eating your hiking partners to survive, but you'll take a wrong turn here or there and waste an hour or even a few hours finding your way. If you do lose the trail, or suddenly realize you're not where you're supposed to be, the first thing you should do is to remain calm. You're not going to die (well, actually, we all are, someday, but that's another, more existential conversation). Try to remember how long ago it was that you were confident you were on the trail or in the right place (i.e., you were confident you weren't lost), and if you can, retrace your steps and go back to that spot—but only if you're sure you can get back there without getting more lost. If you can't remember where you were, get out your map and compass and/or GPS and try to figure out your position, thinking of the last trail intersection you passed or other landmarks: where your path or trail crossed a stream or a nearby mountain you can see and also identify on your map. Use those points to navigate back. If it's getting dark, stay put, get comfortable, and wait for morning (hopefully you've brought a space blanket or emergency bivy sack; see page 84). If you're hopelessly lost, stay put. Blow your safety whistle or yell if you think other hikers might hear you. If no one's around, your best bet will be staying put and waiting for a rescue. You can survive weeks without food but only a few days without water, so find water to drink while you wait. If you've left detailed information with someone about your plans, a rescue group shouldn't have a hard time finding you, unless you wander far from where you'd intended. So stay in one place and stay safe until help arrives.

Do I need zip-off pants?

Plenty of people would say the phrase "hiking fashion" is an oxymoron, and they would be correct. Zip-off pants—pants with zippers at the knees so they can be turned into shorts—have been popular in the outdoor world with a certain crowd for many years. If you like the idea of pants that turn into shorts with a simple zip, or if you have sweaty knees, you should by all means go for it. But you should also know that zip-off pants are not mandatory for hiking. Many apparel companies have now started to make "roll-up" pants to serve the needs of hikers who would like to bare their lower legs midday without having to pack an extra pair of shorts. Wear what you like out on the trail—again, as long as it's not cotton (see below).

What should I wear when I go hiking?

What you wear will depend on the season you're hiking, the weather in your particular area, and your personal style. A good general list of apparel for spring/

summer/fall day hiking includes a synthetic-fabric T-shirt or button-down shirt, a soft shell jacket or light fleece jacket, a rain jacket, synthetic-fabric shorts or pants, wool or wool-blend socks, and sturdy hiking shoes or boots. Depending on the local climate or altitude, it might be a good idea to bring along a light beanie and light gloves. And one thing is for certain: no one's ever died from packing too many clothes, so as you start out in the outdoors it's good to err on the side of overpacking. You'll gradually learn what works for you in each situation and dial in your layering system. Another thing that's for certain: you shouldn't wear cotton (except in really hot desert environments).

Why all the plaid?

Here's the deal with plaid: when you walk into the men's apparel section of an outdoor gear store, you see a lot of it. There are many theories as to why this is, but one functional reason is that plaid hides stains. So if you're out on the trail kicking up dirt, sweating, spilling bits of food or using your clothes as a napkin, your plaid shirt will look less ruined at the end of your hike or backpacking trip. Button-down shirts are also functional for venting when you're walking uphill, or turning up the collar for long days of walking in the sun with your head bent slightly downward at the trail. All that said, you should wear what you want, whether it's a tank top or a tech shirt you got for free from a 5K race you ran— as long as it's a shirt made of synthetic material that will dry quickly.

What do I do if I get a hole in my puffy jacket?

Down jackets keep you warm on the trail and when the temperature drops in the evening, but they are notoriously fragile. The fabric that keeps them light-weight and able to best utilize their fill material to keep you warm is thin and can tear easily if you're not careful. Catching a sharp tree branch or a piece of a rock wall on the sleeve will often pop a hole in the jacket. Another common source of tears is errant embers from a campfire landing on a jacket, melt-ing a small hole in the fabric. The best way to fix a hole in a puffy jacket is to send it to a repair shop and have a professional fix it—but of course if you're a fix-it-yourself kind of person you'll want to know a DIY approach. Sewing the thin fabric isn't a good option for people who aren't expert sewers or don't have ultrafine thread, so the two tried-and-true fixes for holes are duct tape (not surprisingly) and Seam Grip (or Krazy Glue). Both approaches leave somewhat unsightly spots on the jacket—nothing like a 2-by-2-inch square of gray duct tape, or a permanently dark splotch of glue, to accent your brightly colored puffy—but both are effective and widely used by the outdoor community. Hang around enough campfires, and you might assume that a puffy jacket without a hole or duct tape patch hasn't been properly broken in.

Do I need a rain jacket even if it's not supposed to rain?

In the mountains, if you don't pack a rain jacket—no matter what the weather forecast is—you will almost certainly get rained on at some point. If there is literally a 0 percent chance of precipitation on the day you're hiking, you can very likely get away with leaving your rain jacket at home. But it's never a bad insurance policy just to take one, especially if you're going to be hiking in a high or exposed area that might be windy (something that may or may not be mentioned in the weather forecast for your area). Your rain jacket is probably as good at blocking wind as it is moisture, so it makes sense to pack it as a wind layer or emergency layer. If you're mountain biking on a trail with a long descent (or long, downhill-trending section where you're not doing a lot of pedaling), a rain jacket can keep you warm through all the wind chill that your bike's speed generates.

Should I buy a jacket with or without a hood?

There's a saying that many experienced outdoorspeople have abided by for years: "No hood, no good." And this is more than a fashion choice in most situations—the right piece of gear can be the difference between comfort and extreme discomfort (or even survival) in certain situations. A hood on a rain jacket will keep water from getting into the neck of your clothes and soaking your inner layers and your torso, and unless you're never going farther than 2 miles from the trailhead, there's no reason to buy a rain jacket without a hood. On all other upper-body pieces—soft-shells and rain jackets, ski shells and puffy jackets—the hood can be integral to keeping you warm, or just warm enough to stay comfortable. You've probably heard the saying that you lose 90 percent of your body heat through your head. It's only somewhat true. The study that led to that statistic found that when the head was uncovered but all other body parts were covered, subjects lost significant amounts of body heat. When the head was covered just like other parts of the body (i.e., with a hood on a hooded jacket), the body stayed much warmer. This is also essentially the science on how mummy-style sleeping bags work. So even though you might feel a little strange wearing three jackets with hoods all at the same time, you'll be a lot warmer. If you have no hood, that's no good.

What is Gore-Tex?

Gore-Tex is the first invented and most famous of the lightweight, waterproof, breathable fabrics, created in 1969 by W. L. Gore and Associates. It has become, now somewhat inaccurately, a synonym for any waterproof breathable fabric used in the outdoors—similar to our use of the word *Kleenex* to mean any type of facial tissue, not just the Kleenex brand. Waterproof breathable fabrics are important in the outdoors because users need a layer that shields them from precipitation but breathes well enough that they can perform strenuous activities (hiking, skiing). In the almost half century since Gore-Tex was pioneered, other companies have built similarly performing fabrics, such as eVent and NeoShell. Saying they're all pretty much the same is a disservice to all the science and hard work that went into creating these fabrics, but understanding the differences is also fairly complicated. If you don't want to dig deep into the nuances, just remember that when you buy rain gear, get a jacket made with a waterproof breathable fabric—not a heavy one like the burly, nonbreathable stuff that Alaskan commercial fishermen wear.

How do I wash a Gore-Tex jacket?

Your Gore-Tex jacket (or other waterproof breathable jacket made with eVent or NeoShell) is expensive, if you hadn't noticed—so don't just toss it in the washing machine with your jeans (even if your jeans were expensive too). Use a specialized product like a liquid "tech wash" (available at most outdoor retail stores) instead of a detergent soap. Wash the jacket on a permanent press or gentle cycle, and dry it on a low setting or line-dry it.

Waterproof breathable materials are highly specialized and need special treatment to retain their abilities to repel water. Over time, elements like dirt, sweat, oils from your skin, and sunscreen can get into the fabric and necessitate a recharge of the fabric. After your jacket gets enough usage, you'll eventually need to reactivate its waterproof treatment, which you can do by placing it in a clothes dryer on a low setting for a few minutes. If that doesn't work, you may have to re-treat the jacket with another kind of wash-in treatment (also available at most outdoor retail stores).

What if it rains—should I keep going?

It depends on where you are. In the Rocky Mountains, rain is often a sign of more unstable weather coming—meaning that either more rain, snow, or thunderstorms are on their way. In wet regions, such as the Pacific Northwest, rain is often just rain, which is the reality of the local climate. Learn a bit about the regional weather patterns where you're hiking, plan accordingly, and always err on the side of caution. Continuing up into more exposed terrain is always a tough choice when rain begins falling, because no one can accurately predict hyperlocal weather. If you're fixated on getting to a summit and a light rain shower moves in, it's fine to continue on as long as you keep your eye on the weather. Just be prudent: as long as you are able to escape to protected ground if the weather intensifies, you should be fine (but don't overestimate your ability to hike fast downhill on wet rock). If you hear thunder or see lightning, it's time to go down. Even if it sounds far away, lightning can strike 10 to 15 miles from the rainy portion of a storm (see page 54).

What's the difference between third-class, fourth-class, and fifth-class mountains?

The standard accepted climbing grading scale system in the United States, the Yosemite Decimal System, breaks down mountain terrain according to the following scale.

- **Class 1:** Hiking on trails.

- **Class 2:** Scrambling in which hands might be used occasionally for balance.

- **Class 3:** Scrambling in which a rope might be used to protect against falls.

- **Class 4:** Simple rock climbing in which exposure to falls may be a factor and a fall could be fatal. Ropes are often used.

- **Class 5:** Rock climbing in which ropes, belaying, and protective equipment like cams and chocks are used to protect the leading climber from falling. Where technical, climbing ratings from 5.1 to 5.15 are used (see page 119).

Class 3 and class 4 ratings are somewhat subjective, and the difference between the two is often hazy. Some people may find certain terrain rated class 3 to feel much more like class 4, and vice versa. So the ratings of class 3 and class 4 should be observed with discretion.

How do I know if I can climb up something?

It's easy to climb up a slab of granite or a rock gully in the mountains—the important thing is knowing whether you can climb down it. Dozens of tourists have been rescued from technical climbing areas at Devils Tower National Monument in Wyoming and Garden of the Gods in Colorado after scrambling up an easy climb, then turning around and realizing that reversing their steps might be a little scary, or even terrifying. If you have to do a short scramble on your hike that you'll have to climb down later, study the terrain on your way up. Remember where the key footholds and handholds are, and look down while you're climbing up so you'll remember what the terrain looks like from above. And if you get a little nervous when climbing down, try turning and facing into the rock—although it might seem counterintuitive because you feel like you can't see where you're going, it's safer (albeit maybe a little slower). At the very least, your hands are facing the correct way to catch you if you slip, and your toes are way more effective at standing on small holds than your heels are. Take your time, keep your weight on your feet (not your hands), don't take big risks, and make small moves downward.

How do I rappel?

Rappelling is a complicated, high-consequence skill with many variables and should be learned from an expert, but in case of an emergency a carefully rigged and executed Dulfersitz rappel will work. If you absolutely have to descend a cliff that's too steep to climb down, follow these steps:

- **Find an anchor:** Good choices are a tree near the edge of the cliff or a solid boulder (the size of a refrigerator or bigger). This object absolutely must be solid. Although you probably weigh 250 pounds or less, a rappel can place a force on the anchor much larger than your body weight. If your anchor moves or becomes dislodged, you will free-fall to the bottom of the cliff. For this reason, and for easier and safer retrieval of your rope, trees are preferred.

- **Attach your rope to the anchor:** Either tie your rope around the anchor (you won't be able to retrieve the rope if you do this), or wrap your rope around the anchor so that both ends are equal and will touch the ground at the bottom of your rappel (you will rappel on both strands of rope). Clear the area around the anchor of loose debris that might fall down the cliff if disturbed by your rope—anything that falls down, like rocks, can fall on you.

- **Throw your rope:** Gather your rope in one hand and heave it over the edge of the cliff, being careful to not fall over the edge yourself. Throwing it outward from the cliff is the most important thing here, so it can clear any trees or bushes on its way down. If the ends of the rope do not touch the ground at the bottom of the cliff because they've caught up on something on the cliff or the rope has tangled on its way down, haul the rope up and throw it again. If the rope doesn't reach the ground, do not rappel. It will do you no good to rappel halfway down a cliff.

- **Get in position:** Facing your anchor (with your back facing the cliff edge), place the rappel rope between your legs (both strands if you've wrapped it around the anchor). With your right hand, pull the rope under your right butt cheek to the front of your body, then across your chest to your left shoulder. Wrap the rope around your shoulder, and across your back to your right hip, and hold the rope with your right hand.

- **Rappel:** As slowly as possible, walk backward until the rope in front of you is taut. Keep your right hand holding the rope next to your right hip and slowly pay rope out as you rappel down the cliff. Go as slowly as possible, because a quickly moving rope will create high friction, which can burn your clothes or your skin. Remember, your grip on the rope is not keeping it from sliding—the friction created from the angles in the system (through your legs, around your butt, across your chest, around your shoulder, around your hip) is keeping the rope from sliding. So keep the angles in the system by keeping your right hand out in front of your body and you'll be fine.

Never take your right hand off the rope, under any circumstances, until you are safely on the ground at the bottom of the cliff.

Should I hire a guide for a mountain climb?

There are two ways to climb a big mountain: buy all the gear and learn all the skills, techniques, weather forecasting, and conditions assessment yourself over a period of several years and use it to get yourself to the top, or hire a guide and let the guide worry about all that. Guides are trained professionals who have knowledge of the route, systems, and skills needed for the climb and have usually done the climb several times before they guide someone else on it. Guides are inexpensive in the grand scheme of things when you consider all the things they take care of for you. Their job is to keep you alive and to make sure you have success if it's at all possible (and fun)—all you have to do is show up in good physical shape to climb a mountain behind them. With zero mountaineering experience, your chances of successfully summiting Mount Rainier (and, more important, making it down alive) are quite small. With a guide, as long as you show up in dynamite shape and you have decent weather on the date of your climb, your chances of summiting are much higher than your chances of not summiting. Note: You still have to carry all your stuff. Guides will usually carry important shared gear like first aid kits (and sometimes ropes), but you'll be responsible for packing and carrying all your personal gear, clothing, food, and water on the climb.

Should I tip my guide?

If you think that someone taking you to one of the most dangerous places in the world for the experience of a lifetime and ensuring that you arrive safe and sound is a noble pursuit, then yes, you should absolutely tip your guide. Guides, especially in the United States, aren't making piles of money considering the risk involved (although the view from a guide's office is usually about a hundred times better than the view from most of ours), and they rely on tips to make their living. So although it's cool to take your guide out for a beer and a burger after your trip, it's not courteous (or good karma) to consider that a good enough tip—but 5 to 20 percent of the retail cost of your trip is. If you're part of a group, it's common for one person to collect tips from all the group members and then give the money to the guide sometime at the end of the trip and present it as one big group tip (this is also a good way to make sure everyone tips some amount, if they weren't aware of the protocol beforehand).

What should I do in my summit photo?

It's good to have a couple options, depending on your mood, the number of summit photos someone is willing to take of you, and the fact that you may only ever get one photo of yourself on top of Mount Whatever. It's fun to do something unique like jumping in the air or gesturing obscenely with/at your hiking/climbing partner, but it's also good to have one standard "say cheese" snapshot for that time in a couple of decades when you want to reminisce about that time you reached that particular summit. There's no wrong way to take a summit photo just as there's no "wrong" way to cut your hair—you're on vacation, really, so have fun. Just remember to take a few photos of the view *from* the summit as well, because in ten years you'll probably remember what you looked like back then, but you may not remember what the view from the summit looked like.

Should I buy two-way radios?

Two-way radios are great for lots of applications in the mountains—mountain guides who work with one or more other guides in managing large groups who may become separated, ski patrollers, and search-and-rescue personnel. Most recreational hikers, climbers, and skiers, however, don't have a huge reason to carry them—unless they want to carry them for a bit of insurance or just like the idea of being able to communicate from far away. If you're hiking with a friend or two, you generally shouldn't be getting separated to the point that you need a radio to communicate, and if you're climbing, you and your partner should have a communication strategy that works in high winds or other situations where you can't hear each other (e.g., rope signals). Obviously you're free to use radios, and they might come in handy if you take a ski vacation and members of your family don't necessarily ski at the same skill level, but you'll need to wear the radio in a way that you can access it and hear it when someone tries to contact you.

How do I use an ice ax?

Ice axes, besides being really badass-looking walking sticks, are somewhat like a safety belt on snow climbs: used correctly, an ice ax will hopefully save you if you fall on steep snow or ice. Here are the basics of how to use one:

- **Walking stick:** When using your ice ax as a walking stick, always hold it with the pick facing backward.

- **Self belay:** Always carry the ax in your uphill hand, jamming the spike down into the snow (like you mean it), parallel to the direction of your torso, as far as you can in between steps. It has to hold a fall if you somehow stumble and lose your footing, so daintily punching the spike a couple of inches into the surface snow won't cut it.

- **Self-arrest:** If you do fall, get the pick into the snow as quickly as possible and dig it into the snow as far as you can. Ideally, when you fall, you'll be sliding on your chest and legs with your feet going downhill—bring the head of the ice ax up to chest height, grab the bottom of the ax with your other hand so that the handle of the ax runs diagonal across your body, and press all your weight into the pick. Dig into the snow with your toes (kick if you have to)—unless you're wearing crampons, in which case you'll dig in with your knees, because catching a crampon point on ice when you're sliding can instantly break your leg or tear ligaments.

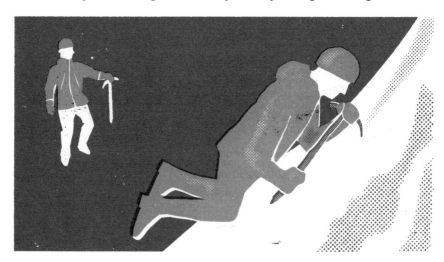

The Eight Best Rock-Climbing Destinations in North America

1. **Red River Gorge, Kentucky:** It has hundreds of steep sport-climbing routes on sandstone cliffs.

2. **Red Rock Natural Conservation Area, Nevada:** One of the most diverse rock-climbing areas in North America, with thousands of high-quality multipitch traditional routes, sport-climbing routes, and boulder problems.

3. **Yosemite National Park, California:** Arguably the most famous rock-climbing destination in the country; thousands of climbing routes on granite faces and monoliths, including 3,000-foot El Capitan and 2,000-foot Half Dome.

4. **Smith Rock, Oregon:** Visit Smith Rock for hundreds of sport and traditional climbing routes on steep golden welded volcanic tuff.

5. **Shawangunks, New York:** Here you'll find historic and unique traditional climbing on quartz conglomerate rock with horizontal cracks and roofs.

6. **Indian Creek, Utah:** It's a world-famous crack-climbing destination; hundreds of dead-vertical routes up parallel-sided sandstone cracks.

7. **Joshua Tree, California:** This desert locale has more than eight thousand climbing routes and boulder problems on granite.

8. **Squamish, British Columbia:** It's North America's premier granite climbing destination with classic routes of all grades and lengths.

How do I navigate in a whiteout?

When visibility is reduced to a few feet in a snowstorm or blizzard, navigation can be a nightmare—without landmarks it's difficult to ascertain your position and know how far you have walked/are walking, and blowing snow can even make it impossible to see changes in slope of the terrain you're walking on. Obviously your best course of action is to not go hiking or riding in blizzards or blowing snow, but if you find yourself in a limited-visibility situation in a bad spot, you can navigate your way out of it.

Knowing where you are on a map is key—if you don't know your position, it's impossible to be confident in where you're going. Try to navigate to a treed area to gain some cover from the storm, or make a plan to get to a lower elevation (it may not be snowing a few hundred feet below you). Be careful of hazards that you might not be able to see because of the blowing snow, such as cliffs, iced-over creeks, or ponds. If you have a GPS, create waypoints and use them to navigate to a safer area. If not, aim a compass (see page 75) toward your objective, and send a friend ahead as far as you can along that bearing without losing sight of him, keeping him as straight on the course as possible with verbal commands ("one step left," "two steps right," etc.) or with hand signals. When he reaches the point where you can almost not see each other, have him stop walking and wait for you until you catch up, then send him walking along the bearing again. Repeat this until you reach a safe spot.

If you are unable to navigate by any means, stay put. Humans have a tendency to walk in circles when we can't see landmarks, so your movement is likely to get you more lost in a whiteout. If you need shelter, dig a hole in the snow, put on all your extra layers, or get in your emergency shelter and under your space blanket, and wait for the weather to subside.

Should I throw a rock off the summit?

You should never throw rocks off the summit of a mountain—remember that the way you came up isn't the only way to the top of the mountain, and rocks sometimes don't stop for a long time once they start going down a mountainside. You don't want to start a rockslide that obliterates an entire family of mountain goats, for example, or worse, hit another human being. In 2007, a hiker on a peak in Wyoming's Wind River Range tossed a rock off a summit, unknowingly hitting and killing a rock climber 300 feet below—a seemingly innocent gesture gone horribly wrong.

EXPERT WITNESS

THREE TIPS FOR MOVING SAFELY ON OFF-TRAIL MOUNTAIN TERRAIN

Adam George, mountain guide, International Federation of Mountain Guides Association

Switzerland-based Adam George has been an internationally certified mountain guide since 2009. He has guided all types of mountaineering, climbing, and skiing adventures, including the North Face of the Eiger, many ascents of Mont Blanc and the Matterhorn, and multiple ski trips of the famous Haute Route.

1. In loose rocky terrain, like talus fields, stay close together, travel at diagonals, and make switchbacks. This keeps people out of the fall line if you dislodge a rock, and any dislodged projectile doesn't accelerate too much between higher and lower climbers.

2. If the going gets steep and you are forced to scramble, remember: don't climb up anything you can't climb down, and it is always more difficult to climb down. Move through these sections one at a time, and try to position yourself where you can offer assistance but won't get taken out in the event someone falls.

3. Descents are where things are most likely to go wrong. Leave plenty of time and daylight for the descent; it almost always takes longer than anticipated. When you're moving down steep terrain, facing into the hillside will be more secure, but facing out will allow you a better view of potential holds. On steep smooth ground, keep your knees bent and your center of gravity over the balls of your feet; resist the temptation to lean too far back.

EXPERT WITNESS

WHAT TO EAT ON A HIKE

Graham Zimmerman, alpinist, Piolet d'Or finalist, ice climber, and rock climber

For a single day in the mountains, I bring food that doesn't require any cooking and foods that I can snack on easily. Items such as simple bars and trail mixes are my go-to. I need to eat a little bit often and drink plenty of water. Often I will eat energy bars a quarter at a time so that I spread my fuel out throughout the activity and keep myself powered up all day long.

For a night out when the weight in my pack is not a huge concern, I will often bring tortillas with simple fixings. I can cook one-minute rice alongside beans in a pot and combine this with cheese and some fresh veggies on a tortilla to make for a pretty excellent meal. This can be complemented with a chocolate bar for dessert to get a little more sugar into the mix. And as always, remember to hydrate!

When we stop to bivy on a big mountain route is when the real fun starts. I have a drink mix that's most of what I consume in the evening. Here are the components that I mix up before I set off.

5 parts vegetarian protein powder

5 parts Carbo Gain maltodextrin

1 part cacao powder

1 part wheatgrass powder

1 part maca powder

Mix a liter of water with a couple of scoops of this stuff and your body will go into full recovery mode. I'll also eat some solid food, but about half as much as I normally would. This is mostly to make me feel happy and give me something solid that's tougher to metabolize, therefore keeping me warm when I sleep.

This solid food will be half dried mashed spuds and half rolled quinoa mixed with salami, cheese, sea salt, and turmeric. Basically a comfort meal with the added benefit of helping you hydrate (salt), working as an anti-inflammatory (turmeric), and giving you lots of protein (quinoa).

The superdrink gets mixed up in a water bottle, and the solid food gets mixed up in an old freeze-dried-meal bag, meaning that the cook pot stays clean and can be melting water the whole time that consumption is going on. Also, all this can be cooked with tepid water simply poured over it. Meaning, no mess and super fuel efficiency—which in the mountains is the kind of world you want to live in.

Ten Mountains to Climb That Don't Require Ropes or Crampons

1. Longs Peak, Colorado (14,259 feet)

2. Mount Whitney, California (14,505 feet)

3. Half Dome, California (8,839 feet)

4. Katahdin, Maine (5,270 feet)

5. Humphreys Peak, Arizona (12,637 feet)

6. Old Rag Mountain, Virginia (3,291 feet)

7. Mount Si, Washington (4,167 feet)

8. Mount Marcy, New York (5,343 feet)

9. Ben Nevis, Scotland (4,409 feet)

10. Mount Temple, Alberta, Canada (11,627 feet)

Should I feed animals in the wild?

Although it's tempting to think about giving little squirrels, pikas, and marmots a bit of your trail snacks, you shouldn't feed the animals. Your generosity causes animals to abandon their natural food sources and become dependent on handouts from hikers; when the hiking season ends, the animals lose their food source. On popular trails and summits, hikers who sit down for a snack experience the effects of years of hikers feeding animals, as they're pestered nonstop by persistent squirrels. Squirrels in the Grand Canyon have been found to carry plague, and animals carry other diseases like hantavirus and rabies, so it's best to keep your distance and keep your peanut butter and jelly sandwich to yourself.

What should I do if I find an arrowhead or ancient pot?

As good as that arrowhead or potsherd might look on your fireplace mantel at home, you should leave it where it is. If you're on public lands, it's actually a crime to remove archaeological artifacts in the United States, under the Archaeological Resources Protection Act. If you're caught, the offense will be prosecuted as a misdemeanor or a felony, depending on the severity of your offense. If you find an artifact, it's best to take a photo, marvel for a minute about how old it is, and leave it where you found it.

What's the difference between trail running and regular running?

Depending on the trail, trail running can be far more strenuous than running on streets/sidewalks or on city park trails. Steep trails can gain upwards of 500 feet in a lateral mile, and running up them can require far more energy than taking most jogging/multiuse trails or sidewalks in cities. The trail surface can also keep you literally and figuratively on your toes—stepping on and over rocks and roots, making sure you don't land on loose debris, and not tripping over obstacles in the trail all require more vigilance than most urban running routes. That's the challenging part. The good news is, time often flies during trail runs because of the varying surfaces and twists and turns in the trail, compared to running laps around a city park or on the street. And, obviously, your chances of getting hit by a car are almost zero—although you'll probably want to keep an eye out for deer and other wildlife, depending on where you run. Another thing that's important to remember is that you might not have cell phone service on a trail run, which can make a huge difference if you sprain an ankle 3 miles from the trailhead.

Should I try trail running?

If you enjoy running, there aren't too many reasons you'd dislike trail running. It takes you to beautiful places, gets you outside in a place with fresh air, is probably more interesting than pounding the pavement in your neighborhood, and might be a better workout (depending on the trail you pick). If you're terribly klutzy with your feet (i.e., you 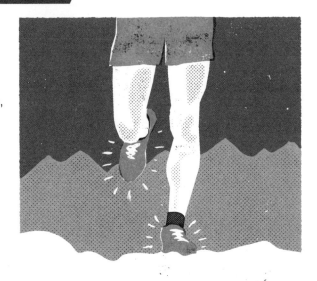 trip on nonexistent cracks in the sidewalk while running), you might have a little trouble with all the rocks and roots you'll encounter during a trail run. But taking that risk is a personal judgment call. Some trail runners say the constant attention to footwork keeps them alert and even seems to leave them less sore than running on pavement or asphalt because running on a dirt trail means you're not landing as hard on your feet.

What kind of shoes should I wear for trail running?

On well-packed trails without many loose sections, roots, or rocks, road-running shoes can work just fine on trail runs. But if you're getting into regular trail running, you might want to invest in trail-running shoes for a few reasons. The outsoles are more aggressively featured and better at gripping varied terrain—some models have stickier rubber that enables them to grip angled rock slabs. The soles of trail-running shoes are generally wider than those of road-running shoes, to help you balance as you run over uneven terrain. Trail-running shoe uppers are usually built with features to protect your feet from rocks, sticks, and other debris, such as tougher materials, toe bumpers, and sometimes waterproof lining.

Should I try rock climbing?

Rock climbing is one of the fastest-growing outdoor sports (if you count people who do it in climbing gyms at least part of the time), for good reason: it is exciting, builds strength and flexibility, gives you fitness goals other than looking good with your shirt off, and, with the explosion of climbing gyms, is something you can learn in a safe (albeit indoor) environment. If you climbed trees as a child, you might love rock climbing as an adult. Even if you didn't climb trees as a child, and you're just curious about the thrill of hanging a few dozen (or a few hundred) feet off the ground, you might like rock climbing. Surprisingly, entry-level rock climbing doesn't require as much upper-body strength as you might think—even if you can't do a single pull-up in the gym, you can learn the right techniques to climb intermediate to difficult routes. With the advent of indoor climbing gyms where you can rent gear and go to learn the ropes, you don't need a climbing cliff nearby to try it out.

How do I get started rock climbing?

Despite what you might have seen in movies, using a rope to keep yourself (and your friends) from falling off a cliff isn't something you can just wing without knowing a few things first. It might seem antithetical to learn to do something like rock climbing indoors, but climbing gyms are the best places to learn its safety concepts and techniques and to try it out before buying all the necessary gear. Plenty of climbing gyms offer an introductory lesson or class for fifty dollars or less per person (including all the gear you need to learn to climb). An introductory course will give you a chance to see if you like the movement and, more important, the exposure to heights, with no pressure or commitment. If you like it, you can usually buy all the gear you need right at the gym, keep going back, and eventually take the climbing outside. Many gyms also offer classes to help you safely transfer what you've learned on artificial climbing walls to real cliffs outside.

What's the difference between rock climbing and mountaineering?

It's easy to confuse the two. After all, no one says, "I'm going to 'mountaineer' Mount Everest"—but that's exactly what you do. Tackling Mount Everest is mountaineering; you'll encounter rock, snow, and ice while traveling up the mountain. Rock climbing is performed only on rock surfaces (or indoor climbing gyms). Mountaineering objectives can involve a section of rock climbing, so most mountaineers learn and practice rock-climbing skills. However, plenty of the world's famous mountains don't involve significant rock climbing—one can climb Mount Rainier, Denali, Aconcagua, and Mount Everest without having any prior technical rock-climbing experience, for instance. Mountaineering usually involves wearing insulated mountaineering boots (often with crampons as well), and rock climbing usually involves wearing slipper-like climbing shoes.

What's the difference between bouldering and rock climbing?

Bouldering is a subcategory of rock climbing, and it's essentially different in four ways.

1. **The routes in bouldering, called "boulder problems," are shorter in height.** Most boulder problems (indoors and outdoors) are shorter than 15 feet tall, whereas most rock-climbing routes are around 30 feet (indoors) and 30 to 115 feet (outdoors).

2. **Ropes are not used in bouldering.** The routes are shorter, so if you fall, you land on the ground. Indoors, cushy mats protect you from injury. Outdoors, you bring your own pads, called crash pads, to land on.

3. **Bouldering is generally more difficult, gymnastic climbing.** The easiest boulder problems are as difficult as intermediate climbing routes (but shorter).

4. **You can do it by yourself.** Since you don't need a rope, you don't need a partner to hold the rope for you. You can go bouldering, indoors or outdoors, by yourself (although it's good to have a partner outdoors to spot you, or make sure you land on your crash pad). Bouldering in a climbing gym is a good way to learn the movement of rock climbing without having a partner.

How do I climb rock faces?

A common misunderstanding of rock climbers, possibly because of the film *Cliffhanger*, in which Sylvester Stallone spends significant periods hanging thousands of feet up with only one hand, is that they have tremendous upper-body strength. Expert climbers often do develop incredible strength in their fingers, forearms, and back muscles, but climbing is more of a total-body effort. Any experienced climber will tell you that rock climbing is all about footwork and learning to stand on tiny footholds—not doing thousands of pull-ups. To move up basic rock-climbing terrain, you'll step up, using your hands for balance, but not death-gripping handholds. Your weight should be on your feet, because your legs can sustain holding your body weight for hours longer than your hands and arms can.

To climb, find a foothold and step onto it, gradually applying all your body weight to that foot. Locate another hold for your other foot, step on it, and distribute your weight as evenly as possible between the two. Find a good handhold for each of your hands, make sure you're comfortable, and then start to look for a new foothold for one of your feet. Move in small steps, not big lunges—small movements are less dynamic and make it easier to stay in control of your balance. Always make sure you have three good points of contact with the rock (two hands and a foot, two feet and one hand, etc.) before you move. On less-than-vertical rock, don't hug the rock face—keeping your butt out away from the rock will deliver more weight to your shoes and help them stick instead of sliding off holds.

What do climbing grades mean?

Climbing has the most confusing system of classifying difficulty. Skiing has the green-blue-black system, which even a four-year-old can understand. Climbing's grading system, called the Yosemite Decimal System, has to be explained historically to make any sense. When the system was first created, fifth-class climbing, which is roped climbing, was assigned a decimal system: 5.1 was the easiest roped climbing, and 5.9 was the most difficult.

This system worked until one day some- one climbed a route so difficult it couldn't be classified as 5.9, so it was decided to be 5.10 (which mathematically makes no sense—but think of 10 being more difficult than 9). So then the tough- est climbs in the United States were classified as 5.10—until someone climbed something more

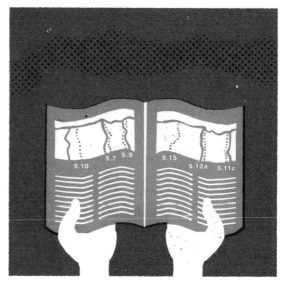

difficult, and it was decided to add letters to the system. If a route was harder than 5.10, it was rated 5.10a. Then, of course, came 5.10b, 5.10c, and 5.10d. After 5.10d came 5.11, then 5.11a, and so on. Now the most challenging climb in the world is rated a 5.15c. Only the upper end of the grading scale (5.10-5.15) uses letters.

If you're confused, just remember to stay at the lower end of the scale when you're learning to climb. Routes at climbing gyms are clearly labeled, and as you're starting out, try a few 5.6s, 5.7s, and 5.8s. Pretty soon you'll be up in the 5.10s, and someday you'll be able to feel the difference between a 5.11b and a 5.11c.

How do climbing ropes work?

Climbing ropes are dynamic ropes, meaning they're built to stretch when force is applied. They don't stretch as much as a bungee cord, but enough so that the force of a climbing fall is distributed along the length of the rope, stretching slightly, so that at the end of the fall there is little or no impact on a climber's body—as opposed to with a nonstretching, or static, rope, which would give a climber a huge jolt at the end of even a short fall (enough to break the climber's

back). If you're first learning to climb, indoors or outdoors, you'll very likely be climbing on what's called a toprope system: the rope runs from your harness up to an anchor and then back down to your belayer. Your belayer will pull in slack as you climb up, keeping the rope tight, so that when you fall you'll only fall a few inches or feet (as the rope stretches). The route ends when you reach the anchor, and your belayer will lower you back to the ground.

Can I climb if I'm afraid of heights?

If you're scared of heights, climbing will do one of two things: help you to learn to deal with your fear of heights, or emphatically establish that you should never get higher off the ground than the top of a 6-foot ladder. Fear of heights is a normal, safe, rational thing, and without it climbing wouldn't be thrilling (for those people who find it thrilling) or empowering (for those people who find it empowering). If you're scared of heights but want to try climbing, you should absolutely try it, and don't be afraid to ease yourself into heights—there are no rules anywhere that say you have to climb to the top of a route. Try getting a few feet off the ground your first time, maybe a few feet higher the next time, and maybe by the end of your first day, you'll get to the top. If being fifteen feet up absolutely terrifies you, lower back to the ground and congratulate yourself for at least trying it out. If you're not sure, it might be better to try climbing indoors for your first time—the trained staff and controlled environment can lend an air of safety to something that feels inherently risky.

When should I wear a helmet?

Helmets are a touchy subject in rock climbing and mountaineering (or really in any pursuit besides professional sports). People wear them when they feel they're necessary, and everyone has their own reasons for choosing to (or choosing not to) wear a helmet. Here are a few things to consider when deciding whether you want to put your noggin under a helmet.

- **Mountaineering:** Any route that's third class, fourth class, or fifth class may have potential for rockfall, whether it's accidentally kicked down a gully by your partner or just standard geologic shifting.

- **Rock climbing:** Helmets are generally uncommon at sport-climbing areas where all the routes are bolted, mostly because of the assumption that crags don't have loose rock. This is sometimes true, but not always. Helmets will protect you from anything falling from above, whether it's a broken handhold, a rock that just came off the top of the cliff for seemingly no particular reason, or a carabiner accidentally dropped from above—as well as if you catch a rope behind your leg when you're leading and flip upside down when you fall, or if you're squeezing underneath a roof (an overhanging section of rock) and underestimate the size of your own head and bang it on the rock (it happens to the best of us).

- **Ice climbing:** At ice-climbing areas, chunks of ice will most likely be falling from above, as climbers swing tools and kick crampons.

- **Terminal velocity:** Even a tiny, tiny rock that drops 50 or 100 feet before it hits your head will hurt.

Eight Important Climbing Terms

1. **Belay:** To provide safety for a climber by essentially holding on to the opposite end of the rope the climber is tied to. Historically, belayers ran the rope around their bodies to provide enough friction to stop a fall—thankfully, belay devices have enabled that same stopping power by redirecting the rope through a piece of metal clipped to the belaying climber's harness.

2. **Crimp:** A small hold that only one pad of your fingers fits on.

3. **Jam:** A crack-climbing technique, in which hands, fingers, or feet are wedged into a crack in the rock, providing enough friction for enough of a downward pull to move the climber upward.

4. **Jug:** A large handhold that you can wrap your fingers around— shortened from "jug handle."

5. **Route:** The specific line of a climb, indoors or outdoors. Routes can be one pitch (30 to 115 feet), or many pitches (routes on El Capitan are as long as 3,000 feet). Each route is graded for difficulty, and each has a unique name if it's an outdoor route (some climbing gyms name their routes, but not all).

6. **Send:** The term for lead-climbing a route, without falling or stopping, to let your body weight rest on the rope.

7. **Smear:** Not as gross as it sounds, a smear is a technique where the friction of your climbing shoe on minimally featured rock provides the foothold.

8. **Toprope:** A climb that has a rope redirected from the belayer to the top of the route to the climber, minimizing the distance the climber will fall should he or she come off the route.

What kind of climbing knots should I know?

Surprisingly, you don't have to know that many knots for basic roped rock climbing. These seven knots will get you through most situations.

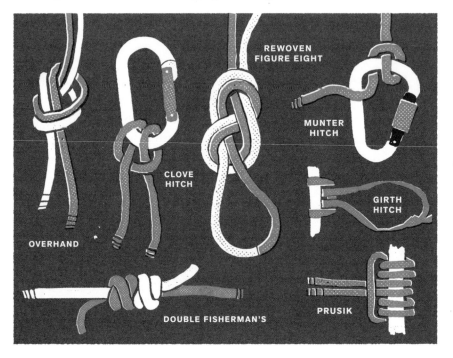

1. **Rewoven Figure Eight:** Used to attach a climbing rope to the climber's harness

2. **Clove Hitch:** Used to tie a rope to a carabiner

3. **Girth Hitch:** Used to tie climbing slings to things, including the climber's harness

4. **Prusik:** Used to ascend ropes and as rappel backup

5. **Double Fisherman's:** Used to tie two ends of a rope or cord together

6. **Overhand:** Used to tie two ropes together

7. **Munter hitch:** Used to belay or lower someone if the climber drops or loses his or her belay device

How should climbing shoes fit?

Climbing shoes have traditionally been designed to be everything but comfortable—something that's been changing for the better over recent years, thankfully. Also traditionally, shoes were worn small enough that they were painful to walk in, sometimes two or three full sizes too small. Climbers figured less loose material meant more sensitivity to small holds. Today, expert climbers tackling technical, overhanging routes still wear tight-fitting shoes, for good reasons. But your first pair of climbing shoes shouldn't be uncomfortably tight or really that expensive. Shoes at the lower end of the price spectrum (one hundred dollars or less) are great shoes to learn to climb in—they're comfortable, all-purpose, and great for learning basic footwork and movement. Pick a pair that isn't breaking the bank, and try them on if at all possible. They should fit snugly, with no extra shoe rubber sticking out at the ends of your toes or the sides of your feet, but not so tight that they're painful or your toes are curled up when you put them on. Leather shoes will stretch a little bit as they break in, and shoes made of synthetic material will not. If you're renting shoes at a climbing gym, you might want to wear socks, but most climbers don't wear socks with the climbing shoes they own.

How can I climb Everest?

Climbing Mount Everest is a commitment in many ways—you have to commit to the physical training, the amount of time required to climb it (typically a total of two and a half months of travel, acclimatization, and waiting for a weather window for a summit attempt), and the expense (usually around $70,000, not including travel to and from Nepal). Most guide companies require clients to have both mountaineering experience and experience at high altitude, so a typical progression to an Everest climb might be a guided climb of Mount Rainier (14,410 feet) in Washington your first year, a climb of Aconcagua (22,837 feet) in Argentina or Denali (20,310 feet) in Alaska your second year, and then Everest your third year. It's not impossible to conquer Everest, it's just expensive in a lot of ways—time and money—so if you want to climb it you definitely have to be serious about the endeavor.

How can I climb Kilimanjaro?

Tanzania's 19,341-foot Mount Kilimanjaro, one of the Seven Summits—the highest mountains on each continent—is an iconic mountain climb, but much more within reach for most people than mountains of similar height like Aconcagua and Denali. Although it's a challenging, high-altitude climb, Kilimanjaro is not technical (there's no snow or ice on the route, and ropes aren't used). All ascents of the peak are guided and employ local guides (usually working with international mountain guide companies). Guided climbs usually take about two weeks (not including travel to and from Tanzania), include a safari, and cost around $6,000. The climb itself is a hike, on a route similar in difficulty to those on nontechnical peaks in Colorado or California. The difference is the elevation—the thin air at 19,341 feet is the great equalizer. Thankfully, the first days of the climb are spent acclimating, and you gradually move higher and higher up the mountain, so your body can learn to function with less oxygen as you get closer to the top. If you train properly (even though there's no snow or ice, the climb still requires some serious leg muscles, endurance, and cardiovascular fitness) and if you have the money, you can do it.

Is there a challenging but doable mountain to climb closer to home?

Climbing the tallest peak in the lower forty-eight states, California's 14,505-foot Mount Whitney, has become a much bigger logistical challenge in recent years. Permits to climb the peak via the Mount Whitney Trail are capped at 160 people per day (100 day hikers and 60 overnight hikers) during the high season and are awarded in a lottery. If you plan ahead and are flexible on dates, getting a permit is less stressful. Once you get the permit, the climb is tough but doable: if you get a single-day permit, you'll have to hike 11 miles of trail to the summit, covering 6,100 vertical feet—and then turn around and descend all that steep mileage back to the trailhead. It's a long day. You can make the challenge a bit less strenuous if you split it up into two days (one day to hike up partway and camp, the next day to summit and hike back out). The good news is, the climb is nontechnical. It's all class 2 (see page 103), which means it's a good trail all the way to the top—even if it's rocky for most of it and in the thin air at high elevation.

Why should I try mountain biking?

Mountain biking can appeal to a variety of people: those who loved riding BMX bikes on dirt as kids, those who like tearing downhill at high speeds, and those who love the cardiovascular workout of pedaling a bike up steep uphill grades. It also appeals to those who just want to ride a bicycle somewhere where there aren't cars, or those who love hiking but would also like the ability to coast over long sections of trails—or would like to move faster in the back-country than they can while hiking. Mountain biking can be challenging from a skills standpoint: for example, trying to pedal uphill around a tight corner while steering your front tire between rocks, or descending a steep downhill section without flipping yourself over your handlebars by squeezing the brakes too hard. But there are also hundreds of mellow trails out there for beginners or anyone wanting to go for a scenic ride in a beautiful place.

Should I use clip-in pedals or platform pedals?

You have a choice when it comes to pedals: platform pedals—the basic, flat pedals that work with any shoe—or pedals that attach to special cycling shoes—which, confusingly enough, are actually called "clipless." Both have advantages and disadvantages for the rider.

Platform pedals are simple to use: you just step onto them and go, and anytime you want to take your foot off the pedal (e.g., when you don't quite correctly navigate through a tricky section of trail and want to put your foot down on the ground for balance, or when you stop to get off your bike), you just do it. The disadvantage of platform pedals is efficiency of motion: a pedal stroke is a full circle, and without your foot attached to the pedal in some way, you're only truly using half of that circle (or less)—the "pushing" part. Still, for a lot of mountain bikers, platform pedals make sense—they mostly go on rides where being able to quickly disengage from their pedals trumps everything else, they have anxiety about being able to clip in and clip out when they need to, or they're strictly riding downhill at a place where they use a ski lift or other means to get to the top of a trail. If you're just starting out mountain biking, platform pedals are a good choice.

Clipless pedals got their name because cyclists used to use "toe clips," a strap-and-cage contraption that attached to pedals. When a system was devised that attached a cleat on the bottom of a cycling shoe to a pedal, toe clips took a backseat, and riders went clipless. It seems strange to call the pedals clipless, since your shoe literally clips into the pedal, but that's the way it is. Clipless pedals are a mechanical advantage for a couple reasons: you can pedal in a full circle, using your foot to pull the pedal backward and upward through the five o'clock to twelve o'clock positions of the pedal stroke, and you can wear stiff shoes with them, which helps transfer more of your pedaling energy into the pedal stroke than a soft shoe. To unclip from your clipless pedals, turn your ankle outward and the clip disengages. Lots of people have trouble with clipless pedals at first, forgetting when they stop that their foot is attached to the pedal until their bike starts to lean over to one side and they crash. You have to train your brain to remember the motion of unclipping so that it becomes automatic (or deal with a few bruises and scrapes from falling over before you learn). Or you can set the pedals to be very loose, so that it only takes a very small motion to unclip—but that can leave you in a position where your shoe might unclip in situations where you don't want it to, like intense uphill pedaling.

What kind of mountain bike do I need?

Thanks to capitalism and engineering, we have dozens of choices when it comes to mountain bikes. We also have the ability to spend anywhere between $400 and $15,000 on a mountain bike—but don't worry, you don't need a five-figure bike to have a good time on the bike.

- **27.5:** Now the dominant wheel size in biking, wheels with a 27.5-inch diameter are a compromise between the traditional 26-inch size and the 29-inch size.

- **29er:** A mountain bike with 29-inch diameter wheels. The good things about 29-inch wheels: They roll over obstacles more easily, and they retain momentum once you're going on a trail. The bad things: They weigh a little bit more, they make it (slightly) tougher to start pedaling once you've stopped, and larger wheels make the bicycles more difficult to maneuver at low speeds (e.g., pedaling uphill around a tight corner).

- **Front suspension:** A mountain bike with a front suspension, or shock, only on the front fork, to absorb the impact of rolling over obstacles.

- **Full suspension:** A mountain bike with a front suspension as well as a rear suspension, combining to absorb the shock of rolling over obstacles and riding bumpy terrain. This bike is more expensive and heavy than bikes with only a front suspension.

- **Fully rigid:** A mountain bike with no suspension; this is the choice of more advanced riders, as the lack of shock absorption requires a much higher skill level to ride rough trails.

- **Single-speed:** Just like it sounds, a single-speed bike has only one gear.

What tools should I take with me on a mountain bike ride?

Unless you're a trained bike mechanic, you're probably not going to be able to fix everything that could potentially go wrong on a mountain bike ride—nor do you want to carry all the tools you'd need in your backpack. But lots of small problems can be fixed with a few tools and a little MacGyver ingenuity. Here's a basic list of what you should have in your toolkit.

- **Baling wire:** Malleable but strong, baling wire can fix plenty of bicycle problems. Clip off a section 6 to 8 feet long and put it in your toolkit.

- **Duct tape:** You always need duct tape. Don't take the whole roll—make yourself a smaller roll 6 to 8 feet long (about the size of a golf ball) that you can pack more easily.

- **Chain lube:** A small bottle of chain lube is great to have in your toolkit for long rides, or when you start pedaling from the trailhead and you hear a squeaking coming from your chain and realize it's been a while since you lubricated it.

- **Multitool:** A compact bike multitool (different from a pliers-style multitool) can solve a hundred problems. Make sure it has plenty of hex wrenches, both Phillips and regular screwdriver heads, and a chain tool.

- **Pump:** A small tire pump should either attach to the frame of your bike or fit in your backpack easily.

- **Rag:** You'll need it for wiping off excess chain lube.

- **Spare inner tube:** It's easier (and faster) in most flat-tire situations to put in a new inner tube than it is to look for the hole that caused the flat.

- **Tire patch kit:** But, of course, you might get two flats on a single ride, so carry a patch kit just in case, because finding the hole and patching it is probably faster than walking your bike all the way back to the trailhead. A patch kit will include patches, adhesive sealant, small squares of sandpaper or other abrasive to rough up the rubber to enable the patches to stick better, and possibly (but not always) tire levers to remove your tire from the wheel. If your patch kit doesn't come with tire levers, make sure you buy a pair.

- **Zip ties:** Zip ties are the duct tape of the cycling world. Throw a half dozen in your toolkit and you won't regret it. A shifter cable hanging loose off your frame or a bottle cage bolt rattled loose and lost along the trail can be fixed in a few seconds with a zip tie.

What do I do if I break a spoke?

You might not notice a broken spoke at first. If you hear it, it will be a loud popping noise coming from your front or rear wheel, which is the sound of the spoke breaking or separating from the wheel. You can carry an extra spoke, but most mountain bikers don't because replacing spokes is pretty labor intensive (you have to remove the tire and tube); plus, a spoke is difficult to pack since it's long and bends easily when not attached to the wheel, and putting it on correctly is an advanced science requiring tightening the spoke to a specific tension correlated with the tightness of other spokes holding the wheel's rim straight. So basically, don't worry about it. If you break a spoke, your wheel will probably be fine for the rest of your ride (unless the wheel was extremely out of true alignment when you started). Stop riding, get off your bike, and stow the broken spoke away as best as possible—bend it around a neighboring healthy spoke, wrapping it so it won't get caught in anything as you continue to ride. Monitor the wheel for significant wobbling, and be vigilant and pay attention to your other spokes. If the wheel is wobbling, walk the bike in. If you break a second spoke on the same wheel, the wheel will become very unstable and it's probably best to walk the bike back to the trailhead instead of risking completely ruining the wheel. Replacing a spoke is inexpensive, but replacing the wheel will cost around one hundred dollars at the very least.

How do I fix a flat tire?

Flats happen, and learning to quickly fix them will give you independence, prevent a lot of walking, and perhaps make you a hero to someone else out on the trail. Here's how to do it.

- Remove the wheel from the bike. Be careful to not touch your brake rotors—they'll be hot if you've been riding and braking a lot. Your front wheel is easier to remove than your back wheel. If it's your front wheel, open the quick-release lever and unscrew it until the wheel is loose enough to remove. If it's your rear wheel, shift gears until the chain is around the smallest cog, and then move the derailleur out of the way as you pull the wheel out of the frame (this can take some practice and even after dozens of times will probably never feel as though you're doing it right).

- Let any remaining air out of the tire. If there's still air in the tube, depress the tire valve until all the remaining air escapes.

- Check the outside of the tire for the hole. Look closely to see if you can spot a small thorn or something else that's stuck in your tire. You may not see anything, but if you do, pull it out of the tire.

- Remove the tire from the wheel. Insert your tire lever where the tire meets the wheel, pry the tire bead away from the wheel, and pop it over to the outside of the rim. Once you've got a few inches of it out of the rim, the rest will come out easily.

- Remove the tube. Push the tube valve through its hole in the rim and pull the damaged tube out. Check the valve stem for damage—if there's a hole in the valve stem, that's probably what caused your flat.

- Find the cause of the flat. This is important, because if you simply replace the tube without finding the thorn or other object that caused the flat, you'll ride a few feet down the trail with your fresh tube and have another flat tire to deal with. Finding the problem can be tougher than it sounds—often the object that caused your flat is almost invisible. Run your fingers around the inside of the tire, slowly, feeling for anything sharp or foreign. If you don't find anything, try turning the tire inside out and looking closely. Remove the object or objects.

- Put the tire halfway back on the rim. Make sure the tire is facing the proper direction (there should be an arrow on the tire itself indicating the direction of rotation), and place one bead back on the rim, leaving the other bead on the outside so you can stuff the new tube in between the tire and rim.

- Put the tube in. Using your tire pump, inflate the tire a little bit to give it some shape. Find the hole for your valve stem and put that part of the tube in first, then push the rest of the tube into the tire.

- Put the tire back on. Make sure one bead is completely seated on the rim correctly, and then begin to seat the remaining bead. Holding the wheel in your lap with the valve at the top, or twelve o'clock position, begin pushing the bead into the rim, your right hand working the tire into the rim in a clockwise direction as your left hand simultaneously works the tire into the rim in a counterclockwise direction. As it becomes more difficult to push the bead into the rim, squeeze the entire tire toward the rim—grip near the valve and work both hands around the circle in opposite directions (right hand clockwise, left hand counterclockwise). This will help create just enough room for the bead to eventually squeeze all the way into the rim.

- Once you have the tire back on, check to make sure the tube isn't sticking out between the tire and rim anywhere—this can cause a "pinch flat" and you'll be right back where you started.

- Fully inflate the tire with your frame pump.

- Put the wheel back on your bike.

How do I do a basic bike tune-up at home?

To repair all the issues you'll have with your mountain bike requires specialized tools and the knowledge to use them properly. You should be able to tackle maintenance of your tires and chain and to perform a basic check of every-thing on the bike to make sure it's working correctly. If it isn't, you should also know when to take it to a bike mechanic for repairs and a professional tune-up.

- **Clean and lube your chain:** To clean your chain, spray it down with a degreaser such as Simple Green and a chain brush. To lubricate it, place a drop of lubricant on the top of the chain at each link, holding a pedal in one hand and turning the crank to move the chain so you can apply lubri-cant along its entire length. Use a rag to dry off excess lubricant.

- **Clean frame and wheels:** Use soapy water and a rag to wipe off the bike frame. Pay attention to the underside of the bike, where you'll likely find the most dirt and caked-on mud. Wipe off the rims.

- **Check wheels and spokes:** Flip your bike over and spin each wheel, checking that the rims don't wobble as the wheel rotates. Check your spokes to make sure none of them are loose. If a wheel wobbles or you find a loose spoke, take the wheel into a bike shop to have it trued.

- **Check tire pressure and tread:** Use a pump with a tire gauge to ensure that your tires are within the recommended pressure (the numbers printed on the sidewall of the tire). Inspect the tread of the tire to make sure no lugs have ripped off and that lug depth is sufficient. Check the tires for holes or thorns in the sidewalls and tread.

- **Check the brakes:** Spin the front tire and pull the brake lever to ensure that the brakes start to grip and stop the wheel at about one-third of a complete pull of the lever. If you have to squeeze the lever farther than a third or halfway to stop the wheel from spinning, take your bike into a shop and have the brakes serviced. Look down into your disc brake and squeeze the brake lever, making sure both sides of the brake calipers are squeezing the pads equally onto the rotors. If not, take the bike into a bike shop for servicing.

Nine Mountain Biking Terms

1. **Berm:** An embankment on a trail; enables a cyclist to lean into a turn.

2. **Chain suck:** The phenomenon of a bike chain not rolling through the drivetrain properly; for one reason or another (mud, worn-out drivetrain, etc.), the chain bunches up and jams.

3. **Clean:** To ride a difficult section of trail without falling or stopping.

4. **Doubletrack:** Two trails that parallel each other; they're often from an old fire road or ATV trail in which two tire tracks run next to each other.

5. **Endo:** A crash in which a cyclist falls (or flies) over the handlebars of the bicycle.

6. **Granny gear:** The easiest possible gear on a bicycle; used when pedaling steep uphill sections.

7. **Rock garden:** A section of trail composed of large rocks.

8. **Singletrack:** A trail wide enough for only one cyclist (or hiker).

9. **Switchback:** A zigzag in a trail, usually built because the trail climbs steeply uphill.

What do I do if I crash my bike?

With normal luck, you'll probably crash your bike several times—hopefully none too serious. When a crash does happen, you may not see it coming, but hopefully you'll be able to look back on the crash, see what you did wrong, and learn something for your next ride. When you crash, here's what to do.

First, check yourself for injuries: Can you stand up on your own? Can you lean on each arm? Can you walk? Inhale a few times, take your time, and slowly get up and check your limbs. If something is seriously broken or smashed, you'll likely be feeling it immediately, but a visual inspection will also help. Depending on which parts of your body took the majority of the impact force, you might have a broken collarbone (a common crash injury), a separated or sprained shoulder, or even a broken hip. In the best-case scenario, you'll have only a few cuts and scrapes.

Next, get yourself and your bike off the trail. If you're okay (or mostly okay), move to the side of the trail and get your bike off the trail as well—you don't want to be in the way of other cyclists, especially if you crashed in a spot where they won't see you lying on the ground until they're right on top of you.

Check your helmet. Is your helmet cracked or punctured, or otherwise compromised? If so, it's no longer useful in protecting your head, so consider that before you hop on your bike and ride the rest of the way back to the trailhead. Your safest option is to walk, but if you're confident your trail is easy riding you can negotiate, ride out carefully.

Then check your bike. Look over your bike for damage that will make it unsafe to ride. Are your handlebars still straight? If not, get out a multitool and straighten them before riding away. Are your wheels straight, or did one or both of your rims get bent in the crash? Spin each wheel and watch it all the way around its rotation to see if it wobbles. If it has a sizable wobble, it may not hold you all the way out to the trailhead, and it's better to walk out. Are your brakes working? As you spin and examine each wheel, pull the corresponding brake lever to make sure it's still engaging and stopping the wheel. Are your shifters working? Ride a few feet down the trail and click through a few gears to make sure your drivetrain is still operating correctly. If your derailleur (the small piece attached to your frame—just below the hub of your rear wheel—that the chain runs through) is bent, don't ride.

How do I avoid going over my handlebars?

Ride a mountain bike often enough, and you'll eventually crash a few times. You may even find yourself flying over the handlebars once or twice. When you're starting out, here are a few pointers to prevent it.

- Use no more than two fingers on your brake levers. Disc brakes are particularly responsive, and you shouldn't need to pull hard to stop your bike—in fact, if you're moving fast at all, it's pretty easy to flip over the handlebars with a good hard squeeze of the front brake lever, so practice "feathering" your brakes, or gently applying pressure. And try to squeeze both at the same time in almost all situations. If you have all four of your fingers wrapped around your levers and you panic and squeeze your front brake lever hard, you'll have a good chance of flying over your handlebars—so don't ever place more than two fingers on the levers.

- Ride within your limits. If you're not confident in your skills, going faster isn't going to make you feel safer. There's nothing wrong with riding at what you think is 70 to 80 percent of your capacity.

- When going downhill, put your body weight to the back of the bike as much as possible. Drop your heels as low as you can. On steep sections, take your butt off your seat and slide behind your seat so your butt is over your rear wheel.

- Keep your center of gravity over the bottom bracket of your bike. Or think, "Heavy feet, light hands" when you ride.

- Keep your elbows slightly bent. When you're tired, you'll probably find yourself riding with your arms straight, placing more weight on the handlebars. Keeping your arms slightly bent will help you absorb bumps with your arms and keep you more in control.

How do I ride over a log?

Riding over obstacles while mountain biking is a matter of "when," not "if"—ride enough trails and you'll eventually have to roll over something bigger than you think is possible. Of course, you can always stop your bike, step off, and walk it over the obstacle, but if you have to do that too many times in

one ride, it can become maddening. For smaller or lower-profile objects in your path (roots, rocks, water bars, manmade steps, or anything 5 inches or shorter), it's often enough to just keep rolling at a moderate speed, adjust your stance so your weight is more on the back wheel than the front wheel (i.e., you're not leaning down on the handlebars), and give the handlebars a pull upward with both hands to help the wheel roll over the obstacle.

If you need to take on a bigger obstacle, say, something 5 to 18 inches tall, you'll need to put in a little more effort. Keep your speed moderate, try to approach the object with your wheel at a 90-degree angle to it (i.e., across the log or step), and start to pull up your handlebars when you are approximately as far away from the object as it is tall (6 inches away for a 6-inch-high obstacle, 12 inches away for a 12-inch-high obstacle, etc.). At the same time you pull up on your bars, pedal forward a half stroke or more—remember, all you're trying to do here is set your front wheel on top of the obstacle, not bunny hop over it. As your front wheel rolls over the top of the obstacle, transition forward on the bike so your weight is over the bars, slightly leaning forward so you're helping the bike carry your momentum over the obstacle. Pedal firmly up and over the object and keep your rear wheel following your front wheel.

What if the chain falls off my bike?

If your bike chain comes off from a crash or other cause, stop and dismount your bike. Shift your front derailleur to the smallest chainring, and shift your rear derailleur to the smallest cog. Lean the bike up against something solid (like a tree) or have a friend hold it upright. Kneel next to the bike, facing the right side of the bike. Push your rear derailleur toward the front of the bike with your left hand, creating slack in the chain. Use your right hand to pull the chain up and set it on top of the smallest chainring, trying to get as many chainring teeth in the chain as possible. Ease the rear derailleur back into position, and the chain should reseat itself on the chainring. If necessary, lift the rear of the bike off the ground so the rear wheel can spin freely, and turn the crank with your hand so the chain moves forward and completely reseats on the crank.

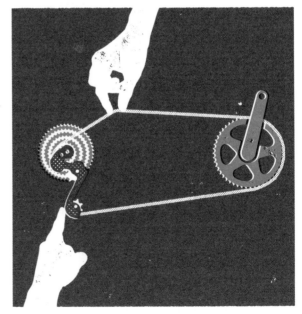

Eight Mountain Bike Rides to Try

1. **Porcupine Rim, Moab, Utah:** This single 30-mile loop on one of the most famous desert mountain bike trails in America includes slickrock, sandstone step drops, and sandy corners.

2. **Zippity Do Da, Fruita, Colorado:** A one-way, 18-mile downhill loop trail with steep descents down ridge tops and long sections of huge rolling hills.

3. **Hangover Trail, Sedona, Arizona:** Less than 4 miles, but heart-pounding exposure to drop-offs and difficult sections make this a test of bike-handling skills—and composure.

4. **Monarch Crest, Salida, Colorado:** A 30-mile ride starting at 11,000 feet, with views for days. The route includes 10 miles of trail that roll along the top of the Continental Divide in the Colorado Rockies.

5. **Big Loop, Gooseberry Mesa, Hurricane, Utah:** The 14 miles of windy, twisty routes through slickrock bowls and tight-turning singletrack feel like a giant skate park in the desert.

6. **Tsali Trails, Bryson City, North Carolina:** Features more than 30 miles of tree-lined swoopy singletrack in the Appalachian Mountains.

7. **Bull Mountain and Jake Mountain Trails, Georgia:** A network of more than 50 miles of trails with steep climbs and a swoopy singletrack. You'll have to carry your bike over the stream crossings.

8. **Comfortably Numb, Whistler, British Columbia:** A monument to human trail building, this test piece rolls up hand-built ladders, bridges, rock cliffs, and other features for almost 14 miles.

Can I mountain bike if it's rainy?

Maybe. Your biggest concern with rain is not getting wet when you ride but potentially ruining the trail for everyone else. In dry climates like Colorado's and Utah's, and in other alpine and desert environments, riding on a wet trail can wreck it, leaving mountain bike tire ruts through sections of trail—which, once they dry, aren't fun to navigate a bike through. In the Pacific Northwest, where the soil is more loamy and trails have absorbed moisture and human impact for years, biking in the rain is usually totally fine and won't cause permanent damage. If you're in doubt, ask a local: find a bike shop and ask an employee what trails are ridable in the rain (if any are). If locals don't ride when it's wet, don't ride when it's wet.

IN THE WATER

4

Humans were not born with gills or fins, but we've done a pretty good job figuring out how to use water for our recreational pastimes. We've invented myriad ways to enjoy our oceans, rivers, and lakes, from riding 20-foot-tall waves on a surfboard to navigating football field–sized whitewater rapids in a raft. Whether it's wave riding or sailing, there's a special feeling that comes from floating on water and pulling ourselves across it, or harnessing its energy to propel us forward.

This chapter covers how to survive and thrive in the water: swimming, surfing, stand-up paddling, whitewater kayaking, rafting, or flatwater canoeing. You'll learn what kind of watercraft is right for each situation and all the basics, from putting a boat on your car to driving a boat on water, from what to do when you flip a kayak to how to execute a perfect rollover, from how to save someone who falls overboard to how to get yourself safely out of a rip current.

Where can I recreate on water?

Although most of us are raised swimming in swimming pools nowadays, there's a lot of fun to be had playing in more "wild" water—the creeks, rivers, ponds, lakes, and oceans around us. (And there's probably less pee in it too.) Creeks and rivers are great for swimming (in swimming holes or in calmer sections), kayaking, canoeing, fishing, and sometimes stand-up paddleboarding. Ponds and lakes are calmer waters by nature and are even easier to swim in or paddle on, and they are great for fishing, whether from the shore or from a small boat. And thankfully, the majority of most coastlines remain public, so swimming, surfing (as well as other wave-riding activities), and fishing are easy to access. Of course, there are no lifeguards in most wild water situations (except at popular beaches), so be aware of dangers before heading out: rip currents, rapids, wake from big or fast boats, and even sharks.

What are some basics of water safety?

Aside from the fact that there are usually no lifeguards, swimming in the wild can be quite adventurous—or even dangerous. Some basic safety principles will help keep you alive.

- Moving water is more powerful than it looks. People have underestimated the flow of a river and stepped in, then become overpowered by the current or slipped, and been carried downstream and drowned or pulled over a waterfall. Don't chance it; respect flowing rivers.

- Consider the water temperature. Cold water can sap your energy, and icy-cold water can drop your body temperature to hypothermic in a matter of a few seconds or minutes. It might be fun to leap off a cliff into a mountain lake with chunks of snow and ice floating in it, but make sure you can get to shore easily before you jump in.

- Scout your landing area. If you're going to hop off a cliff or a boat (or even a bridge), make sure you know what's at the bottom and how close the bottom is. While it's exciting to make a leap of faith without looking first, it's far safer to swim into your intended landing area, dive down, and estimate how deep the bottom is. Slamming into the bottom of a pond or river or a rocky shelf in a lake can break bones.

- Don't get overconfident. In a lake or pond where there are no lifeguards, it's easy to get in trouble by swimming out too far and becoming exhausted or freezing. It's better to swim near shore than end up sinking in the middle.

- Wear a life jacket. If you're in a boat, wear your life jacket from the outset. After you fall out of the boat, it's too late to try to put on a life jacket.

How do I hold my breath underwater?

Holding your breath underwater seems simple, but there are ways to maximize your breath holding.

- Before you submerge your head, be as calm as possible. Don't go from paddling your arms and legs frantically to dunking your head underwater—your heart rate will be higher, requiring more oxygen and thus more breaths. Less motion equals less oxygen needed.

- When you're ready, take a big breath in, and exhale it out—all the way out. Take one more big inhale, and go underwater.

- Stay calm underneath the surface of the water. Make sure you're not sinking, but don't paddle your arms and legs around too much.

- As you start to feel like your lungs are bursting, try letting out small sips of air—not full exhales, just create some room. Obviously, don't breathe in.

Stay close to the surface of the water, and when you start to get uncomfortable, swim up and pop your head out to get some air.

How do I swim?

Most kids spend half their summer every year for five or six years learning how to swim, but you probably don't need that much instruction. If you aren't trying to win an Olympic medal and instead you just want to survive in the water, here's what you need to know.

Get in the water and lie on your stomach. Extend your arms; cup your hands and keep them under the water in front of your body, paddling from just below your shoulders to just above your waist, one hand at a time—as

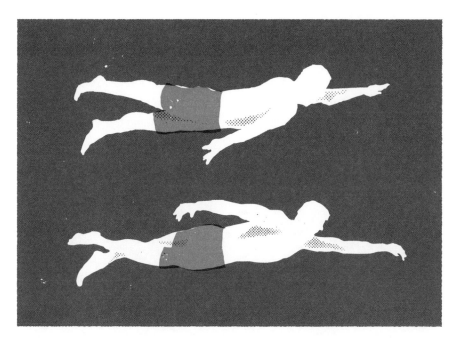

you paddle your left hand downward from your shoulders to your waist, simultaneously bring your right hand back up from your waist toward your shoulder so you can start the next paddle stroke. You should be scooping water toward your waist with the downward-paddling hand, and pulling the opposite hand through the water minimizing drag as it moves from your waist up to your shoulder.

As you paddle with your hands, simultaneously kick your feet under the water, moving from the hips (as opposed to the knees). Keep your toes pointed as you kick. Kicking will help keep your body in a swimming position (lying down as opposed to pointing straight down in the water) and keep you more buoyant than just paddling with your hands, not to mention use energy more efficiently than frantically trying to paddle using only your upper body.

Try to keep your body relaxed so you can move calmly and efficiently, not aggressively.

Once you become comfortable with the basic swimming technique, if you would like to move more quickly through the water, experiment with taking longer strokes with your arms and kicking your legs more forcefully to propel you forward.

How do I tread water?

Knowing how to tread water is useful if you just need to stay afloat in one spot. The first thing to remember: Relax. You shouldn't have to work too hard to keep your head above water once you learn proper treading technique, and a relaxed state of mind will keep you from expending too much energy on anxious movements.

Move your legs as if your feet are on bicycle pedals—but pedal, don't sprint. Keep pedaling.

Imagine you're looking down at your head from above—straight in front of your face is twelve o'clock, directly behind you is six o'clock, and so on. With your arms fully extended, left hand at nine o'clock and right hand at three o'clock, cup your hands facing forward and sweep them toward each other in a giant semicircular motion, almost meeting at twelve o'clock. Turn your cupped hands so they're facing away from each other and reverse the motion in an outward semicircle, stopping your sweeping stroke when your left hand is at nine o'clock and your right hand is back at three o'clock. Continue simultaneous leg and arm movements, and remember to relax. And keep your head pointed forward, not up.

How do I save someone who is drowning?

As easy as it may be to imagine yourself heroically diving into the water to reach someone who's struggling to stay afloat and drag them to safety, swimming to the person should actually be your last resort. If you see someone in danger of drowning, follow these five steps, in this order:

1. **Call for help.** Yell to anyone nearby to help you with the swimmer who's struggling—the more people, the better. Pulling a full-grown adult out of the water isn't easy.

2. **Try to reach the person.** Your first concern should be that the struggling person doesn't pull you into the water too—he or she will likely be panicking. Is there anything nearby that you can extend from shore to water to help pull the swimmer to safety? A tree branch, towel, or pool-skimming net can work. If you don't have anything, or the person is not close enough, get in the water and hang on to shore or a boat with one hand and extend your other hand to the swimmer.

3. **Throw something to the swimmer.** Most pools and most larger boats have a life preserver ring tied to a rope for just this purpose. If you can find one, throw it toward the swimmer. Don't worry about hitting him with it, or throwing it past him—he can always grab the rope if the actual life preserver ring flies over his head, and better too long than too short of a throw.

4. **Row.** If you're in a boat, try to maneuver it closer to the swimmer so he or she can grab on.

5. **Go.** As a last resort, swim toward the person. The person will likely be struggling, and in his or her efforts to stay afloat may drag you underwater as well, so be careful. If you have a towel, bring it with you so the swimmer can hang onto it while you tow him back to safety.

How do I get out of a rip current?

Rip currents are small ocean currents that typically flow away from a beach toward breaking waves. They can be hard to identify, and dangerous in that they can pull unsuspecting swimmers out to sea. Rip currents generally move perpendicular to a beach and might appear as a line of foam or debris steadily moving out

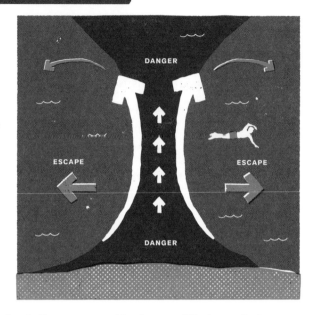

to sea. If you are swimming in the ocean and feel yourself being pulled away from the beach, you may be in a rip current.

To escape it, stay calm. You are not stronger than the ocean, so there's no use fighting directly against the current by paddling into it toward the beach. You'll want to paddle parallel to the beach to get out of the flow of the rip current. When you're able to break away from it, swim toward the beach at an angle facing away from the rip current (i.e., don't swim parallel to the current and accidentally find yourself back in it). If you're unable to break away from the current, stay calm and let it carry you out to sea a little ways—rip currents usually weaken as they travel away from the shore. Tread water as it carries you away, and when it weakens, swim parallel to shore to escape it, and once you escape it, again, swim toward the beach at an angle away from the rip current.

If you're unable to escape the rip current under your own power, tread water, face the beach, and yell for help while waving your arms above your head.

How do I ride waves?

The most straightforward way to understand wave riding is probably the most minimalist: bodysurfing, which is pretty much gliding down the front of a wave as it rolls into shore. To bodysurf, find a beach where the entry to the water is gradual, where you can wade in and then start swimming. Take a few minutes to watch the waves come in. You're looking for waves preferably 5 feet tall or shorter, that break in a slope down from top to bottom as you look at them from the shore rather than slamming down all at once (you're going to ride the wave, so if it's crashing straight down you'll crash straight

down too). Walk into the water until it's up to somewhere between your waist and chest, and watch for a wave to come in. If you see a wave you don't want to surf, turn sideways and duck into it, swimming through the back side of the wave as it passes. When you see a wave you want to surf, wait until the wave is about 5 feet from you, push yourself off the ocean floor and paddle hard toward shore, letting the wave carry you in on your stomach. That's body-surfing. Walk back out and pick another wave, this time trying to position yourself so your hips get above your head as you ride the wave into shore. As you graduate into deeper water and bigger waves, you can wear a pair of swimming fins to work up speed to catch waves. Once you understand bodysurfing, you might want to try bodyboarding or surfing.

How do I stand up on a surfboard?

Lying on your stomach on your surfboard, paddle out to where waves are breaking. Once you reach the spot where you think you can catch a wave, turn around so you're facing away from the wave. Straddle your board and sit up on it, watching waves come in. Decide on a wave to catch, and commit to it—pop down onto your belly again and paddle. You are now paddling to

get up to speed with the wave, so as it comes in behind you, paddle hard and fast—much harder and faster than you might think. Get motivated. Dig deep, figuratively and literally. If you've paddled fast enough to catch the wave, you'll feel it begin to push you toward shore. Just as you start to pick up speed, pop up onto your feet—front foot pointing forward toward the nose of the board, back foot turned out between 45 and 90 degrees. If you've done everything right, you will now be cruising on top of a wave toward shore. If not, thankfully, the ocean will never run out of waves, so paddle back out to your spot and wait for the next set.

How do I drive a boat?

Driving a boat with a small outboard motor is easy. But the first thing you'll notice is that it's not a car—you can't really slam on the brakes and come to a stop when you want to.

To start the motor, sit down next to the motor and put the shift lever in the neutral position (between forward and reverse). Turn the throttle control arm to the "start" position and pull out the choke. Pull out the starter cord, waiting until you feel friction from it, then firmly and quickly pull it again. If the engine doesn't start, repeat until it does. Once the engine is running, slowly push the choke back in and turn the throttle control arm to "run."

To drive, keep your hand on the throttle control arm. Remember that pulling the throttle control arm to the left side of the boat will turn the boat to the right, and pulling the throttle control arm to the right will turn the boat to the left. Move the shift lever to "forward" and gently turn the throttle handle to begin moving the boat. Ease out into the water and gradually turn the throttle handle more to give the boat speed.

To moor the boat, don't aim the boat directly at a dock—aim to slide in alongside the dock. Remember, there are no brakes on a boat, so come in slowly as you approach where you want to pull in. If you're unsure about speed, shift the motor to neutral as you approach, and get a sense of how fast the boat loses speed. If you need to, shift back into forward and turn the throttle to give the boat a little more speed. You'll have limited steering control when the motor is in neutral, so aim the boat exactly where you want to go before shifting to neutral. If you've done everything right, you should slide into the docking position and the boat will oh-so-gently bump, or even kiss, the dock as it comes to a stop.

How do I stay safe in a boat?

First, wear a life jacket. Make sure everyone on board your boat is wearing a life jacket. Yes, it looks kind of funny. Yes, it can save your life.

Know the right-of-way. Obviously you should operate your boat defensively, use speed conservatively when around other boats, and avoid collisions at all costs. If you're approaching another boat head on, stay toward the right, just as you would when driving a car on an American road. If you're approaching another boat at an angle other than head on, the other boat has the right-of-way if it's coming from your right; if it's coming from your left, you have the right-of-way.

Always know the weather: check the weather forecast before you go out, and don't get on the water if severe weather is a possibility. High winds and/or storms can make being on a boat cold and wet, and at worst choppy water can make capsizing a real possibility.

Carry a means of communication with you in case of emergency, and more important, know whom to call if something goes wrong. Find out if you will have cell phone coverage where you are going, and if not, arrange for a marine radio to be on board.

Finally, don't drive a boat if you're drinking alcohol—just as you wouldn't drink and drive a car. Think of a boat as being like a car that's much more difficult to control and that you can also fall out of so that you drown. Plus, there are no seat belts.

How do I transport a canoe on top of my car?

Unless you happen to live in a waterfront house, you'll have to get your canoe to the water somehow. The best way to transport a canoe on a vehicle is on a rack on top of your car—a rack is sturdy, is easy to strap the boat to, and minimizes contact with the vehicle's roof (which minimizes damage). If you don't have a roof rack, you'll want to use foam pad racks (which look basically like modified foam blocks and are sold at most outdoor and boat stores) to protect the roof of your car. The foam pad racks will attach directly to your canoe and sit between the canoe and the car's roof.

To transport your canoe, the best-case scenario is to have two people to load the canoe onto your car. You'll be putting the canoe upside down on your car roof or roof rack, so lift one end and have your friend lift the other

end, and carefully hoist the boat over your heads and onto the top of the car (or onto the rack). If you are by yourself and can't get anyone to help you, pick up the canoe and carry it by the bow seat (again, with the boat upside down), and carefully slide it onto the roof/roof rack.

Center the canoe on the top of the vehicle, front to back and side to side—you'll be strapping one tip of the canoe to the front bumper and one tip to the rear, so make sure it's positioned optimally before you start tightening the straps. Run two straps over the middle of the boat around your roof rack from one side of the vehicle to the other—or if you're not using a roof rack, roll down all four windows of the vehicle and run one strap through the front windows and one strap through the rear windows. Tighten those straps, and then strap the bow and stern to the front and rear bumpers of the vehicle, respectively—and make sure you're strapping the boat to something sturdy (and preferably metal) on the car, not just a lip of plastic on the front or rear bumper, which will bend or break once you start driving.

Should I try canoeing?

Canoeing is a great entry point to experiencing water by boat—maneuvering a canoe is fairly intuitive and simple, the seating is comfortable, and you can usually fit a cooler full of food (and possibly other refreshments) in the boat with you. Canoes are usually easy and fairly inexpensive to rent and can make for a fun and relaxing day out on a lake, pond, or calm river. Just don't stand up in the canoe, and make sure you don't have serious communication issues with the person you pick to be your paddling partner in the canoe.

How do I get into and out of a canoe?

Getting into a canoe requires a bit more balance and control than, say, sliding into the front seat of a BMW. Canoes are easy to tip over, which is not that fun when you are by yourself or the first one in the boat, and kind of a jerk move if your friend is already in the boat and you flip it and dump both of you in the water. So approach the canoe with respect and humility.

To get in from land, move as close to the boat as possible so you don't have to take a giant step into the canoe. Stay low, stay centered, and move slowly. Carefully step one foot into the keel of the canoe (the bottom centerline running from the front to the back), grab both gunwales  (rails along the top of the boat), and carefully step your other foot into the keel. Once you're in the boat, either kneel on the keel or sit back onto a seat. If you have gotten in without flipping the canoe, congratulations. But don't get overconfident—it might just be a matter of time before you (or your partner) flip the boat and go for a swim. To get out of the boat, reverse the steps, and remember to stay low and centered as you put your feet on solid ground.

Ten Useful Watersport Terms

1. **Bow:** the front end of a canoe, raft, or kayak

2. **CFS:** an acronym for cubic feet per second, a measure of the volume of water flowing in a river or creek

3. **Eddy:** a spot in a river or creek where water is deflected and flows upstream; also the place to "pull over" to get out of the main current

4. **Hole:** a spot in a river where water flows over a rock or object, drops down, and flows back upstream onto itself, creating a continuous cycle

5. **PFD:** an acronym for personal flotation device, also known as a life vest or life jacket

6. **Portage:** to carry a canoe or kayak on land around a section of river or creek

7. **Scout:** to assess a rapid by getting out of a boat and examining it from the shore of a creek or river

8. **Stern:** the back end of a canoe, raft, or kayak

9. **Strainer:** a tree or tree branch that hangs in a river or creek, allowing water to flow underneath but trapping boats

10. **Wave:** a spot in a river or creek where the water flows over a large rock, the gradient briefly goes uphill, or the river/creek constricts, pushing water up out of the flow

How do I paddle a canoe?

Once you're in the canoe, you need to make it go forward or backward, or it's going to be a very boring day on the water. Here's how to move a canoe by yourself and with a friend.

If you're by yourself: Grip the paddle; hold one hand on the top grip, and the other hand 12 to 18 inches above where the paddle shaft joins the blade.

Paddle with your torso, not your arms: when you paddle, envision your arms as just holding the paddle, and your torso powering the paddle. To take a stroke, turn your upper body toward the side of the boat opposite your paddle blade—you're "winding up" your body. Dip your paddle in the water and rotate your torso the opposite direction, or "unwind" it to propel the boat forward. To maximize your paddling efficiency, keep your hands where you can see them—don't stroke so far back that your lower hand disappears out of your field of vision. Keep your feet as wide as possible in the boat and use your lower body to stabilize and balance the boat as your upper body works to propel the boat forward. As you paddle, keep an eye on where you're going—when the boat starts to turn too far to one side, switch the paddle over and paddle on the opposite side of the boat. Continue alternating to keep the canoe straight.

If you're with a partner, you both need to paddle as close to in unison as possible or the boat will spin. If you're in the back of the boat, watch your partner up front, and try to dip your paddle in the water to start your paddle stroke at the same time they do. Paddle on the opposite side of the boat they do (if they're paddling on the left side of the boat, you paddle on the right). Try to agree on a cadence and communicate when you want to paddle slower or faster or you want to switch sides of paddling. In general, the back person in the canoe determines the steering of the boat, and the front person sets the paddling cadence and watches for rocks and other obstacles and hazards.

How do I turn a canoe?

If you're paddling a canoe by yourself, turning the canoe is simple: paddle forward on the opposite side of the boat where you'd like to turn—or paddle backward on the same side you'd like to turn to (which will kill your forward momentum). To turn faster with forward strokes, dig your paddle in and take long strokes (but remember to stay in balance).

If you're paddling with a partner, the basic method of turning is for the front person to paddle forward on the opposite side you want the boat to turn (left side if you want to turn the boat right, right side if you want to turn the boat to the left), and for the rear person to paddle backward on the side of the boat you want to turn toward (right side of the boat to turn right, left side of the boat to turn left).

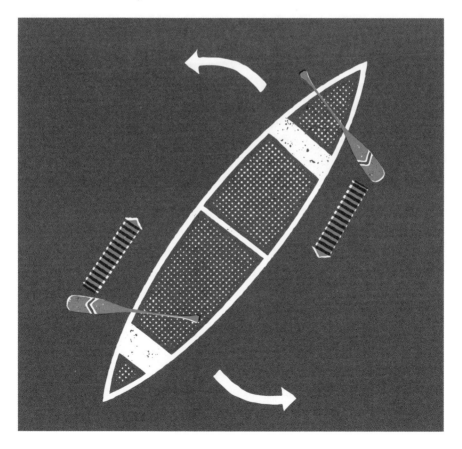

How do I portage a canoe?

When it comes down to it, paddling a canoe is way more fun than lifting it over your head and carrying it. But at some point, you may have to portage the canoe, whether it's to go from one lake to another or to avoid a dangerous rapid in a river or creek.

If you're canoeing with a partner, portaging is fairly straightforward: on shore, grab a carrying handle, and carry the boat to your destination. For longer distances, you'll want to lift it over your heads and carry it upside down on your shoulders (this method is also advantageous in that you can see the ground around your feet and watch out for roots, rocks, and obstacles). So empty the boat out first. If you're by yourself, you'll basically flip the boat over and wear it as a (huge) hat—which is maybe easier than it

sounds. With the canoe facing up on the shore, stand on one of its long sides near the middle of the boat. Tip the boat slightly so the hull (the bottom of the boat) is resting against your legs. Squat slightly, grab the center yoke (the bar that goes across the center of the canoe) with one hand and pull the boat up onto your thighs. With your other hand, stretch over to the other side of the boat and grab the gunwale near the yoke. Then, as quickly as you can, flip the canoe over your head so the yoke lands on your shoulders. Once the canoe is on your shoulders, the tricky part is over. Walk to your destination carrying the canoe, being careful to not trip on anything. When you reach the water again, reverse the process. Don't drop the boat on the ground, but drop it onto your knees first so you don't bash it on something.

How do I get back in if I fall out of my canoe?

If you fall out of a canoe and you're by yourself, you're probably going to have two problems: the canoe has capsized (flipped upside down), and you are not in it. If your canoe has not flipped, skip to step 2.

1. If your boat is upside down, your gear is very likely slowly dragging it to the bottom, so give up on keeping your stuff and detach it from the boat. Locate your paddle immediately—otherwise, once you get the boat righted, you're going nowhere—and tie it to the boat. Your boat will be filling with water, so get it flipped over as soon as humanly possible. Swim underneath the canoe and try to lift it out of the water—if you're lucky or very strong, you'll be able to do this and flip it back over. If not, you'll have to flip the boat back over and it will be full of water. Bail water out of the bottom of the boat by using a bail bucket or your hands. As you remove water from the boat (however slowly it may seem), it will gradually regain its ability to float.

2. Once your boat is right side up and floating again, it's time to jump back in without reflipping the boat. Swim toward one end of the boat, grab both gunwales with your hands, and heave yourself up onto the boat, ideally getting most of your head, shoulders, and rib cage between the gunwales. If you don't get high enough at first, slide off the boat and try again until you do. Once you're partially in the canoe, rotate your legs around toward the middle of the boat and roll into the boat. Then find your paddle and get moving again.

How do I back up a canoe?

Paddling backward is a difficult skill to master, and even more difficult (and sometimes frustrating) with a partner, so before paddling backward, decide if it's really necessary or if it would be easier to just paddle forward and make a U-turn.

To back up the canoe if you're paddling by yourself, simply paddle backward, alternating sides of the canoe every other stroke. You won't easily be able to see where you're going, so try to turn and look over your shoulder, and assess your direction every stroke or two. Use smaller strokes (as opposed to big sweeping strokes) to keep the trajectory more stable.

With a partner, your roles are opposite what they are when you're paddling forward: the front person is now in charge of steering the canoe, and the rear person is now the eyes of the canoe, looking out for obstacles behind. Match your cadence and paddle backward in unison, with the paddles on opposite sides of the canoe.

How do I pack a canoe?

Yes, there is lots of space in a canoe. Does that mean you can bring everything you want? Consider a few things:

- **Water:** No matter how well you paddle, your stuff is likely to get a little wet, from you getting in and out of the boat, and from drips off the paddles as you switch sides. A small amount of water will gather at the bottom of the boat, so it's not a great place for, say, a sleeping bag that isn't packed in something waterproof. If you don't want it to get wet, pack it in a dry bag.

- **Weight:** A heavy boat is harder to maneuver, and if you're on a nonmoving body of water (like a lake), your muscle power is pulling the boat, so loading it with heavy gear will make it more strenuous to move. Also, if you have to portage your canoe, you have to portage the gear in it as well, so keep that in mind.

- **Balance:** When loading your canoe, keep it balanced. Load the heavy stuff in the middle of the boat and the light stuff toward the ends, and keep the weight distributed left to right as well. You don't want to spend a day paddling a canoe that's leaning to the right or the left all day.

- **Flipping the boat:** There's always a chance you might flip your canoe (no matter how good of a paddler you are, or think you are), so there's always a chance you might lose some of the gear in the boat. Think about whether or not you're willing to risk it before you pack your signed first edition of *Fifty Shades of Grey*. If you're taking a cooler, take one with a secure latch—if the boat flips and your cooler goes in and the latch opens, you lose everything.

- **Tie it down:** Make sure everything in the boat is attached to the boat in some way, to minimize the chance of losing it if the boat flips.

What happens if I hit a rock in a canoe?

If you're canoeing in a river or creek, be especially vigilant about hitting rocks with your canoe. Rocks may be large and visible, or they may be hiding underneath the water with only some surface ripples to indicate they're there. Keep your eyes on the water ahead as much as you can, scanning the water for obstacles. If you see a rock, move to avoid it sooner rather than later, and be prepared to make a last-second sweep stroke (a wide pulling stroke on the side of the boat opposite the direction you want to turn) to avoid the rock. If everything fails and you do hit the rock, chances are you'll be fine—most contemporary canoes are made of materials that don't easily puncture or rip. But if you do notice your boat taking on water, it's time to pull ashore and either attempt to repair it or abandon your boat and take a ride on another canoe. Even though hitting a rock won't likely tear a hole in your boat, the more times you hit objects (like rocks), the shorter your canoe's life will eventually be—canoes are tough but not indestructible.

In addition to the potential damage they can cause your canoe, rocks can jar you enough to throw you off balance and out of the boat, flip your boat, or, in some circumstances, provide a surface that your boat can get pinned against by the current of water rushing downstream.

Why should I try kayaking?

Kayaking and canoeing are often compared, since they are human-powered boats used on lakes and rivers. Both are fun ways to explore flatwater and beginning whitewater (although advanced whitewater paddling is done almost exclusively in kayaks nowadays). A kayak, however, is a boat you sit in (or "wear," as some say), as opposed to a canoe, which you sit on top of. So a kayak can feel more cramped, since your legs are under the boat deck. Kayakers use double paddles, which are more efficient than the single paddle used in canoeing, and beginning paddlers will find a kayak easier to steer. Kayaks have better ease of paddling, because they have smaller surface area in the water. Kayaks are a little more comfortable to use in rougher water, and they're generally lighter (but not always) than canoes.

Would I like flatwater kayaking or whitewater kayaking better?

Paddling whitewater rapids is arguably the "sexier" type of kayaking, but if you're just starting out as a paddler, flatwater paddling is probably easier to learn. Flatwater kayaks (commonly called "sea kayaks" or "touring kayaks") are generally longer and easier to maneuver. Whitewater kayaks are more responsive for action-packed sections of rapids but tiring to paddle for longer distances. It's not a bad idea to rent a kayak and try one type first to see if you like it. If you believe you'll want to do both and don't want to buy both a whitewater kayak and a flatwater kayak, several companies sell medium-length boats that work well for both types (although not quite as well as having a separate boat specialized for each type).

What kind of kayak do I need?

The kind of kayak you should buy depends on what you want to do with it—sadly, the color and the look of the boat are both irrelevant. Here's what each kayak is best for, listed in order of boat length from shortest to longest.

- **Whitewater kayak:** Whitewater kayaks are designed to be agile in bumpy water—that is, rapids. The boat is short and the cockpit is tight (to keep you inside when you roll). Think of whitewater boats as being more for "sprinting" than "long-distance" runs. They're not ideal for covering lots of miles on calm water because they're challenging to keep straight over a long stretch—they're better at quick turns and short bursts of paddling.

- **Recreational kayak:** This kayak generally has a bigger cockpit but is shorter than a full-on sea kayak. Recreational kayaks are a good choice for beginning paddlers or paddlers who spend most of their time on calmer water—lakes, ponds, and lower-intensity creeks and rivers.

- **Touring kayak:** A touring kayak has a large, comfortable cockpit, with lots of hatches to store gear. The boat's design plus optional features like rudders make it track well (i.e., it's easy to keep in a straight line), and it is ideal for flatwater adventures on lakes and ponds. Touring kayaks are great for paddlers who want to do longer trips—all-day or multiday adventures requiring carrying camping gear on the boat.

- **Sea kayak:** A sea kayak is similar to a touring kayak in that it is a long, stable boat that tracks well, but it is designed to be lower in the water and to have smaller hatch openings to deal with rougher ocean waters.

How long should my kayak paddle be?

Paddles for touring and recreational kayaks generally range between 210 and 240 centimeters (metric system measures are standard). If you're a beginning kayaker of average height (between 5 foot 6 and 6 foot), you'll probably want a 230-centimeter paddle. If you're shorter than 5 foot 6 or have a narrow boat (less than 23 inches wide), try a 220-centimeter paddle, and if you're taller than 6 foot or have a larger boat (more than 26 inches wide), try a 240-centimeter paddle.

What should I wear kayaking?

When you're paddling a kayak, you're going to get wet—at the very least, your feet will get wet and sometimes your legs and upper body too. You'll inevitably end up with a little water inside the cockpit of your boat, usually not enough to immerse (and soak) your butt, but sometimes enough. When paddling, depending on how aggressive your paddle stroke is, you'll get a few drops of water trickling off your paddle into your lap or onto your shoulders, head, and arms. So you'll want to wear quick-drying clothing: a swimsuit or shorts made of nylon (or other synthetic material), and if you're wearing a shirt, one made of synthetic fabric. If you're kayaking on a lake, remember there won't be much shade out in the middle, and sunlight will reflect off the water and onto your body, so wear sunscreen (or a long-sleeve shirt), sunglasses, and maybe a brimmed hat. Your feet will almost always get wet when you're putting your boat in the water, so wear shoes that you don't mind soaking and that drain quickly—river sandals are great for this, but an old pair of running shoes will work fine. And of course you should always wear a life jacket.

How do I carry a kayak?

The advice for carrying a kayak is—as for any heavy lifting—use your legs, not your back. If you're carrying the kayak for any significant distance, it's a good idea to wear your life jacket so you have a bit of padding on your shoulder where the boat will rest.

Stand next to the kayak, facing the bow, and lay your paddle down over your outside foot (this is so you can lift it up with your foot to your awaiting hand after you've lifted the kayak onto your shoulder). Roll the kayak onto its side so the cockpit opening is facing your knee and the boat is leaning on your leg. Squat down and pull the kayak up by the edge of the cockpit opening so it slides up your leg and onto your thighs (which should be parallel to the ground if you're squatting down far enough). With the cockpit still facing you, turn the boat and push one arm

and shoulder into the cockpit—you'll carry the boat on that shoulder. When you're stable, stand up, keeping your core muscles tight. Remember that paddle that's resting on top of your foot? Carefully shift your weight to the nonpaddle foot, get your balance, and lift your paddle-holding foot up until you can grab the paddle with your free hand. When it's time to put the kayak down, set the paddle down, turn the kayak so you can set it on top of your thighs as you squat, and gently slide it back onto the ground.

How do I get into a kayak?

The best way to get into a kayak is very carefully—flipping a kayak over before you've even started can be a wet, confidence-sapping endeavor (although not the end of the world, of course).

Pick a spot to get in your kayak—a shallow spot without big rocks under the water, or a bank that gradually eases into the water at a slight angle. The safest way to get into your boat, which might be a good idea for your first time, is sitting on land at the edge of the water, getting in your kayak, and having a friend push you into the water (or using your hands to push yourself in, which can be a little tiring). If you'd like to do it by yourself, pick a spot, and slide

the boat into the water so the cockpit is in shallow water where you can step into the kayak without doing a giant high-step. Hold on to the kayak with one hand, grab your paddle with the other hand, and walk around to the side of the kayak you'd like to get into (both sides of the boat are the same, so pick whichever one you prefer). Set your paddle on the top of the kayak just behind the cockpit, holding on to it with your fingers and wrapping your thumb around the rim of the cockpit hole. Step into the cockpit hole with the foot that is closest to the back of the boat and steady the boat with both hands. Slide your butt onto the top of the kayak and sit behind the cockpit hole (not in the cockpit yet). Put both hands on the paddle and steady yourself, and bring your other foot up and into the cockpit. You should now be sitting on the deck of the boat just behind the cockpit, with both feet in the cockpit. When you're balanced, push up onto your hands and slide your hips into the cockpit, being careful to not wobble the boat as you get in. Once you're seated comfortably, find the proper position for your feet. The foot pegs will be on the outer walls inside the cockpit, and you'll use them to hold yourself in place once you start paddling. Adjust them so your knees are slightly bent, not straight, and not bent so far that they will be pushing against the deck of the kayak when you paddle.

How do I put on a spray skirt?

A spray skirt is the piece of fabric designed to keep water out of the cockpit of your boat. You'll be surprised at how much water can drip off your paddle and onto your lap or fill the boat during even a brief rain shower.

Step into the spray skirt and pull it up under your life jacket. Tighten the top bungee cord around your lower rib cage—any opening at the top will let water

in, so make sure it's snug. Sit down in your kayak, taking care to not sit on any part of the spray skirt. From the seated position, lean forward and pull the back of the spray skirt around the cockpit coaming, the lip surrounding the cockpit hole. Carefully work both hands forward along the coaming, pulling the spray skirt over the lip as you work up toward the front of the cockpit.

Near the front, it will become more difficult to attach the spray skirt as it nears its stretching capacity—keep tension on it, holding it down around the lip and pushing it forward equally around both sides until you can pop it over the front of the cockpit. It may take you a few tries at first, so be patient.

How do I paddle a kayak?

Sit in the kayak with the paddle in hand. Set the middle of the paddle shaft on top of your head and grab the shaft with both hands—your elbows should be bent at 90-degree angles when they're in the proper position. Set the paddle on your lap and turn it so the blades are perpendicular to the water. To paddle, insert one blade in the water as far forward as you can and pull it back toward you, with the opposite end of the paddle higher than your shoulders so the shaft is at about a 45-degree angle to the water surface. Don't try to muscle the paddle through the water too much—you'll burn out rather quickly and waste energy. Take moderate strokes, and when you're pulling backward with your bottom hand (the end of the paddle that's in the water), simultaneously push forward with your top hand, making it a full-upper-body effort. To increase your speed, increase the angle of the paddle shaft to the water—the top blade passing almost over your head as the opposite blade passes through the water closer to the side of the kayak.

Once you're moving, your main objective when paddling is keeping the kayak straight. Pay attention to see if your boat is slightly turning as you paddle, and adjust accordingly (paddle harder with one side, paddle less hard with the other side, etc.).

How do I turn a kayak?

There are two ways to turn a kayak when paddling. The quickest way is to plant one blade of your paddle in the water (the right side if you want to turn the boat right, the left side if you want to turn the boat left) and hold it in place or push forward against the water. This will, unfortunately, stop or slow down your kayak significantly, so if you don't want to lose speed, use the "sweep stroke" instead:

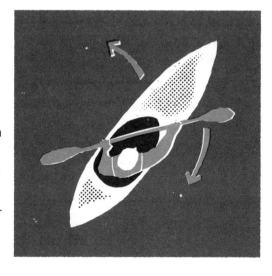

instead of your standard paddling motion, put one blade of your paddle (opposite from before: the left side of the paddle if you want to turn the boat right, the right side if you want to turn the boat left) in the water, farther from the edge of the boat than your normal paddle stroke, and pull the paddle backward in a semicircular motion.

How do I back up a kayak?

Getting a kayak to go backward is simple: just paddle backward, pushing the blade forward in the water instead of pulling it toward the back of the boat. One caution: just as in a car, you can't go from forward to reverse when the boat is moving, so if you're moving forward, slow the boat down to a stop before you start to paddle backward. Trying to abruptly go from forward to backward might throw your boat off balance.

How do I roll a kayak?

The best way to learn to roll a kayak is to get in a waist-deep swimming pool with a partner who is willing to spend an hour helping you practice. When you have that, work on the basic moves to roll.

Hold the kayak paddle with a normal grip, and rotate over to hold it parallel to the kayak on the left side. Look and make sure that the right blade (next to your right hand) is facing upward and that the blade edge closest to the kayak is tilted slightly up. Lean forward over the deck of your kayak and keep your head tucked into the deck. Hold your knees firmly against the bottom of the deck, and brace your heels against the bottom of the boat so you are holding

your lower body in place as securely as possible. Now it's time to flip your boat. Lean your upper body to the left and the kayak will flip over. You're now upside down and your head is underwater, and you must do one thing immediately: calm down. Obviously you can't take a deep breath (again, your head is underwater), but take one second and get

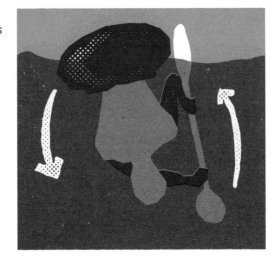

oriented. Once you've established that you're not going to panic, lean as far forward in the boat as possible, tucking your face into the deck of the kayak again. Your hands should be as far forward as you can get them, holding the paddle slightly away from the side of the boat, and sticking out of the water. It's time to roll. Use your upper body to pull the right blade of your paddle in an extended U-shaped (or rainbow-shaped) stroke from the front left side of the boat to the rear right (your left hand will punch upward and out of the surface of the water while your right hand plunges deeper into the water), straightening your body as you do it. Focus on leaning your upper body back as far as you can while pushing your right knee into the top of your boat. As the kayak rolls over, keep pulling the paddle with your right hand and pushing it with your left hand, pulling the kayak under your shoulders as you lean forward. If at any point you realize your roll will not succeed, signal to your partner to help you flip back over, and try again.

How do I do a wet exit?

Of course, you'd love to go your entire paddling life without getting in a situation where you go upside down in your kayak and can't get rotated back to the surface. But it may happen, so it's good to know how to get out of an upside-down boat (and to practice once or twice). Here's how.

When you're upside down with your head underwater, remember to lean forward as far as possible to avoid hitting your head on anything that might be on the bottom of creek, river, or lake you're kayaking in. If you're using a spray skirt, pull on it. Reach for the grab loop, which is at the front of your cockpit opening—you can open your eyes to look for it, but it's better to learn to find it by feel in case water conditions impair your vision. Pull it off, pushing the loop forward to separate it from the cockpit coaming, with one hand (your other hand shouldn't leave your paddle, which you'll need when you resurface). Then pull the loop toward you to remove the skirt and open the cockpit. Next, move your hands back to the rim of the cockpit next to your hips, and push yourself out of the boat (or push the boat off your hips). As you slide out of the cockpit, pick one side of the boat and lean toward it so you don't come up directly underneath the boat. Hang on to the boat with one hand as your head comes out of the water, and don't let go—you're going to need the boat.

What kind of safety gear should I carry in a canoe or kayak?

Along with a general first aid kit/survival kit like what you'd take on a back-packing trip (see page 92), a few specific items should be in your canoe or kayak whenever you put it in the water.

- **PFD/life jacket:** Should you get separated from your boat, you can sur-vive much longer with the extra buoyancy provided by a life jacket to keep you afloat than you would treading water or swimming without one.

- **Spare paddle:** Hopefully you'll never snap a paddle in half, break the blade on a rock, or lose your paddle to a fast-flowing section of river—but if you do and you have an extra paddle in your boat, you won't be screwed.

- **Paddle float:** On a kayak trip, a paddle float is a must for reentering your kayak without help from a friend.

- **Bilge pump and sponge:** A bilge pump is a simple hand-operated device that sucks up and removes water from the cockpit of your kayak or canoe. A sponge will get any remaining small pools of water and is great for dry-ing out your boat at the end of a paddling day on a multiday trip.

- **Emergency whistle and signal mirror:** If you end up in a situation where you need to signal for a rescue, these two items are far more effective than just waving your hands and yelling at passing boats.

How do I keep my stuff dry on a river trip?

Though putting your things in a ziplock bag will keep them dry during a short rainstorm when you're on a day hike, it probably won't keep them dry on a river trip—especially if the boat flips and your stuff is submerged under calm water (bad) or whitewater (the worst). To keep your things dry, you'll want to keep them in a dry bag, which are available at most paddling shops and general outdoor shops. A dry bag is made of tough, waterproof vinyl that is rolled at the top to seal out water. Dry bags are soft-sided, so if you're at all worried about something fragile breaking in a boat flip—such as an expensive camera or lenses—you'll want to pack it in a waterproof plastic case (which will be more expensive but worth it when protecting your gear).

How do I pack a dry bag?

Correctly packing a dry bag comes down to two principles: knowing its volume limits and securely sealing it. To make the dry bag's seal watertight, you have to be able to fold the opening a minimum of three times. If you fold it only once or twice and water washes over it at some point (or if your boat flips and the dry bag is submerged), your stuff will get wet. So don't pack too much stuff in it. To securely seal the bag, fill it with your stuff (leaving plenty of room at the top), fold the opening shut, and squeeze the excess air out of the bag. Hold the top of the bag so no additional air can get in, and fold the top once, twice, and a third time (and more times if possible), and clip the handle shut. Clip a carabiner to the handle, and clip the carabiner to a strap on the boat for some extra security in case the boat flips.

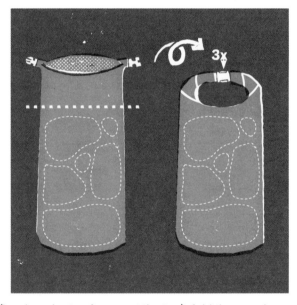

How do I get back in a flipped kayak?

First things first: Flip your kayak back over. If there's a significant amount of water inside the kayak, flip it back over, and, swimming hard, try to lift it out of the water one or more times to get the water out of the cockpit. If it's windy at all, figure out which way the wind is blowing, and turn yourself and the boat so your back is to the wind—if you're downwind, the breeze will keep pushing the boat on top of you. Position yourself on the right-hand side of the kayak, just behind the back of the cockpit.

Take your paddle float and inflate it, and slide it onto one end of your paddle. Then position your paddle so the other (nonfloat) blade lies flat on the boat deck just behind the cockpit, perpendicular to the boat. Slide your arm over the paddle and grab the back rim of the cockpit, holding both the cockpit coaming and the paddle shaft in your hand.

Grab the opposite side of the boat, or the cords running across the back deck of the boat, with your left hand. Heave yourself up and over the boat, trying to land your stomach and chest on the back deck of the kayak. As soon as you can, kick your right leg over the paddle and hook your foot over the shaft of the paddle. Quickly do the same with the other foot. Rotate your body, keeping your stomach and chest on the boat deck, and slide your legs one at a time into the cockpit—toes downward.

When you have both feet inside the cockpit, slide your left hand down next to your left hip and grab the paddle shaft. Use the paddle to balance yourself as you corkscrew your body into the cockpit (rolling your left shoulder backward and your right shoulder forward as you slide your hips down into your seat). Empty any remaining water from your cockpit, remove your paddle float, and put your spray skirt back in place.

How do I pack a sea kayak?

Your first thought when peering inside the hatches of a sea kayak might be, "Look at all that room! I can take whatever I want." Well, true, there's quite a bit of room in there. But it's not limitless, and the space you're packing your gear in is a little strange—the compartments narrow to points at the ends of the boat, and of course you can't really take anything you can't fit through the hatch opening (so sorry, no gas grill). Packing a kayak is a little like packing a backpack, except instead of carrying all your stuff in one big bag, you'll carry it in a bunch of little bags. Some tips:

- **Get dry bags for all your gear.** Yes, the hatches are supposed to be waterproof. There may be a time they aren't, and you don't want to have to find that out by pulling out a soaking wet sleeping bag after a long day of paddling.

- **Use a variety of colors of dry bags.** There's nothing more frustrating than having to dig through all your bags to find something like a spoon or stove. And if all your dry bags are blue, for example, you can't tell them apart.

- **Get smaller dry bags as opposed to bigger ones.** Yes, putting a bunch of items in one big dry bag is easier, but you still have to stuff that big dry bag into a hatch, and a large full dry bag will be difficult (if not impossible) to cram into the hatch opening. Buy several dry bags, none bigger than 15 liters (maybe one that's 20 liters), and pack all the gear and food you're taking on your trip to make sure it fits. If it doesn't, buy more dry bags.

- **Keep items you'll need in an accessible location.** Don't put your lunch in the bag that you push all the way into the bow of the boat and then stuff other bags behind it in the hatch. If you do, you'll feel like you're unpacking your entire boat when you stop for lunch. Keep food accessible near the opening of the hatch, and keep a dry bag with your camera and other items like sunscreen in the cockpit of the boat with you—but make sure it's clipped to something in case you happen to flip your kayak.

What do I do if I fall out of a whitewater raft?

When you fall out of a boat, the most important thing to do is stay calm. But unlike when you see a bear (see page 47), or realize you're lost in the woods (see page 97), staying calm in whitewater is more complicated, because you might not be able to do the one thing that helps calm us:

take a deep breath. But the river is going to do what it wants with you, so you have to figure out how to function in it, and how to get back onto the boat.

In whitewater, you will continue moving downstream whether you like it or not, so turn so you're on your back floating downstream feetfirst. This is the whitewater swimming position. Your life jacket will keep you afloat—your job is to make sure your feet don't get caught under rocks or tree limbs under the surface. If your feet get stuck the river will continue to push you downstream, eventually pushing your head underwater. Float on your back, feet pointed up, and paddle your hands backward to slow yourself down.

If you are near the raft, grab the rope that runs along the outer edge of the boat, hang on, and face the boat. Don't try to climb in. Someone in the boat will reach over, grab your life jacket by its shoulder straps, and heave you back into the boat—this works best if you're not flailing around.

If you're not near the boat, stay in the whitewater swimming position, and wait for a boat to come to you. If a boat can't get close, someone on the boat may toss you a "throw bag," a stuff sack full of rope (the other end of which someone on the boat is holding on to). Grab the rope, not the bag, and continue floating faceup. The person holding the other end of the rope will haul you in. Don't turn to face your rescuer until you're close enough to grab the boat.

How do I fit a lifejacket/personal flotation device?

More than anything else you wear on a whitewater outing, your life jacket needs to fit properly—if it comes off your body, it's useless. Before you put it on for the first time, make sure all the straps on the flotation device are loosened as much as possible. Put the life jacket on and tighten the straps evenly, making sure the strap below your rib cage is particularly snug. Once you have all the straps tightened, ask a friend to lift up the life jacket by the shoulder straps—if it easily slides upward, or your nose touches the zipper in front, the life jacket is too big and you should find a smaller size. Remember, if you fall out of a raft or kayak, you will be pulled back onto a boat by a rescuer who will be grabbing your shoulder straps, so if the life jacket slides up and over your head, your rescuer will fall back in the boat with an empty life jacket in his hands and you'll still be sitting in the water.

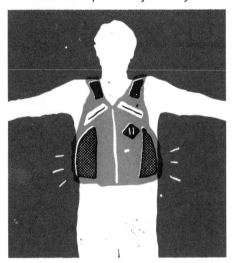

Why should I try whitewater rafting?

Whitewater rafting is a great social activity; it can be as thrilling as a roller coaster ride (but much less dry and much more wild) and as scenic as a walk in the woods (with a few more obstacles). Rafts can fit as many as nine or ten people, all riding through adrenaline-coursing whitewater at the same time, sharing the experience. Perhaps best of all, you don't need any equipment to try rafting—just find a guide service that offers one-day or half-day whitewater trips, and book a spot on a boat. Once you know you like the activity, you can commit to a multiday trip that combines the adrenaline of whitewater rafting with wilderness camping on the riverbanks.

How do I rig a whitewater raft?

Your whitewater raft will have two large boxes that spread the width of the boat between the tubes: the seat box and the cooler. Both are intended to carry the heaviest items on the boat—the seat box holds kitchen supplies like pots and pans, and the cooler will be full of food and ice. Both the seat box and the cooler should not sit on the floor of the boat; hang cam straps from the raft frame so that they run under the cooler, and keep the bottom of the cooler off the floor of the boat. Do the same with the seat box.

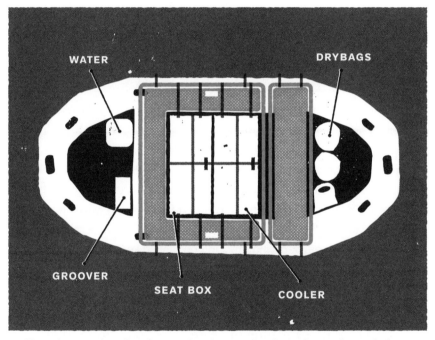

If you have a drop bag in your boat, put other large heavy items in it, such as camp chairs or a Dutch oven. That leaves only the stern and the bow compartments free—you can put remaining items like water jugs, a groover box (portable field toilet), and camping gear in dry bags in those compartments. If you have larger dry bags or duffels, place your smaller bags at the bottom of the stern and bow compartments, and put the big bags on top of the small bags. Don't worry if the gear sits higher than the outside tubes of the raft.

Once the boat is loaded, begin strapping everything into the boat. Remember, you're not just strapping it in to prevent it from flying out of the top of the boat—your rigging job has to withstand the raft flipping upside down and water rushing through it, so secure everything down, and make sure each item has a tightened cam strap running not only over it but through a handle (including your cooler). Dry bags should be clipped to cam straps with carabiners or have a cam strap laced through their handles.

Keep any personal gear you need to access throughout the day within reach and easy to find; use carabiners to clip your items to something solid on the boat.

What should I wear on a whitewater raft trip?

You're going to get wet, so you'll want clothes that can dry quickly: wear a swimsuit or nylon shorts, and if you want to wear a shirt, wear something noncotton that dries quickly. Wear shoes you don't mind getting wet or river sandals (not flip-flops that can fall off) that secure with one or more adjustable straps across the foot. If you wear glasses or sunglasses, secure them with a cord that you can tighten around your head—one big wave and they can instantly be washed off your face and down the river. Most raft guiding companies will rent quick-drying tops and booties to keep clients warm and dry when appropriate.

What do the different classes of whitewater mean?

Most rivers are rated on the International Scale of River Difficulty, a system created by the American Whitewater Association. The scale has six classes (or grades).

- **Class I:** Fast-moving water with riffles and small waves. Few obstructions to water flow, no hidden obstructions, low risk to boaters who fall out of their boats.

- **Class II:** Straightforward rapids with wide, clear channels evident without scouting. Some maneuvering of boats may be necessary, but avoiding obstructions should be easy for trained paddlers.

- **Class III:** Rapids with moderate, irregular waves that may be difficult to avoid and that can swamp an open canoe. Complex maneuvers in fast currents often necessary, as well as boat control in tight passages. Large waves and strainers (trees or tree branches present in the current that allow water to flow through but will trap a kayak) possible but easily avoided. Strong eddies and powerful current effects possible, scouting advisable.

- **Class IV:** Intense, powerful but predictable rapids requiring precise boat handling in turbulent water. May have unavoidable waves, holes, or constricted passages requiring fast maneuvers. Scouting rapids or passages may be necessary. For kayaking, a strong roll is recommended.

- **Class V:** Extremely long, unobstructed, or very violent rapids that expose a paddler to added risk. Drops may contain large, unavoidable waves and holes or steep, congested chutes with complex routes. Eddies may be small or hard to reach. Scouting is recommended, and rescue is often difficult.

- **Class VI:** Class VI runs are rarely attempted, experts-only, and high-consequence. Once a class VI rapid has been run several times, its rating may be lowered to class V.

How do I row a whitewater raft?

Class I and II rivers are beginner-friendly, and knowing a few basic strokes will give you a command of your raft with some practice. But captaining a whitewater raft through class III or class IV rapids is a skill that takes dozens of days of training—because if you can't correctly read whitewater and understand what it will do to your raft as you pass through it, anything you can do with the oars in your hands is basically just a suggestion. For any class of water, these oar strokes will be the ones you need to know.

- **Backstroke:** Hold the oar blades above the water, push the oar handles forward, dip the blades in the water, and then pull the oar handles toward your chest. As you pull the oar blades through the water, the raft moves backward. For a powerful backstroke, push through your feet and use your entire body.

- **Push stroke:** The push stroke moves the raft forward, but as you'll notice, you have much less power than doing the backstroke because it's harder to use your entire body. To push stroke, pull the oar handles to your chest with the blades out of the water, dip the blades into the water, and push the handles forward.

- **Ship:** When you pass between rocks or near a steep riverbank, you will need to get your oars out of the water so you don't damage them. You'll line them up parallel to the sides of the boat by either pushing them forward all the way (you will probably have to stand up) or pulling them backward all the way (you'll lean far back).

- **Turn:** Dip both oar blades into the water. You will push one oar handle and simultaneously pull the other one, and the boat will turn quickly in the direction of the oar you're pulling.

Where should I sit if I'm not rowing?

If you're in an oar boat, one person will be doing the rowing and the rest of the boat passengers can relax—or, as often happens, hang on for dear life. If you sit in the front of the boat, you'll get the brunt of any waves the boat hits, so you'll get wet. But the front of the boat is often a better place to sit to distribute weight to make the boat easier to steer for the captain. Sitting in the back of the boat has the advantage being a little drier, but it can be a tougher place to hang on if things get a little rowdy. Going through a hole, for example, can pop the back of the boat up in the air and launch passengers up or forward. And if you get launched out of the back of the boat, you can hit the captain, which can be bad since the captain is in charge of rowing the boat through the rapids. Unless you're deathly scared of getting wet (in which case you might ask yourself if whitewater rafting is really for you), sit in the front of the boat.

Can I take photos when I'm on a raft?

You can take as many photos as you want, but be aware of a few things.

- Your camera may get wet—or even soaked through—if it's not protected in a case when your raft goes through a rapid. If you don't have a case, shooting photos only in between rapids is safer for the camera.

- You need to use your hands to hold on to the boat. If you have a camera in one hand, that's a hand that can't hold on to the boat, and you might fall out. If you fall out and you have a camera in your hand, your camera will fall out too. And it will get soaked through if that happens, assuming you actually hold on to it and don't drop it into the river.

- If you lose your grip on your camera, it can fly out of your hand and hit someone in the chaos of the boat going through a rapid. Cameras aren't soft, and thus it would not be fun to have a camera hit someone in the head at any speed.

- If you lose your camera, you will lose all your photos of your trip.

- A dry, secure camera will survive the trip, and so will your photos. Keep your camera in a waterproof case or pouch, and keep it secured when you're not shooting photos. Zip it into one of your life jacket pockets, or strap the case directly to the boat frame.

Can I bring booze on a river trip?

For river trips, more than for any other outdoor sport, alcoholic beverages are almost a given: rafts can carry more comfortable camping gear than any other human-powered craft (more than your backpack, more than your mountain bike, more than you on skis, etc.), so boaters are known for lush camping, including liquor and beer. But there are two simple rules: (1) carry no glass, and (2) take your empty cans with you. Typically, liquor that's packaged in glass bottles is simply poured into plastic containers before a raft trip—the plastic containers are unbreakable and as such won't leave shards of glass all over the floor of your raft or campsite (and more important, you won't lose your booze as things get banged around). Just be sure to label each when you pour it in a new container—use duct tape and a black marker to write which spirit is which, because it's easy to mix up gin and rum and vodka, or whiskey and tequila, if they're not labeled. And nobody wants a margarita made with whiskey or a Bloody Mary made with rum.

Where do I pee when I'm on a raft trip?

As gross as it sounds, when you're on a raft trip, you pee in the river. That's right—dilution is the solution to your pollution. If you pee on the ground at campsites on rivers that are popular among boaters, it doesn't take long to make an entire campsite smell like pee and ruin it for everyone. Urine is sterile, and in moving rivers it is carried away quickly.

How do I take a Grand Canyon raft trip?

If you want to see the Grand Canyon from a raft, you have a couple of options, both of which require a week or several weeks off work.

1. Befriend a person or a group of people who regularly do their own independent raft trips and can organize the logistics for a multiweek raft trip. As lofty as this sounds, there's no test or exam you have to pass to be on a Grand Canyon raft trip—many groups have only a handful of people who are 100 percent comfortable rowing a boat through big whitewater rapids, and the rest of the group members instead bring other attributes or skills to the trip, such as cooking, fixing things, taking care of the toilet (really), or taking pictures. The biggest issue in getting on a private trip is acquiring a permit. Permits

are awarded in a weighted lottery system and sometimes take several tries to obtain. Private raft trips in the Grand Canyon last from seven to twenty-eight days.

2. Pay for a spot on a trip with a commercial guide company. Most commercial guide trips will take you through the canyon in twelve to twenty-one days. A commercial trip is more costly than a private trip, but guides take care of plenty of things, including all logistics, cooking, bathroom maintenance, rowing, and sometimes even setting up tents, which makes the extra cost worth it.

Regardless of which option you pick, you get to see the Grand Canyon from the bottom, from a boat, and it's a life list trip for outdoorspeople around the world.

Five River Trips of a Lifetime

1. **Middle Ocoee River, Tennessee:** America's most popular raft trip can be done in two hours; it's 5 miles with seventeen major rapids up to class IV and is advertised as "90 percent whitewater."

2. **Grand Canyon, Arizona:** The 280-mile, fourteen-day (minimum) Colorado River trip is the biggest water in America, with forty-seven major rapids rated "Grand Canyon class 5" or higher (the Grand Canyon has its own whitewater rating system, 1–10 instead of I–V).

3. **Middle Fork of the Salmon River, Idaho:** It takes five to six days, and has more than one hundred rapids over its 105-mile stretch that cuts between vistas of Idaho's mountains. As a bonus there's trout fishing and hot springs.

4. **Upper Gauley, West Virginia:** Forty-plus rapids from class III to class V+ are covered in just 11 river miles, including the 14-foot-high Sweet's Falls.

5. **Upper Youghiogheny, Maryland and Pennsylvania:** Five miles of continuous rapids up to class V; there are twenty rapids in all.

How do I stay upright on a stand-up paddleboard?

Actually standing on a stand-up paddleboard is straightforward, but staying up is another matter, as balancing in changing water conditions can be difficult. Boat wake or choppy water can upset the board, and if you don't react correctly to it you can lose your balance and fall off (which of course is not the worst thing in the world).

To paddle, walk your board into a spot in the water that's deep enough that the board's fin doesn't hit the bottom of the lake or river. Flop yourself onto the board, and ease yourself up onto one knee and then both knees. Place one hand on the paddle's top T-grip and the other near the middle of the paddle shaft (it doesn't matter which hand is which; you'll be switching

hands every stroke). The paddle blade should angle away from you into the water. Take a stroke, then switch hand positions and take a stroke on the other side of the board. Get a feel for how you will balance the board by staying on your knees for several strokes, and when you feel ready, step up onto one foot, then the other. Stand facing forward, with your feet shoulder width apart.

To turn the board to the right, paddle on the left side of the board. To turn it to the left, paddle on the right side of the board.

If you fall off, don't worry, just hang onto the board and flop yourself back onto it and repeat the process. Your paddle will float if you lose hold of it, but make sure it doesn't float away from you; otherwise you'll have to paddle with your hands until you can get it within reach.

How do I skip a rock?

Skipping rocks is a great way to while away a few minutes whenever you're close to a lake or pond. Learn to do it properly, or you're just another chump chucking rocks into the water to watch them splash.

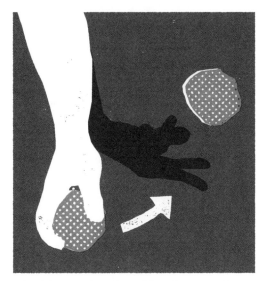

First, pick a rock to skip. Look for a mostly flat rock with a smooth bottom and top, and one that's more triangular in shape than round on the sides. Bigger is better—roughly the size of a credit card is ideal.

Make a "C" with the thumb and forefinger of your throwing hand, and make the rest of your fingers into a loose fist. Hold the sides of the rock with your thumb and forefinger and rest the bottom of the rock on the knuckle of your middle finger.

Orient your body so the foot opposite your throwing hand is pointing toward the water. Lean back onto your other leg, pull your throwing hand back, and throw the stone—you're aiming across the water, not down into it. Imagine the stone being light and bouncing along the top of the water as you throw it firmly (but not hard). Let the rock roll off your forefinger as you snap your wrist toward your body. Watch your rock gloriously skip across the water and try to count the number of skips, or, alternatively, watch your rock crash through the surface of the water, find another skipping rock, and try again.

5

IN THE BACK-COUNTRY

Sleeping on the ground will never be quite as comfortable as sleeping in a bed indoors—but if you can learn to love it, camping out has many side benefits: great views of the sunset and sunrise, campfire conversations, an unobstructed look at the stars in the middle of the night, and the unique satisfaction of sipping from a mug of hot coffee the morning after a chilly night spent in a sleeping bag. Knowing a few basic skills and tips can make a night outside more comfortable so you don't feel as though you're roughing it.

This chapter will give you a sense of where to camp, how to find a good campsite, the gear you need, what to eat and how to cook it, how to light a campfire (and more important, how to put it out), how to pitch a tent, and everything you need to plan your first camping or backpacking trip. Follow these tips and you'll find that sleeping in a tent is like staying in a million-star hotel.

Why should I try backpacking?

Backpacking can definitely seem like a lot of work. After all, you're carrying everything you need for a few days and nights on your back, and that can be pretty heavy to haul around steep trails for miles and miles. And, of course, there are no bathrooms or electricity in the backcountry. But if you're the type of person who believes all good things come at a price, it's worth it. What you trade in comfort you get back in solitude and scenery: statistics show the majority of national park visitors never get more than a mile from their cars, and if you're willing to put in a little sweat equity and carry your tent, sleeping bag, and food into the backcountry, you'll be rewarded with an escape from people—and likely a great view of an alpine lake or mountains, or a secluded forest campsite. If you're interested in hiking and you're interested in camping, backpacking combines both: simply put, you're just hiking to your campsite.

Where can I go camping?

There are two basic designations for camping: campgrounds and dispersed camping (see page 13).

Developed campgrounds include privately owned campgrounds and RV parks, national park campgrounds, state park campgrounds, county park campgrounds, municipal campgrounds, US Forest Service campgrounds, and Bureau of Land Management campgrounds. Almost all developed campgrounds charge a fee per night of usage, from five dollars to forty dollars. Generally, developed campgrounds will have—at minimum—established campsites, fire rings, picnic tables, water spigots, and bathrooms or vault toilets. Some developed campgrounds have amenities like bathrooms with running water and electricity (and sometimes showers), trash receptacles, grills, campground staff, and even laundry.

Dispersed camping is a term for primitive camping that's allowed anywhere on public land managed by the US Forest Service or the Bureau of Land Management. Dispersed camping covers both car camping and backpacking or backcountry camping—as long as you can get your stuff there, you can sleep there. Dispersed camping is entirely without the amenities and infrastructure of developed campgrounds—for example, you might find a flat spot with a fire ring just off the side of a dirt road on Forest Service land, or you might backpack two or three miles from a trailhead on Bureau of Land Management land and pitch your tent in a flat spot.

When using a dispersed camping site (or creating your own), you are expected to take all trash with you and bury human waste.

Can I camp next to a river or lake?

You can camp near a river or lake, but it's bad form to camp right next to it (even if you really, really, really want to take a photo of your tent next to a lake for Instagram). To protect the area for future users (remember, someone protected it for you), camp at least 200 feet from a water source. You don't have to be exact, just respectful: walk about seventy-five big steps from the edge of a lake (that's roughly 200 feet) and find a spot near there, or better yet, find an existing campsite and use that.

How do I find a campsite in the backcountry?

When you're backpacking, finding a place to sleep isn't quite as simple as pulling off the freeway at the next motel or Googling "hotel" on your smartphone—but it's pretty easy. You're going to need water to cook break-fast and dinner, so the most logical place to camp is near water—luckily for you, most other people who have gone backpacking before you are just like you, so they've probably established campsites near water sources. When planning your trip, look at the map and figure out a few possible goals for your first night, based on how far you can reasonably hike (whether that's 2 miles or 10 miles). Lakes and ponds are the easiest places to find campsites, as there's usually flat land somewhere nearby. Creeks and rivers are also good water sources but sometimes don't reliably have flat spots nearby—the blue line signifying a creek on your map can be pinched in a steep gully, with nowhere nearby to pitch a tent. But if the contour lines on your topographic map are far apart near a creek, there's a good chance there's some flat land.

Hike to your water source—again, a lake or pond is your safest bet—and when you arrive, explore the perimeter of the water for established campsites—they should be about 200 feet away from the water's edge and should have one or more flat spots free of vegetation where tents have been pitched in the past (and where you can pitch your tent). It's best to use established campsites for a couple reasons: it minimizes damage to the area, and it's easy—you don't have to stamp down grass and pull out rocks to clear a spot for your tent. Additionally, if you're lucky, someone has pulled a downed tree over to the campsite and made it into a good bench for you to sit on while you're emptying your pack and/or cooking dinner.

In a pinch, of course, you can camp somewhere not near a water source, but remember, the only water you'll have to make dinner and breakfast (and coffee!) is what you've got in your backpack, so plan wisely.

How can I tell if a spot is flat enough to sleep on?

You'll never find a spot in the backcountry that's truly flat, not in the way you can measure with a carpenter's level when you're working on your house. If you think a spot looks flat, it's probably pretty close. One trick that will help: Before you set up your tent only to find out it's slanted downhill at an unacceptable angle, lie down in the exact space where you're going to put your tent. If it feels too tilted, find another spot. If you think it might be okay but you're not sure, go ahead and set up your tent but don't stake it down. Set it in the exact spot, and if it looks tilted too much, try turning it or moving it to the right or left a little bit—the visual will help you decide. If you're still not sure, unzip the door and get in the tent and lie down—if you're sliding (even a little bit) in one direction or another, it will probably be a pretty miserable spot. Look for a better spot nearby, and if you can carry your tent over to the new spot without breaking it down, go for it.

How close to someone else's campsite can I set up my tent?

It's safe to assume—unless the person indicates otherwise—that everyone you see in the backcountry has gone there to get away from people. A person may be friendly and chatty when he sees you on the trail, but unless he specifically invites you to camp right next to him, it's probably better to keep your distance. If at all possible, set up your tent out of sight from other tents, and if that's not possible, give the other tents 150 feet or so of space. If you're in doubt, it never hurts to ask before you put up your tent, with a simple "Would it be okay with you if I set up camp over here?" Most people aren't territorial about campsites or interested in hogging the view of an alpine lake—but it's courteous to ask first.

Is it okay to listen to music at my campsite?

It's okay to listen to music at your campsite, with a couple of caveats: be aware of how close the next campsite is, and whether there are people camping there who may or may not like to listen to your EDM all night—or really at all. Most people head to the backcountry to escape noise, and although it might be hard to imagine, plenty of people have different musical tastes than you do and might find your choice of dinner music undesirable. But if you don't have close neighbors at your campsite, there's no reason you can't listen to some music. Just make sure it's not reaching everyone else at the campground. After you turn on the music, take a walk away from your campsite and see if you can hear the tunes from other spots in the campground, especially near other people's campsites. If not, you're probably okay. If you can hear it, the courteous move is to turn the music down (or off). Just remember not to mess with the volume after you've had a beer or three, because obviously your judgment will be altered somewhat. Whatever you do, try not to be that person that everyone in the campground hates.

How do I light a campfire?

First, build a fire ring or find an existing fire ring near your campsite to keep the fire from getting out of control. A dozen or so fist-sized rocks should be enough for a fire for two people, and double that number for three or four people. The diameter of your fire ring shouldn't be bigger than about 2 feet—you are building it to stay warm while camping for an evening, not roasting a whole pig over it. There are three components to a campfire.

1. **Tinder:** Has to be dry, has to catch fire easily, and will burn quickly (so grab a lot of it). Dry green cottony fungi works, as do dry leaves, dead grass, small shards of leftover firewood (often easily found surrounding campfire rings at campgrounds), dry bark found around downed trees, and wood shavings (which you can whittle and/or splinter off your fuel wood).

2. **Kindling:** Imagine your fire having to work its way up to big chunks of wood. It has to burn the small stuff first (the tinder), then medium-sized stuff, which is the kindling: pinky-diameter or smaller pieces of wood. Again, your kindling has to be dry or it won't burn. So don't go snapping small branches off live trees. Look for downed trees or broken-off branches, and gather a bunch—two large fistfuls or more.

3. **Fuel wood:** Fuel wood is wood that will burn hot and long once you've gotten your actual fire going. When gathering wood, look for pieces the diameter of your wrist or bigger. Don't go too big—you're not looking for a Yule log. Grab a few pieces that are wrist sized and some bigger than that. Look for dry wood.

Now, imagine a fire having to climb up stairs—the first step is the tinder, the second one is the kindling, and the third step is your fuel wood. Place the tinder and kindling in the shape of a teepee: tinder on the bottom and the kindling on top of that in a small teepee—twigs and sticks balanced against each other in a cone shape, with enough space in between the twigs so that air can move through the teepee, and enough space on a few sides that you can reach the tinder with a lighter or lit match. Once you've got a good teepee of tinder and kindling, light the tinder in three or four spots. Watch closely to see if the fire is spreading from the tinder to the kindling—gently blow on it from a few directions to help it get oxygen. When blowing on the fire, don't be afraid to get close—down on all fours, face close to the ground. Once you're convinced the fire is taking to the kindling, start to put on your fuel wood—again, build a teepee, and start with your smallest-diameter fuel wood. As the small fuel wood starts to burn, go ahead and add the larger-diameter fuel wood.

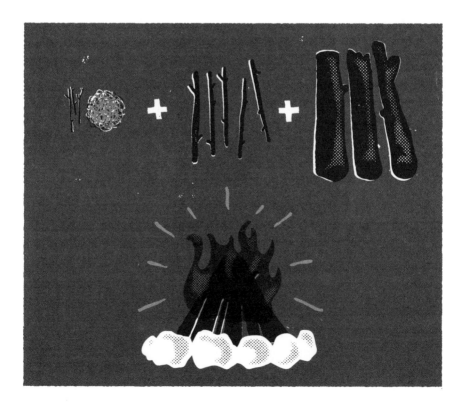

At some point, your teepee will probably collapse on itself—don't sweat it, just make sure that when you add wood you arrange it so the wood can get some oxygen on the bottom as it burns. Lay pieces of wood at angles on each other, and keep a stick handy to adjust wood in the fire as it burns to keep oxygen flowing through it.

Should I carry matches or a lighter?

It's really a matter of personal preference, but the best thing to take to light a fire is actually two things: matches and a lighter, or two lighters. Unless you've got a 100 percent reliable lighter, either matches or a lighter can fail (or just be impossible to light in certain windy or rainy conditions), and then you're without a fire for the night—unless you've mastered making a fire without ignition. With both matches and lighters, make sure they're in a waterproof container, because even getting them damp can make them impossible to light. A prescription pill container can work as a carrying case, or a sturdy ziplock bag (just make sure it doesn't get holes poked in it as it starts to rack up the miles riding inside your backpack). Outdoor gear stores usually sell several types of waterproof or "light anywhere" matches, which can be nice but are often unnecessary—a book of matches from a restaurant or bar is usually fine as long as you keep it dry.

Can I make a fire on a rainy day?

A few sprinkles or even a major downpour doesn't have to put the kibosh on having a campfire. If it's just sprinkling intermittently, your campfire might not get wet enough to go out, so light it and see what happens. If it's going to downpour, you have two issues to deal with: finding dry wood and keeping your fire from getting soaked. If there's a lot of rain in the forecast for your camping weekend, consider bringing a tarp and lots of cord to string up a shelter to keep your fire from the rain. Remember, heat rises, so when you're stringing up a tarp above where your fire will be, give the fire some respect and distance so it doesn't burn through the middle of your tarp. Anchor the tarp to four trees, making sure it's taut so rainwater won't gather in the middle of the tarp and weigh it down, and slightly angled so the rain will drip off one edge of the tarp. If the tarp is roughly 7 or 8 feet above the ground, it should be high enough that it won't be in danger of getting burned by the fire, as long as you're not building a ridiculously large fire. If you're buying a tarp specifically for the purpose of sheltering a campfire, take into account the fact that you and your friends will probably want to stand or sit around the fire, and ideally you'll be out of the rain too—so get a tarp big enough to cover both the fire and a circle of chairs around it (15 by 15 feet should be big enough for a group of up to six people). And don't forget the dry wood—keep it in, or underneath, your car, or if you have enough space under your tarp keep a stash there.

How big should my campfire be?

It's fun to make big fires—just admit it. But a big fire is unnecessary unless you're trying to keep twenty-five people warm, which you're probably not. On a camping trip, make your fire size proportional to the number of people in your group. If everyone's huddling around the fire, it's a little too small. If you find everyone keeps scooting his or her chair back away from the fire because of the heat, it's too big. And remember, unless you brought a trunk full of firewood, the fire lasts only as long as the supply of wood lasts. So keep your campfire as small as comfortably possible, and you'll be able to sit around your caveman TV much later into the evening.

Should I burn my garbage?

Although throwing your garbage in a campfire to get rid of it might seem like a good idea (then you won't have to carry it out, right?), you'll probably find that most of your backpacking garbage doesn't burn well and you won't be saving that much weight either. Plastic food bags and energy bar wrappers don't weigh that much after they've been emptied, so it's best to just bring them out with you. Don't attempt to burn aluminum foil in a campfire either—it never completely burns, and it leaves pieces of aluminum in the ashes, which eventually blow all over the forest and spread trash everywhere. A 1-gallon ziplock bag should fit a week's worth of trash on a backcountry trip.

Devote a little energy to minimizing trash when you're packing your food before your trip—get rid of cardboard boxes and put things in plastic bags whenever possible. That box of macaroni and cheese will take up less space in your pack if you transfer it into a plastic bag before the trip, and it will be in less danger of bursting open inside your pack and spilling everywhere.

How do I put out my campfire?

Smokey Bear will tell you to make sure you put your campfire out every time, for good reason: some of the most catastrophic forest fires in the past few decades have been human caused (some intentional, some unintentional). To make sure your fire is completely out, break up any still-hot coals into smaller pieces (use a stick so you don't burn your hands), spread them around the fire ring, and then pour water on the coals to make sure they're completely out. If you're conserving water, you can pee on the coals, but be warned: urine on hot campfire coals produces a pretty bad smell. Another

good policy: Be careful not to put a large piece of firewood on the fire as things at camp are winding down for the night. You don't want to be the last person up waiting by yourself for that thing to burn down, and it's an amateur move to leave a big piece of unburned wood in a campfire ring for the next party to find.

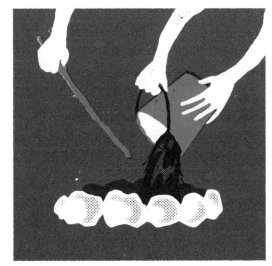

Is it okay to leave apple cores and banana peels on the trail?

Fruit is biodegradable, so it's okay to leave it on the trail, right? Yes, it's biodegradable, but no, it's not okay to leave it out where you're hiking. Orange peels and apple cores take six months to decompose in the outdoors, and banana peels take up to two years—and they don't exactly blend in with the natural environment when you toss them off to the side of the trail. So keep a small trash bag in your pack and carry everything out with you.

The Eight Backpacking Trips of a Lifetime

1. **Grand Canyon Rim-to-Rim, Arizona, USA:** A three-day backpacking trip down to the bottom of the Grand Canyon and up the other side

2. **John Muir Trail, California, USA:** A classic twenty-one-day trek across the Sierra Nevada, including Yosemite

3. **Inca Trail, Peru:** A four- to five-day trek to the fifteenth-century Inca dwelling of Machu Picchu

4. **Routeburn Track, New Zealand:** The premier mountain hut–to–mountain hut hiking route in the mountains of New Zealand's south island

5. **Hiker's Haute Route, France/Switzerland:** The famous hut-to-hut hiking route across the Alps connecting the famous mountain towns of Chamonix and Zermatt

6. **Alta Via 1:** The weeklong hut-to-hut trek across the Italian Dolomites

7. **Everest Base Camp:** A ten- to fourteen-day trek through the giant mountains of the Himalayas to the base camp for Everest climbers, elevation 17,600 feet

8. **Torres del Paine trek, Chile:** A five-day trek through the famous granite spires of Patagonia

What do I need to go car camping?

Car camping is the most beginner-friendly type of tent camping—you can pretty much take whatever you want, as long as it fits in the vehicle you're driving to the campground. And you don't need the highest-tech or most expensive gear to do it. Here are the basics.

- **Stove:** You can, of course, choose to cook over an open campfire, but it usually leaves your pots and pans coated in a layer of black soot, and a fire is tougher to keep at a consistent temperature, so stoves are easier and more reliable. Most department stores with a sports section sell camping stoves that work great. If you think you might like to try backpacking, buy a one-burner stove—it will work for car camping and also for backpacking (because there's no way you'll haul a big two-burner stove anywhere in a backpack). With the stove, you'll also need fuel, so be sure to buy the corresponding fuel to whichever stove you buy (propane or isobutane, usually).

- **Pots:** If you don't want to spend money on specific camping pots and pans (usually you'll only use one or two pots, or a pot and a pan, when you go camping), just grab a pot or two from your kitchen and toss it in your car—as long as it isn't a precious gift from your deceased grandmother and you can't bear to think of getting it dirty or scratching it while camping. If you do want to buy pots, consider getting a set in which a smaller pot rests inside a bigger pot—these sets are great for packing and are also ideal if you decide later to try backpacking.

- **Flatware:** Again, your flatware from your kitchen at home will work just fine. Or you can buy a set of plastic/Lexan spoons and forks from an outdoor store for a couple dollars. Just don't forget to bring some, or you'll be eating your pasta with your fingers.

- **Plates and/or bowls:** The plates and bowls you have at home are probably breakable and not designed to handle a bumpy car ride or much abuse in the outdoors, so it's best to buy some hard plastic, steel, or titanium bowls and/or plates made for camping. If you're choosing between plates or bowls, bowls are usually more versatile for camp food (you can eat oatmeal out of a bowl but not off a plate, for example).

- **Food:** Generally, if you can cook it in a pot or pan, you can cook it while camping. You won't have an oven, so things like lasagna and cookies are probably out. But everything else is fair game: hot dogs cooked over the fire, pasta dishes, soups, oatmeal, pancakes, and even tacos are great camping meals. If you're nervous about what to cook, bring something simple that cooks in a single pot, like macaroni and cheese.

- **Water/water container:** Many campgrounds have running water, but it's not that likely that the water pump will be right next to your campsite It's good to have a 3- to 7-gallon jug in your car that you can either bring filled with tap water from home or fill at the campground—you'll be doing lots of cooking, washing dishes, and washing hands, and you'll probably use more water than you think.

- **Coffee-making apparatus:** If you're a regular coffee drinker, camping isn't the time to try to go without it. Bring instant coffee or another way to make your morning coffee (see page 231).

- **Firewood:** If you want to have a campfire, it's best to bring some firewood to the campground (if it's allowed). Some campgrounds will sell firewood, but don't count on it. Pick up a bundle or two from a grocery store or gas station on your way. It's also a good idea to bring a hatchet to split up thick chunks of wood.

- **Camp chairs:** You might get lucky and find a fire ring with perfect-sized logs surrounding it, but for long-term campfire sitting a good canvas camp chair is best.

- **Tent:** You don't need to spend a thousand dollars on a tent, but if you buy a lower-end tent make sure it has a rain fly—inexpensive tents are often sold separately from their corresponding waterproof rain flies, and without the rain fly you might be in for a wet night.

- **Sleeping bag:** Again, you don't need to spend a pile of money (see page 217), but the more you spend, the higher quality your bag will be, and usually the less likely you'll be to freeze. Consider the low temperature for the nights you'll be camping, and buy a sleeping bag rated to well below that (e.g., if the low is in the 40s, get a sleeping bag rated to 20°F or even 15°F).

- **Sleeping pad:** It's tempting to buy a thick air mattress for camping, since they're theoretically the most comfortable. But be warned: All that air underneath you will act like a refrigerator when it cools down in the night, and sleeping on 5 or 6 inches of cold air can be very uncomfortable. Thinner sleeping pads will be less comfy but warmer, so they're better for sleeping overall. If you're worried about a sleeping pad being too thin, bring a thin foam mat to place underneath it to double up the cushioning.

Should I bring a flashlight or a lantern?

When it comes to lighting your campsite, the most functional thing you can pack is not a flashlight or a lantern—it's a headlamp, a light worn on a strap around your head. The light points where your head points, and you don't have to hold it in your hand like a flashlight, so you can do things that require both hands, like carrying firewood, cleaning dishes, or cooking. Lanterns are nice to light up tables or cooking areas and they add ambience to campsites; although they used to require fuel and sometimes hard-to-replace parts, many lanterns nowadays are battery powered or rechargeable by USB or AC outlet. Flashlights are fine if you don't want to spend the money on a head-lamp, but once you convert to using a headlamp while camping, you may find yourself using it at home more often than a flashlight too.

How do I pack a cooler?

Fill it with beer. Done.

Actually, there are a few techniques to help you get the most cooling possible from your cooler. First, when you start packing the cooler, try to have it be as cool as possible. If you're at home, an hour before you want to pack the cooler, throw something out of your freezer (a few ice cubes or a bag of frozen vegetables) into the cooler and shut the lid—this will cool it down. Second, be organized and get the cooler loaded all in one go: put down some ice, put your beer on top of that, add some more ice, some food, then a little more ice, then shut the lid and load it into the car. Taking an hour to pack it and repeatedly opening and closing the lid will lower the temperature. Third, the ice that turns into water is almost as cold as the ice itself, so don't get overzealous with draining the cooler—do it only when necessary. Fourth, keep the cooler cold once you're outside. Put the cooler in the shade during the day, and minimize opening and closing it—when you get up to get yourself a beer, ask if anyone else wants one. That's just the nice thing to do anyway.

How do I cook in a Dutch oven?

A Dutch oven is a heavy, three-legged cast-iron pot with a lid that can revolutionize your camp cooking if you're willing to put in the effort to lug one around and also to learn how to use it. If you can cook something in a slow cooker, you can cook it in a Dutch oven, and if you can bake something in a regular oven, you can probably bake something similar in a Dutch oven.

To use a Dutch oven, you'll need a campfire, a bag of charcoal, a set of tongs, a pair of leather gloves, and, for best results, a recipe that's designed specifically for Dutch oven cooking. For your first time cooking in a Dutch oven outdoors, try something simple like canned biscuits or a chocolate cake from a simple box mix. The Dutch oven works by cooking from both above and below, so you'll need an area of a campfire where you can build a small nest or seat of hot coals in which to set the Dutch oven.

Heat up the charcoal in a side spot of the campfire bed, coat the inside of the Dutch oven with a small amount of cooking oil, and mix up your chocolate cake mix or open your biscuits. Put the cake batter or biscuits in the Dutch oven, and place the Dutch oven on top of the hot coals. Put the lid on the Dutch oven and place some hot charcoals on top of the lid, building an even layer. Monitor the cake/biscuits every few minutes to see how they're cooking—it's a good idea to rotate the Dutch oven in the bed of coals to make sure it's cooking evenly throughout the process. Once the cake/biscuits are done, clean out the Dutch oven with only water (no soap). Once you've mastered an easy recipe like cake or biscuits, you can make more complex meals like soups or stew.

What kind of tent should I buy?

There are a bajillion different tents on the market, costing from $25 to $10,000 (really). As with everything else, the more you spend, the higher the quality of the product you can expect to get, but how much do you need to spend if you're not going to Mount Everest and camping locally? Generally, spending a minimum of $150 to $200 will get you a tent that won't leak or break on you with regular use. To decide which type of tent you need, you'll want to consider how you're going to use it: Will you take your whole family camping and need enough space for six people, or will it just be you and one other person sleeping in the tent? If you're going to be backpacking, a giant six-person tent you can stand up inside is not going to be very useful, because it will weigh 30 pounds and you won't want to walk too far with it in your backpack (if you can even fit it inside your backpack). A good, basic tent that's good for backpacking as well as car camping would be a small, two-person tent that weighs around or under 5 pounds—big enough to sleep two people but not luxuriously huge (more of a sleeping room than a living room). At 5 pounds, it can be packed in a backpack and not feel as though it's crushing you. A basic but quality two-person tent will cost $150 to $300 and will come with poles, a rain fly, and stakes, and you can confidently take it on weekend car camping trips as well as weeklong backpacking trips and be sure it won't burst a leak or blow over in gusty winds. For an extra $25 to $60, you can also buy a tent footprint, an extra layer of fabric that clips onto the bottom of your tent to protect the floor of the tent from punctures. Make sure you buy the footprint that corresponds to your exact tent brand and model—any other footprint likely won't integrate with the shape of your tent.

How do I pitch a tent?

If you can, it's best to just convince your friend to set up your tent while you sit down and rest or take a nap, but if you can't do that it's good to know how to pitch it yourself. Tent designs are varied, and each one has its own specific setup protocol, but most contemporary tents are extremely user-friendly and won't take more than five minutes or so to set up. In general, the basics of pitching a tent are as follows.

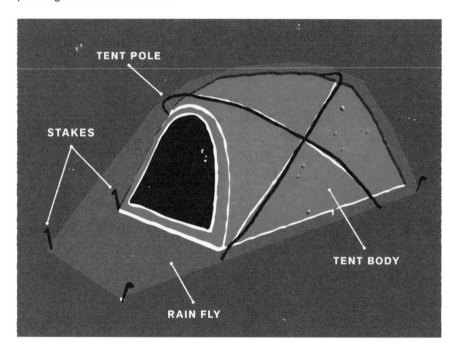

- **Locate all the parts.** Tent body, rain fly, tent poles, tent stakes. As you're setting up the tent, make sure the lightweight tent body and tent fly are weighted down and won't blow away in a gust of wind.

- **Lay out the tent body.** Figure out which side is the bottom and which side is the top (the top will be made mostly of mesh), and lay it out where you'd like to sleep for the night—a flat spot free of sharp sticks and rocks.

- **Set up the poles.** Almost all tent poles are made of a number of short sections connected by bungee cords and will snap together quite easily as the end of one section fits inside the end of the next section. Be careful that each pole section is fully inserted into its neighbor—if not, it's possible to break the tent pole.

- **Insert the poles into their proper places in the tent.** The poles will slide into either nylon sleeves or plastic clips, and the ends of the pole will pop into grommets near the bottom of the tent. As you do this, the tent will begin to take shape.

- **Attach the rain fly.** The rain fly will attach to the tent body via clips or hooks. Make sure that it's attached securely and evenly and that the doors of the rainfly match up with the locations of the doors on the tent body.

- **Stake it down.** First stake down the tent body, then the doors, then the guylines. Make sure the tent is as taut as possible—any loose sections of the tent will make a lot of noise if the wind picks up in the night, and setting it up correctly in the first place is far better than getting out of your warm sleeping bag in the middle of the night to readjust the stakes and guylines because the tent is flapping in the wind.

What do I do if the ground is too hard to get tent stakes into?

If you're camped on hard-packed dirt or a flat rock surface, driving tent stakes into the ground can be difficult or impossible. Fear not, and consider a few options.

- Move your tent to a spot with softer ground so you can put in the tent stakes.

- If you're in a spot with sufficient tree cover that acts as a solid windbreak, you can probably get away with staking down only the doors of your tent. Keep your gear inside the tent to weigh it down, or carry two or three heavy rocks inside the tent to weigh it down when you're not inside it (your body weight will hold it down when you're in it), and set the rocks outside the door when you turn in for the night.

- Stake it down with rocks. If your tent has a sufficient number of guylines, you might be able to use only the guylines to secure it. Find the biggest rocks you can carry and place them around your tent. Wrap each guyline around a rock and tighten it so there's no slack. Pay attention to your tent's position—if it's sheltered from the wind, you might be okay with minimal stake-down points. If it's not, consider moving. Just because there's no wind at 4 p.m. when you're setting up camp doesn't mean there won't be 35 mph gusts at midnight. Move the rocks back when you're done.

- Tie your guylines to nearby trees.

How do I set up guylines?

When you pulled your brand-new tent out of the bag for the first time, you probably noticed some cords attached to the rainfly in a few spots and thought, "What are these?" They're guylines. If utilized, they help stabilize your tent in windy weather, help the tent ventilate, and keep the rainfly from touching the tent body and building condensation. You will also likely trip over one of them at some point. But they're useful, and in a storm they can mean the difference between your tent poles snapping and your tent poles staying intact. A few pointers:

- When you bought your tent, it probably came with too few stakes to utilize all the guylines (this is a regular, if mysterious, practice). The tent also was probably built with several tabs that can optionally be used to tie guylines to, but no cord to make guylines with. Do yourself a favor, and before you leave the store, buy four or five additional tent stakes and 40 feet of thin cord so that when you get your tent home you can utilize all those guyline options.

- You don't have to tie guylines to every single spot on your tent, but a minimum of four guylines will do wonders to keep it upright in gusty weather. If your tent's rainfly has tabs or loops where the fly runs over the tent poles (and it should), utilize those spots first—they oppose each other and basically pull the tent in four different directions to anchor it down and add stability.

- You stake a guyline down just as you do a tent: pull the cord taut and push the stake into the ground at about a 45-degree angle, with the top of the stake pointing outward away from the tent.

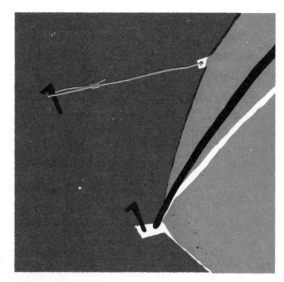

- After you stake down the first guyline, do the opposing guyline next (the one diagonal from the corner of the tent you just staked down). Then do the last two guylines.

- Guylines are wonderful, but they are not super-powered—don't set your tent up in an exposed place (a mountain ridge with no windbreak, for example) and expect guylines to keep you safe. Use them as a safeguard, not a substitute for good judgment.

- You'll likely have to adjust the tension of your guylines during a stormy or windy night. The best way to do that is to have them tied with an easily adjustable knot like a trucker's hitch (see below).

How do I tie a trucker's hitch?

The trucker's hitch is a knot that was traditionally used to tie down loads to truck beds, and it works just as well to secure your tent to the ground. The magic is that it's adjustable after it's tied, so it's great for guylines that need to be retightened throughout the night. Tying a trucker's hitch might seem complicated at first, but it will become your new best friend once you master it.

- Tie one end of your guyline cord to your tent, pull the cord out toward the ground, and put a stake in the ground at about the halfway mark on the cord (this is not necessarily the final spot where you'll stake down your guyline). Pull the cord out and loop it around the stake so you are pulling the loose end of the cord back toward the tent.

- On the strand of guyline between the tent and the stake (not the loose end), tie a figure eight on a bight knot about halfway up.

- Take the loose end of cord and run it through the loop of your figure eight on a bight knot. Pull the cord tight, and secure it to both strands of cord with two half-hitch knots.

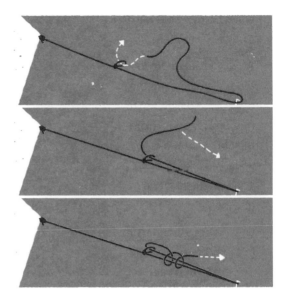

- You now have a trucker's hitch. Find the optimal spot for your tent stake, and vary the length of your guyline accordingly—you want the guyline as taut as possible, but with enough room to adjust it when it needs to be tightened later. You may have to untie the trucker's hitch and start over if your initial figure eight on a bight knot is too close or too far from the tent.

What do I do if I break a tent pole?

Almost all decent backpacking tents come with an emergency pole repair sleeve, a cigarette-sized aluminum tube that slides onto a broken section of tent pole to stabilize it. If your tent didn't come with one (check the bag the stakes came in), you can buy one at most outdoor stores for about five dollars.

When you snap a pole, carefully pull it out of the tent. It will probably have sharp edges, so make sure you don't snag it on anything that it can tear— which is pretty much every inch of fabric on your tent. Slide the repair sleeve up the pole until it's centered on the broken spot, and use a small strip of duct tape on each end to hold it in place.

If you don't have a pole repair sleeve, the best you can probably do is use a tent stake (you can very likely spare one from your tent unless you're camped in an extremely windy spot) or a very stiff stick to splint the pole where it's broken—wrap it tightly with a few feet of duct tape.

How do I rig a tarp?

A tarp is the most minimalist and often the cheapest camping shelter option—besides sleeping in a cave. All you need is a 10-by-10-foot tarp, 50 feet of lightweight cord, and eight tent stakes. There are many different configurations to rigging a tarp, but the simplest and most stable is the A-frame pitch.

To rig your tarp, find two trees with a flat space between them (or at least a space flat enough that you can sleep on it without rolling downhill all night). Tie a long length of cord between the trees so it's taut and about 4 feet above the ground in the middle. Flip the tarp over the cord so the cord splits the tarp in half, and tie short sections of cord to each corner grommet. Stake the corners of the tarp down so it forms an A-frame roof over the ground, and when the tarp is taut, tie cord to the other grommets along the edges of the tarp that are touching the ground, and use your remaining stakes to stake them out.

Rain will come in the ends of your tarp, so don't set up your sleeping bag so your head is near either end—put your sleeping bag more toward the center of your A-frame so you're covered.

Can I sleep outside without a tent or tarp?

If you really do want to sleep out under the stars, as in when you open your eyes in the middle of the night, you see stars, you can ditch your tent. But if you ditch your tent, you'll want to take into consideration a couple of things, the first of which is (maybe quite obviously) the weather forecast—if it rains, you're going to get soaked if you're sleeping in an unprotected sleeping bag (almost no sleeping bags are made waterproof enough to withstand much of a rain shower). So pick a night where there's a minimal chance of rain and go for it. But also remember that you won't have any protection from bugs if you don't have the mesh of a tent between you and any mosquitoes or other insects that might like to feast on your blood or just crawl around on your

face. If you're squeamish about spiders or other creepy-crawlies, you might consider the alternative of sleeping under the stars, which is setting up your tent but leaving the rain fly off. That way you're still sleeping under the stars, obstructed only by a layer of see-through mesh.

Can I cook in my tent?

If it rains, or if it's so cold you don't want to get out of your sleeping bag to cook dinner or breakfast, you might think it makes sense to bring your stove inside your tent to cook. Don't do it. Cooking inside a tent on a canister stove can easily produce enough carbon monoxide to kill you, not to mention melt or burn your sleeping bag, sleeping pad, and the tent itself. Cooking inside a tent on a white gas stove is an even bigger risk for fire. If you absolutely have to cook without leaving your tent, place the stove outside under the rain fly under one side of your tent door, and leave the other half of the door open. If your tent has a second door, open the door on that side for ventilation. Be careful with hot liquids and hot pots near the tent—just touching the tent fabric with something hot will melt a large hole in it.

How do I brush my teeth when I'm camping in the backcountry?

Brushing your teeth in the backcountry will teach you how little water you actually need to get your teeth clean. Use a small amount of toothpaste and a tiny amount of water on your toothbrush, and when you're done, blow the toothpaste spit out of your mouth in several bursts, pursing your lips tightly so the spit vaporizes as much as possible (nobody wants to see a pile of toothpaste spit in the backcountry). To rinse your toothbrush, pour a little water out of your water bottle onto the bristles, or pour an ounce or two of water into your mouth and forcefully spit it through the bristles to rinse it out. Yes, your brush might not get 100 percent clean, but your teeth will.

What happens if I get a hole in my tent?

If you get a hole in the rain fly of your tent, it's not an issue—until it rains, and that could be the next night of your trip. In that case, your first instinct might be to duct-tape the hole, but the old maxim that duct tape fixes everything is not exactly true. It can work for a short time, but for a real repair job that will actually hold, it's best to carry and use a field repair kit (which costs around eight dollars and weighs a couple of ounces). A field repair kit should contain a small tube of a product called Seam Grip or an equivalent, and a couple patches made of waterproof material. This will repair small holes in your tent fly. If you manage to rip a hole larger than about 2 inches in diameter, duct tape might be your only option (along with really hoping it doesn't rain) until you can seek out a professional repair when you get home.

If you rip a hole in the body of your tent, including the floor, use the same repair kit to fix it. If you rip a hole in the mesh of your tent, it's not as much of a big deal in the field (unless you're camping in an area with tons of mosquitoes or other insects that will fly in through the hole). Either leave it as is or patch it with duct tape, and when you get back home find a mesh repair kit in an outdoor store or online and fix the hole.

How do I put up a hammock?

Hanging a hammock is simple, right? You just hang it up between two trees and voilà, you're done. Not so fast. There's actually some math that goes into it, and your particular hammock should come with instructions specific to the measurements of the hammock. Here are the basics you'll want to know:

- Always use webbing straps to attach a hammock to trees. These are simple strips of webbing with loops at the ends to run cord through. Find two trees roughly 12 to 25 feet apart and around 8 inches in diameter or slightly smaller. Wrap one of your two webbing strips around the tree trunk at about shoulder height so that the webbing wraps around twice and the loops are facing the direction where you'll hang the hammock (the space between the two trees).

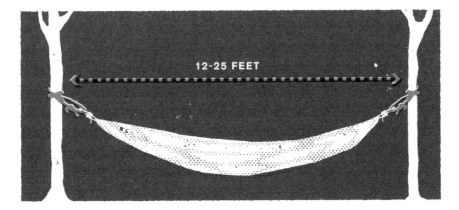

- Your hammock has a cord on each end (one on the foot end, one on the head end). Pick an end and estimate how much cord you'll need to hang the hammock evenly between the two trees, and tie it to the webbing with a couple of half-hitch knots (see page 207). Don't worry; this isn't your final position, so don't tie the knots too tight—just enough to keep it in place while you figure out the exact position of the hammock.

- Wrap your second strip of webbing around the other tree, and run the cord from the opposite end of the hammock through the loops in the webbing. Tie a couple of half hitches in the cord just as you did with the other side, and step away from the tree and eyeball the hammock. Is it hanging with an even amount of cord on each side? If not, adjust your half hitches until it is. The hammock should be hanging at a height where you can sit down in it from a standing position—if it isn't, move your webbing straps up or down the tree trunks as appropriate.

- Once you've got the hammock in the correct position, secure it to the webbing. Untie your half hitches and begin lashing the cord to the webbing. Pull the cord taut and wrap the tail (the loose end) under the section of cord running from the webbing to the hammock, then bring it back up and across the cord. Run the tail through the webbing, between the two loops, and bring it back toward the hammock, pulling it tight. Repeat this process four times, pulling the tail tight each time. Tie up the loose end with a couple of half hitches. Lash the cord on the other end of the hammock in the same fashion.

What's a bivy sack?

Bivy sack is short for *bivouac sack*, a minimalist waterproof shelter that is used instead of a tent or tarp (or sometimes in combination with a tarp). It's the same shape as a sleeping bag and is large enough to fit a sleeping bag inside. If you choose to use a bivy sack in lieu of a tent or other shelter, you are likely doing it to save weight in your backpack. The advantages are that it is lightweight and easy to pack (no tent poles, no stakes), and the disadvantages are that the inside of a bivy sack is a small place to spend a long rainy day or night—you generally can't sit up in a bivy sack, and if it's raining you will want it zipped almost all the way up with you inside it (don't worry, you'll still be able to breathe). You also lose the ability to shelter your gear from the rain—with a tent, you can always shove your pack and cooking gear inside during a rainstorm, but in a bivy sack you don't have that space. But bivy sacks can be great if you're on a trip with little chance of rain and you want to keep your backpack as light as possible—even the heaviest of bivy sacks weighs only 2 pounds, compared to most tents, which weigh 3½ to 6 pounds.

Should I keep the tent in the bag it came in?

Your backpacking tent probably arrived in a nice sleek bag, and you might think that it would make a nifty little package to strap to the back of your backpack. It might, but then you're putting a bunch of weight on the outside of your pack, and that weight will pull your pack backward. Plus, the tent poles will be on the outside of your pack, and if you accidentally set your pack down hard somewhere, the poles are in an unprotected spot and can bend or break (not good). It's better to remove the tent body, rain fly, poles, and stakes from the bag, leave the bag at home (or bring it along to use as a bear bag—see page 252), and pack the tent in your backpack in pieces—or split the tent in half and give part of it to your backpacking partner to carry (one person gets the poles and fly, the other gets the stakes and the tent body). When you get home, store the tent back in the bag.

How do I clean out my tent?

In the backcountry, hopefully you're able to keep from spilling food and liquids in your tent (because bears like that sort of thing). So most of the things you want to clean out of your tent should be dry solids—pieces of grass, dirt, and small rocks that got into the tent as you were moving in and out of the door. The easiest way to clean out the tent is to wait until the next morning when you're packing up camp. Take your tent stakes out of the ground, remove the rain fly, unzip the door (or both doors), pick up the tent by the poles, lift it over your head, and shake it, letting the dirt fall out the open door. If you want to do an even better job, take out the poles, turn the tent body inside out, and brush the dirt off the floor with your hand.

Once you get home, if you need to do further cleaning, set up the tent in your garage, front yard, or living room, and wipe it out with a wet paper towel or rag. You shouldn't need to use any sort of cleaning product unless you spilled something nasty in there—but if you do, use a little soapy water, which won't damage the fabric of your tent floor.

What do sleeping bag temperature ratings mean?

Strangely, sleeping bag ratings have always been a bit nebulous. For years, there was no universal rating system, and one manufacturer's 30-degree rating (meaning that you could comfortably sleep in the bag in weather 30°F or warmer) was something far different than the next manufacturer's 30-degree rating. Thankfully, many (but not all) sleeping bag manufacturers have started to use the EN (European Norm) methodology, which is used to test sleeping bags and establish their true insulative value. However, the rating is not printed on the sleeping bag—you'll find it on a tag attached to the bag. The EN system lists three ratings for each sleeping bag.

1. The Comfort Rating (for women) is the lowest outside temperature at which an average woman will stay warm inside the sleeping bag.

2. The Lower-Limit Rating (for men) is the lowest outside temperature at which an average man will stay warm inside the sleeping bag.

3. The third rating, the Extreme Rating, is the lowest outside temperature at which an average woman can survive in the sleeping bag.

How does that relate to a manufacturer's rating of sleeping bags? For one sleeping bag that the manufacturer itself rated as 15 degrees, for example, the EN ratings were as follows:

- Comfort Rating: 27.1 degrees

- Lower-Limit Rating: 15.6 degrees

- Extreme Rating: -17.5 degrees

Should I get a down or a synthetic sleeping bag?

Most sleeping bags will fall into one of two categories, according to the type of insulation they contain: down (plucked from geese), or synthetic (some type of synthetic insulative fiber). There are advantages and disadvantages to both.

Down sleeping bags are almost as a rule more lightweight and compressible than synthetic sleeping bags. Because down is extremely compressible, down sleeping bags pack smaller in your backpack. They're also more expensive, starting at around $250 for a low-end bag and running nearly $1,000 for a high-end, custom-made sleeping bag. A major disadvantage to down sleeping bags is that when down gets wet, it loses its insulative capability, so if your bag gets soaked somehow, whether by a rainstorm or a leaky water bottle or a fall during a river crossing, you'll be in trouble. Many companies have started to make "hydrophobic" down, which is not waterproof but will resist soaking and dry more quickly than regular down. This can be good in damp camping conditions but still takes a long time to dry in the event of a full soaking. Down sleeping bags are a great choice for adventurers who are conscious of the total weight of their backpack (backpackers and climbers in particular) and people who spend most of their nights camping in dry environments like the desert or the Rocky Mountains.

Synthetic sleeping bags are usually less expensive than down sleeping bags but are heavier and bulkier (although gear companies are perpetually making lighter and more compressible synthetic bags). Synthetic insulation, unlike down, will hold some of its insulative properties when it's wet, so synthetic bags are a good choice for adventurers who spend more time in wet environments where they're likely to deal with rainy or snowy weather multiple days in a row. Synthetic bags are also appropriate for people who are less worried about weight or space (kayakers or whitewater raft enthusiasts) or who are just more concerned with warmth in all conditions (snow and rain) than they are with weight and space.

What's the difference between a $50 sleeping bag and a $250 sleeping bag?

Yes, you could save a lot of money on camping gear by buying it all at a discount department store that also sells toasters, jumper cables, and Christmas decorations, but it might not last that long or work that well. The primary difference between a $50 sleeping bag and a $250 sleeping bag is performance. An inexpensive sleeping bag is likely to be a rectangular-shaped bag with a large opening at the top. This lets in lots of cold air, which makes you cold and probably means you'll have a night without sleep and a general dislike of camping. A mummy-style bag of any quality will insulate better than a rectangular bag simply because it has a much smaller opening at the top and less dead air inside for your body to heat up. A $50 bag will also probably not have quality insulation or zippers, and zippers can be the bane of your existence if they don't work correctly. If one breaks, you can pay half of the cost of your $50 sleeping bag getting a new zipper put in it.

And, as with a lot of inexpensive things, durability will be an issue. If you want to go camping five times in your life, buy a $50 bag. If you want to go camping twenty-five or more times, spend some extra money and get yourself a quality sleeping bag.

How do I wash a sleeping bag?

A sleeping bag might seem straightforward to clean (isn't it just like a duvet?), but it requires a little extra care so you don't ruin your investment. You don't need to wash your sleeping bag every single time you use it. Unless you really stank it up somehow, washing it once every twenty or thirty nights of use (or once a year) will keep it from getting too funky. It's best to avoid washing it in a top-loading washing machine because the cords on your sleeping bag can get caught on the spindle and wreak havoc on the bag, and the agitator can rip apart the stitching. So use a front-loading machine. If you don't have one, head to a laundromat and use a front-loader there. Wash the bag in cold water, on a gentle cycle, using a nondetergent soap. When it's done, put it in a dryer set on no heat (not low heat—no heat) with a couple of tennis balls or dryer balls. Without something bouncing around the dryer to break up the clumped down (or synthetic insulation), it will just stay clumped and take days to dry—plus you'll have to break up all the clumps by hand. Your sleeping bag works only as long as it has loft and the insulation is evenly spread throughout it, and improperly drying it can ruin the distribution of insulation.

How do I store my sleeping bag at home?

Your sleeping bag should come with two bags with drawstring closures: one big (possibly mesh) bag of about the same dimensions as a queen-sized pillowcase, and one "stuff sack," which you should use to compact the bag and carry it in the bottom of your backpack while you hike. Storing the sleeping bag in the stuff sack for prolonged periods of time can nearly permanently compact the down so it has almost no loft (or it can take weeks for it to regain the loft once you pull it out of the tightly compacted storage)—so keep it in the bigger, mesh bag at home, or better yet, store the bag completely rolled out if you have enough space to lay it down somewhere or hang it from its foot end.

How do I store my tent when I get home?

When you get home from your backpacking trip, it's a good idea to set up your tent in your garage, backyard, or living room for a day to make sure it's 100 percent dry before you put it away—mildew has caused the premature death of many tents. If it's clean and dry, store the tent in the bag it came in when you bought it. Some people like to neatly fold and roll up the fly and tent body, wrapping them around the tent poles before sliding them into the bag, and some people just stuff the tent in the bag around the poles. Neither way has been proven to be superior for any significant reason—although folding it generally leaves the tent with fewer wrinkles and creases (or at least neater-looking wrinkles and creases) the next time it comes out of the bag for camping use.

What should I do if my sleeping bag gets wet on a camping trip?

If your sleeping bag gets wet on a camping trip and you're camping for another night, you'll have to do your best to dry it out. If it's a synthetic sleeping bag, find a sunny spot and ideally a tree branch to hang the bag over so the sun and the breeze can dry it out. If you can't find a tree branch that will hang the bag facing the sun, lay it out on a dry rock. If it's a down sleeping bag and it got wet, do the same thing—hang it on a tree branch in the sun. If the down insulation in the sleeping bag got wet enough that it has clumped inside the bag, break up the clumps by pinching them with your fingers. As the bag dries, keep working to break up the down. It may take several hours for the bag to dry, especially in a humid climate.

If your sleeping bag gets wet and it's the last day of your camping trip, don't worry about getting the bag dry before you head home. Pack it away, and when you get home hang it up to dry or put it in a clothes dryer on a "no heat" (not "low") setting. If it's a down sleeping bag, make sure to place two tennis balls in the clothes dryer to bounce around and break up the clumps of down.

How do I sleep (comfortably) in a sleeping bag?

There's no sleeping system that can really approximate your bed at home, and the sooner you understand that, the better off you'll be. Instead of trying to replicate a bedlike experience, learn to sleep in a sleeping bag with a few basic tips. Understand that you'll be zipping yourself into a bag, and you won't be able to spread out your limbs and starfish like you can in a bed. That's the bad news. The good news is, a decent sleeping bag will keep you warm as the temperature drops to below freezing. Follow these tips to make your sleep more comfortable.

- Make a pillow by putting your extra clothes inside a stuff sack and put it under your head, either inside your sleeping bag hood or outside it.

- Zip up your sleeping bag, get all your limbs inside, and make sure you're not breathing into the bag itself (condensation on the inside will make you cold). To prevent this, when you roll onto your side, roll so the bag rolls with you, not so your head turns facing away from the opening. The smaller you make the opening around your face, the warmer you'll be—in extreme cold, your nose and mouth might be the only things poking out.

- If your socks are wet or damp when you go to sleep, either put on dry socks or just take your socks off your feet (they'll dry overnight inside your sleeping bag).

- If you wake up in the night and you're too warm, work your way out of the bag in increments: often just popping your head out is enough to cool you down to a comfortable temperature. If it's not, unzip the zipper six to twelve inches and see if that works. Then try sticking one arm out, and so on.

- You'll likely wake up in the night more times than if you were sleeping at home. That's normal; just accept it as part of sleeping outdoors.

What kind of sleeping pad should I buy for underneath my sleeping bag?

There are three basic choices when buying a sleeping pad: foam, self-inflating, and air pad. A foam pad is the least technologically advanced, lowest cost, lightest weight, and usually lowest comfort of all the options—it's basically just a ½-inch-thick strip of closed-cell foam, which is fine for a lot of people. You can also skip the foam pad and find a campsite with some natural cushion under it (such as pine needles or grass). A self-inflating pad is generally an inch or more thick and will fill itself with air at least partially—but you'll need to blow it up by mouth to get it completely inflated. Self-inflating pads are more comfortable than foam pads and generally warmer and more durable than air pads (but a little heavier than both foam pads and air pads). An air pad that you inflate by blowing air into it with your mouth is the most cushioned and usually the most lightweight option—think of a pool air mattress, but a bit more high-tech and durable. It's generally 2½ inches thick or more, which is a luxurious amount of padding in the backcountry, but it can be cold unless it has an insulating material inside its cells (all that air underneath you cools quickly overnight and can lower your body temperature, even through your sleeping bag). Many models of air pads puncture more easily than self-inflating pads, so they're not the best for "sleeping out" without a layer of protection underneath them.

How do I roll up a sleeping pad to be as small as it was when I bought it?

When you buy a self-inflating sleeping pad, it's tightly wrapped in vacuum-sealed plastic. This is the smallest it will ever be. Let go of any delusions that you will ever stuff an object that size in your backpack again. It's impossible. The sleeping pad you bring home from the store was packed by a machine, and you are no machine. Don't try to compete with it; instead, compete with yourself. See how small you can roll up your sleeping pad. To do this, unscrew the air valve and let the air seep out. Start slowly rolling the foot end of the pad toward the head end (or from the end opposite the air valve to the end with the air valve). Squeeze the air out as you go, and roll slowly enough that air has a chance to escape and doesn't gather in the rolled part. When you reach the end and you've rolled up the pad completely, close the air valve so no air can get back into the pad. Unroll it again, fold the pad in half lengthwise (or in thirds, depending how it was originally packed), and start rolling from the feet end again. As you get closer to the top, you will have to open the air valve to let more air escape. Do that, and when you have the pad completely rolled up, close the valve again and tighten a strap around the pad to keep it compacted in your pack.

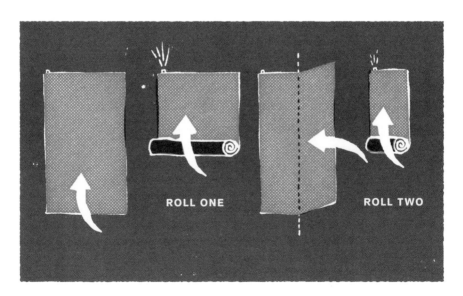

ROLL ONE   ROLL TWO

How do I patch a hole in my sleeping pad?

If you somehow get a hole in your sleeping pad, you'll know. Halfway through the night, you'll notice that you're feeling much closer to the ground or that your hip seems to be sitting on something quite firm when you roll over (that's the ground). To patch the hole, you need two things: a patch kit and the ability to find the hole.

When you bought your sleeping pad, hopefully it included a patch kit. If not, look up the manufacturer and purchase a patch kit from them—a patch kit is lightweight, inexpensive, and insurance against uncomfortable nights trying to sleep in your tent. The patch kit should consist of a small tube of adhesive and a few patches that match the material of your pad (if you buy the patch kit from the manufacturer of your sleeping pad versus buying another brand's patch kit, it will match).

Finding the hole is the true crux—especially if you're in the backcountry. Unless you have superpowers, you probably won't be able to find it without sinking the pad in a body of water—the air pressure inside a sleeping pad isn't usually enough that you can hear a hissing noise indicating air escaping. So when you have a chance, either before you leave camp or when you arrive at your next night's camp (or when you pass by a pond or lake sometime during the day), inflate the pad and dip it into a calm body of water, watching for bubbles indicating the leak. When you find the leak, apply the adhesive around the hole (don't be shy) and stick the patch on. Open the air valve on the pad, and leave the pad out to dry as long as the manufacturer's instructions indicate. If you discover the hole on the last day or night of your trip, fix it at home: just fill up your kitchen sink or bathtub and find the hole, then patch it.

Should I share my tent with my friend?

Your relationship with your friend can, of course, dictate this—whether you want to get that close to him or her. But there's no reason to have a hang-up about spending the night in a small tent with another person. It's actually way better than sharing a bed with someone, since you're both zipped into sleeping bags and no one can awkwardly, accidentally, try to spoon you in your sleep. One tent split between two backpacks means about 2½ pounds for each of you, whereas each of you bringing your own tent means 5 pounds each—that's a lot of extra weight and bulk. Although it's most economical to carry one tent, there are a few reasons why you'd want to take separate tents: your friend is a chronic snorer, or taller than 6 foot 6 and needs to lie diagonally in a tent, or maybe you're on a trip that's a week or longer and you each just want your own space.

How do I have sex in a tent?

Assuming you already know how to have sex, there are a couple of things that are different about doing it in the great outdoors as opposed to indoors:

- **Air temperature:** Just because you're warm and toasty inside your sleeping bag doesn't mean you can unzip it, get completely naked, and be comfortable. If it's chilly outside at all, you might consider waiting until morning, when the sun will warm the air temperature significantly.

- **Fluids:** Washing a sleeping bag isn't as easy as throwing a set of bedsheets in the dryer, so think about that when you're about to get busy. If it's warm enough, it's a good idea to shove both parties' sleeping bags aside, out of the way of any bodily fluids. Also consider that a wet spot inside a sleeping bag might be unavoidable when you zip yourself up in the bag afterward. Bring a wet wipe or two to clean up any stuff you don't want sticking to your tent when you pack up camp.

- **The ground:** The ground is often harder than you might first think, especially on the back and knees. Try to push your sleeping pads together and eliminate gaps, and make sure knees aren't rubbing against bare ground during the act itself.

How do I find firewood?

If you're in an area where firewood gathering is permitted (i.e., Forest Service land, Bureau of Land Management land, or anywhere that doesn't have a sign reading "Firewood Gathering Prohibited"), firewood gathering should be pretty easy. Grab a wide selection of different thicknesses of wood—a few twigs for kindling, a few finger-sized pieces to burn after that, then some "quarter-sized" pieces, or limbs about the diameter of a quarter, and then a few larger ones. If you're in a heavily used backcountry area and can't find firewood near your campsite, remember that most humans generally try to conserve energy and thus won't go too far from camp to look for firewood. Grab a strap or piece of cord to bundle together any pieces of wood you'll find, go farther out from your camp, and climb higher (most people don't want to walk uphill to find wood). As you pick up pieces, strap them together, and when you've found enough, head back to camp and start your fire.

How do I split firewood?

Unless your fireplace is the size of a taxicab, you don't want to be throwing a log as thick as your waist on your fire (no matter how trim your waist is)—big chunks of wood are hard to get lit, and when they finally catch they take forever to burn. So at some point you'll need to split at least a few chunks of wood in order to build a fire.

For thick, round sections of wood 6 or 8 inches in diameter, you'll want to use a splitting maul, a long-handled ax with a heavy, wide head. Take your chunk of wood and set it upright (it's nice to have a chopping block underneath, but not mandatory). Inspect the top of the wood, where your ax blade will be hitting it: you want to aim your blade so it drives itself into the wood parallel with the grain, not perpendicular to it. Don't worry about picking a specific line on the top of the wood and hitting it exactly—you won't, and it's not important. Just concentrate on lining up the blade and the grain. Don't hit a knot, because you won't get through it (the tree will almost always win that battle).

Stand facing the wood you're going to split. Hold the maul with your nondominant hand (in this case, we'll say your left hand) near the bottom of the handle and your dominant hand near the blade, with the blade pointing away from your thumb (or down toward the ground as you hold the maul parallel to the ground in front of your body). Bring the blade end of the ax back past your right hip and swing it up over your head, simultaneously sliding your right hand down the ax handle to join your left hand.

With both hands near the bottom of the handle, swing the maul into the wood. Don't try to hit it as hard as you can—you will rarely get through a big chunk of wood in one swing, and you want to remain in control—firm, but controlled. Your elbows should be almost exactly straight when the ax blade hits the top of the wood. Aim for the center of the wood or slightly off center toward you (not away from you)—if you miss the center by too far toward the back, your ax handle will hit the wood, and most ax handles can't endure too many hits like that. The blade will get stuck from time to time—when it does,

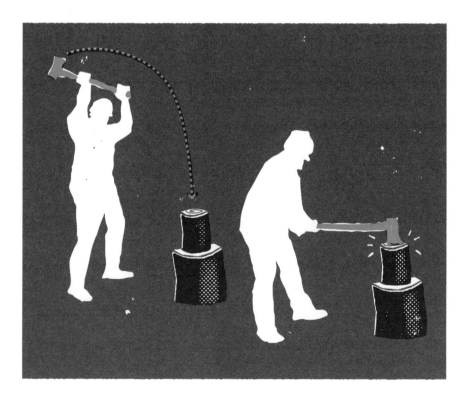

slide one hand up the ax handle close to the blade and wiggle it out (you may even need to step on the wood with one foot and work it out using both hands). Keep swinging the maul into the same spot on the wood until it splits.

For smaller chunks of wood, you'll want to use a hatchet, holding your small chunk of wood in your nondominant hand, using an abbreviated swing into the wood: lean over the chunk of wood, holding it in one hand and swinging the hatchet no higher than your head. Obviously be careful to avoid hitting your nondominant hand with the hatchet, and if you want to be extra-safe, stand the wood up in a stable spot and don't hold it with your other hand when you swing the hatchet. If the hatchet gets caught in the wood on your first swing, you may not even want to bother pulling it out—simply swing the hatchet with the chunk of wood attached to the blade and slam it into the ground until the hatchet splits through the wood.

What kind of ax should I buy (a big one or a hatchet)?

As sexy as it is to whip a heavy splitting maul over your head and swiftly drive it through a chunk of wood, for general camping purposes it's probably unnecessary, especially if you're buying firewood from a gas station on your way to the campsite or making a fire from firewood you've gathered from the forest near your campsite. A small hatchet, or one-handed ax, will suffice to split your firewood into smaller pieces when necessary or to trim small branches from downed logs. Look for a hatchet with a 12- to 20-inch-long handle and toss it in the trunk of your car, where it will be for your next camping trip.

Do I need a saw?

For general backpacking purposes, you will probably never need a saw. If you're building a campfire in the backcountry and you are burning pieces of wood you can't snap in half by bending them over your knee or standing on them, you're probably gathering wood that's too big. If you're car camping and bringing in your own firewood, a hatchet will probably do more of what you need (i.e., splitting logs into smaller pieces). That said, if you foresee some sort of need for one, get one that's specifically designed for backpacking—they break down so they're easy to pack, and they add much less weight to your backpack than a regular saw (some weigh less than a pound).

Should I take a machete hiking?

If you want to draw suspicious stares, or scare the crap out of other hikers, or have everyone talk about you after you pass them on the trail, you should definitely take a machete hiking. If you are reading this book, you will absolutely not need a machete when you go hiking. If you do need a machete where you go hiking, your trip is far beyond the scope of this book, and we will probably read about it in the pages of *National Geographic*, because your hiking is not in a fun place where trails are at least somewhat cleared prior to your hike, and you are hacking at vegetation with a machete to gain passage to something in the name of science or exploration.

Can I cut down a tree for firewood?

Putting your lumberjack/Brawny Man fantasies aside, cutting down trees for campfires is generally a bad idea for many reasons. Cutting down a live, green tree for firewood doesn't usually work because the wood is so wet it won't burn properly. Cutting down large dead trees can be dangerous unless you're experienced at accurately felling them—meaning you can get them to fall in the exact spot you want, so that they don't get hung up on neighboring trees or land on the hood of your car. And on Forest Service land, you can cut down trees for firewood, but you first have to have the proper permit. So bringing your own firewood, or gathering wood from near your campsite, is your best bet. If you want to hack away at a tree for a while, you should have no problem finding one on the ground that's already been felled by Mother Nature.

How do I poop in the outdoors?

Pooping in the outdoors is a rite of passage: when you learn how to do it, the world opens up to you. You are no longer limited to short one-day hikes during which you will not have to worry about going number two. If you can poop in the woods, you can sleep in the woods, wake up the next morning, do your business, and hike for a second day, and repeat the process. So how do you do it?

First, you dig a hole. For this, you'll need a small backpacking trowel, procurable at any outdoor gear store. With your backpacking trowel in hand, select a spot—ideally it's private, 100 feet away from a trail, and 200 feet from water—and start digging. Make sure the hole you dig is at least 6 inches deep in order for your poop to decompose properly (and to bury it under enough dirt to keep its smell and sight hidden). It's not a bad idea to anticipate your bowel movement and "pre-dig" a hole near your campsite for when the time comes.

Once you have a hole 6 inches deep, it's time to do your business. Squat down and aim toward the bottom of the hole. If you need help balancing, extend a hand backward (watch out for the hole). And relax.

Congratulations. You've now pooped in the woods. Spread the dirt back over your hole and tamp it down. If you missed a little bit, grab a stick and nudge your stuff into the hole before burying it.

What do I do with my toilet paper?

You probably never give much thought to your used toilet paper. But in the woods you have to give a little more thought to where it goes, because you can't just flush it away. Here's the deal: not using toilet paper at all in the backcountry is the true mark of the expert outdoorsperson. Yes, for real. Sticks, rocks, leaves, even the occasional snowball work just as well, once you figure out your technique. This means you don't have to carry toilet paper with you when you go backpacking.

However, few people achieve, or even aspire to, this expert level of outdoors pooping. So here's what you do: take only white, nonperfumed types of toilet paper in your pack, and either bury it deep in the cathole you dug to poop in or pack it out with you in a sealed plastic bag. Try to minimize your toilet paper usage—don't bury half a roll of it every time you poop, and maybe experiment with using a few squares of toilet paper only for "buffing" after you've tried using some sticks/rocks/leaves first. Of course, you'll want to make sure you don't wipe with poison ivy, poison oak, or poison sumac (see page 63).

Do not under any circumstances burn your toilet paper to get rid of it. Yes, it would disappear faster that way, but if you do it incorrectly (or if there's a gust of wind at the wrong moment), you could burn down the forest, which is not worth the risk.

How do I toast a marshmallow?

The most important thing to remember in toasting a marshmallow over a campfire is that there's really no right or wrong way to do it—just a matter of preferences.

Grab a stick about the length of your arm or slightly longer (unless you want to toast your forearm as well as the marshmallow), preferably with a semisharp end. If one end isn't sharp enough to poke into a marshmallow without ruining it, take a minute and whittle the end down a little bit with your pocketknife.

Poke the stick into your marshmallow, and hold the marshmallow over the fire, keeping it in the edges of the flames. Watch the marshmallow and rotate it as it turns golden brown on each side. When you've achieved your level of toastedness (light brown, brown, dark brown, or black), pull the marshmallow out of the fire and give it a few seconds before biting into it.

An alternative method: Stick the marshmallow all the way into the fire until it catches on fire, then pull it out of the fire and blow it out. It'll be singed, but gooey on the inside.

What's the best way to make coffee in the backcountry?

Coffee is a very touchy subject among outdoorspeople, and everyone has his or her own opinion on how to make it best. Here are a few options and their pros and cons.

- **Starbucks Via (or other instant coffee):** Simple, easy, no wet grounds to pack out, no mess.

- **Cowboy coffee (see page 232):** Simple, easy, but gritty.

- **French press:** Makes wonderful coffee, but carrying the apparatus can be bulky, and there are lots of grounds to deal with.

- **French press mug or French press attachment for cooking pot or Jetboil:** Makes wonderful French press coffee and is less bulky than a regular French press, but there are still lots of grounds to deal with.

- **Pour-over:** Also makes wonderful coffee and isn't very bulky but leaves lots of grounds (and filters) to deal with.

- **Aeropress:** Makes great espresso; is somewhat bulky but leaves less waste/grounds to deal with than other options.

- **Abstaining from coffee:** Ridiculous!

I absolutely love my French press—can I take it backpacking?

Here's the great thing about backpacking: you can take whatever you want to take, no matter what anyone says. The only bad thing is that everything you want to take adds weight to your pack, so you have to make some choices or deal with a crushingly heavy pack. If you want to bring your special coffee-making apparatus because it's the only way you can wake up, and when you get your coffee everyone on the trip will be better off, then do it. Think about jettisoning something else unnecessary if you need to make room for that moka pot (an extra pair of socks, a paperback book, deodorant, etc.). And when you hand your buddies a cup of wonderful espresso 5 miles from the nearest road, say, "I told you it was going to be worth it."

How do I make cowboy coffee?

There are a hundred fancy, even precious, ways to make coffee in the back-country, but everyone should know how to make cowboy coffee—it's the simplest possible way to make a cup of coffee. First, decide how many cups of coffee you're making and pour the appropriate amount of water into the cooking pot. Bring the water into a rolling boil over your heat source (stove or open fire), remove the pot from the flame, and stir in the equivalent amount of coffee grounds. Let the pot sit for five min-

utes and allow the grounds to settle to the bottom, and then carefully pour the coffee into cups. You (or someone in your group) will get a coffee ground or two in your teeth at some point, so sip with awareness.

How do I cook over a fire?

Humans have been cooking over fire for thousands of years, and you can still reconnect with your ancestors by doing the same thing, even if you're heating up some pasta instead of a saber-toothed tiger you killed with your bare hands. There are three ways to do it.

1. **In a cooking pot over coals.** Get a good campfire going and stoke it so a small bed of coals is exposed. Place your cooking pot (with the lid on) directly on the coals, making sure to keep the handle pointing away from the fire (because you need to be able to pull the pot out of the fire later without burning your hand). Keep an eye on whatever you're cooking, as you can't really turn the heat down—to turn your coals to a "low" setting, just pick the pot up and hold it a small distance above or to the side of the coals.

2. **Wrapped in foil.** With a small amount of aluminum foil, you can cook fish, meat, even leftover pizza or burritos. Just prepare a bed of coals the way you would for a cooking pot, place your foil-wrapped food on the coals, and monitor it. Keep something handy to flip the item over when it's cooked on one side—a pair of sturdy sticks can work great.

3. **On a stick.** Using a sharp stick, you can cook hot dogs, sausages, bratwurst, vegetables, or any other food you can stab and hold over a fire. Just as you would cook a marshmallow, keep rotating it and make sure it's thoroughly cooked before you eat it.

What size backpack do I need?

The size of your backpack depends on how long you're going to be out on the trail or in the mountains. Packs are sold according to volume, usually measured in liters. If you're only going out on a one-day hike, a 30-liter or smaller pack should be plenty—unless you plan on taking a whole watermelon and the entire *Hunger Games* series on your hike. If you're going on an overnight hike, you'll need room in your pack for a tent, a sleeping bag and pad, a stove and pots, and a water filter, so you'll need a bigger pack—something in the 55- to 60-liter range. If you're staying out for four or five days or longer, you'll need a pack in the 60- to 85-liter range.

How should my backpack fit?

Finding a backpack that fits is a bit different from finding jeans that fit—and believe it or not, it doesn't have much to do with how tall you are. Backpacks are sized on the basis of your torso size, or the length of your spine from your iliac crest (the top of your hip bones on the sides of your body) to your C7 vertebra (which is the bone that sticks out farthest from the base of your neck when you're standing up with your chin to your chest). Get a friend to help you measure the distance between these two points by holding a measuring tape (not a ruler) between your C7 and the spot where your thumbs meet when you hold your hands on your hips with your middle fingers running across your iliac crest. This measurement will indicate your torso size.

Once you know your torso size, you have a starting point to find the right backpack for you. If your torso size puts you in between backpack sizes (i.e., it places you at the top end of a "medium" pack but at the bottom end of a "large" backpack), try the smaller-sized pack first. More and more companies now make backpacks specifically designed for women, so explore those options when shopping for a backpack—you might have to check the tags to tell the difference between men's and women's models.

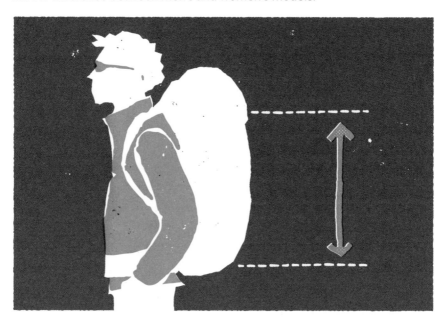

The best way to fit a backpack is to work with a sales associate at an outdoor gear store, but if that's not an option, here's how to do it at home.

- Load the backpack with some weight, padded by towels or pillows. Stuff a pillow at the bottom of the pack, and then put ten to fifteen pounds of books or gear in the pack, and fill in the rest of the air spaces in the pack with clothes or towels. Cinch down the compression straps (the straps on the actual pack that compress the load inside, not the shoulder straps and waist belt). Loosen the shoulder straps, waist belt, and sternum straps all the way out. Pick up the pack and slide your arms through the shoulder straps.

- Tighten the waist belt first, making sure to pull both straps evenly and keep the buckle in the middle. Your iliac crest should split the waist belt, and the bottom of the waist belt should be high enough so it doesn't interfere with your hip joints when you step up.

- Tighten the shoulder straps next, pulling them so they're snug but not putting pressure on the tops of your shoulders—your waist should be supporting most of the weight in the pack, and the shoulder straps should more just hold the pack in place. Look in a mirror at your side profile; if there is air between the shoulder straps and your shoulders, either tighten the shoulder straps or adjust the harness to move the top attachment point for the shoulder straps down.

- Tighten the pack's load-lifting straps next—they're the straps that rise from the tops of your shoulder straps to the pack at an upward angle. Don't crank them down too much, just enough that the pack doesn't wiggle around when you lean forward or move side to side.

- Tighten the sternum strap last—again, don't cinch it too tightly, just enough to keep the shoulder straps at a comfortable width across your chest.

- If you've done everything correctly, the weight should rest on your hips and the pack should not feel as if it's crushing your shoulders. No fully loaded backpack is going to feel *that* great to carry, but it should be comfortable enough that you don't feel as if you have to take it off every half hour on the trail. If your pack doesn't fit correctly, exchange it for a different size.

How do I pack a backpack?

There are a few goals to keep in mind when you're packing a backpack for an overnight trip.

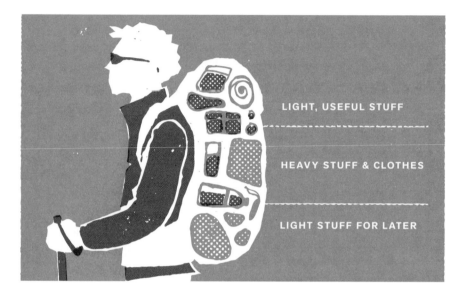

1. Get all your stuff inside the pack with a little room to spare.

2. Balance the pack so its weight isn't pulling you to one side or the other.

3. Get most of the heavy stuff as close to your back as possible—not up at the top of the pack, or at the back of the pack where it will pull you backward. To do this, put the light stuff that you're not going to use during the day—tent, sleeping bag, sleeping pad—at the bottom. On top of that, put your stove, fuel, and food and most of your water (if you're using a hydration reservoir like a Camelbak, the reservoir pocket will be against your back already) in the middle section of the pack. Use your clothes to fill the spaces left in the pack (but keep your rain jacket as close to the top as you can, because you might need it while hiking). Once you've got everything as tightly packed as possible, throw your snacks and a water bottle on the top, close the pack, and cinch down all the compression straps. You should have a tight, balanced package.

How do I lighten my backpack?

Your pack could always be lighter. Always. You can do two things: choose to deal with it psychologically, or take steps to minimize the weight wherever possible. There are entire books written about the subject of ultralight backpacking and a thousand different opinions about what the best tactics are. Here are three basic things that will help get you started on the path.

1. **Adjust your definition of "comfortable."** Leave your pillow at home and your extra pair of socks too. Learn to sleep under a tarp instead of packing a whole tent. Take a lighter-weight sleeping bag, and chop your foam sleeping pad down to two-thirds your body length; use your empty backpack as padding for your legs when you sleep. These are just some suggestions. You can probably think of some others too.

2. **Buy a luggage scale.** Geeky, yes, but weighing and knowing the weights of every single piece of gear will help you quantify what's worth the weight and what's not.

3. **Make spreadsheets.** This is also geeky, but it's effective. Once you have a luggage scale to weigh all your stuff, type every item and weight into your spreadsheet so you can obsess over where you can spare an ounce or two.

Should I clip things to the outside of my backpack?

There is a tendency for beginner- to intermediate-level backpacking enthusiasts to clip items to the outside of their backpacks. This is either a phase all backpackers go through or some sort of idea we picked up somewhere that we should have at least one piece of gear clipped to the outside of our pack. There are no real rules about this sort of thing, but your pack should be big enough to hold all your stuff. If it's not, maybe you're taking too many things, or maybe you need a bigger pack. Either way, you will find that keeping items inside your pack leads to fewer missing items than does clipping things to the outside of your pack. Backpacking is not a fast sport—if you have items you think you will need to access throughout the day while you're hiking, put them near the top of your pack. Unclipping a couple of buckles and loosening a drawstring to get to that item takes a few seconds, and you'll be less likely to arrive at camp to find that, say, the coffee mug you clipped to the outside of your pack or the bandanna you were sure you had securely tied to one strap has gone missing somewhere along the trail.

How should I train for backpacking?

Compared to training for a marathon, backpacking isn't something a lot of people prepare for physically. But if you've got a big trip coming up, a little effort can go a long way in making your outing as comfortable as possible. Hiking, of course, is the best training for backpacking, because it gets you used to utilizing your stabilization muscles, as compared to walking on a treadmill or riding a bicycle (although any cardiovascular exercise is great for general fitness). If you can fill up a backpack with a few pounds of extra weight and go for a hike, it should help ease you into the first day of your backpacking trip, and putting on your 30- or 40-pound pack at the trailhead won't be such a shock. Take a few short hikes with the actual pack you'll be using on the trip, if possible, to get your hips and shoulders used to the weight they'll be carrying. If you strap a 45-pound pack to your hips and shoulders at the beginning of a multiday trip and you haven't so much as worn a 10-pound pack all year, you may be in for quite a surprise.

What's the best way to keep my pack dry while backpacking?

There are two different strategies to keeping your pack dry: keep the entire thing dry, or just keep the stuff inside it dry. The first school of thought uses a pack cover, which is a piece of waterproof fabric with an elastic band that covers your entire pack except the part that actually touches your back—it looks and functions like a giant shower cap. The only problem is, it leaves open the part between your back and the backpack, so in downpours some rain can get in and soak your stuff. The second school of thought, keeping the stuff inside dry, uses a simple piece of gear: a trash bag (or a more durable trash compactor bag), lining the inside of the backpack and holding all your stuff, and sealed at the top. The second school of thought subscribes to the theory that your pack itself actually doesn't need to stay dry, which is true—just make sure that if you go the trash bag route you remember to remove all the items from the external pockets of your backpack and put them inside the trash bag, or they'll get soaked too.

Can I ever drink water in the backcountry without treating it first?

Plenty of hiking and climbing guides in the Sierra Nevada and other places drink water from mountain streams without treating it. The rationale is that at a high-altitude or other remote location animal activity that would contaminate a stream isn't present at a high enough level to actually worry about. That theory is of course never a guarantee, and if you're a better-safe-than-sorry type of person you'll want to treat your water every chance you get. The advantage of not treating your water is simply convenience (you don't have to carry a filter or chemicals with you), and the advantage of treating your water is the assurance that you won't get Giardia or another parasite or virus. Mountain water sources aren't tested for contamination, so all claims that the water is fine at high altitudes are anecdotal or informally studied. If the testimony of someone who's been hiking in, say, the Sierras for years without treating drinking water and has never gotten sick is proof enough for you, then go for it. If you're not sure, it's probably best to treat the water before you drink it.

How do I find water to drink?

Your water filtration system won't be of much use if you can't find any water to filter with it. If you're backpacking on a somewhat popular route, or are reading about it in a guidebook, there should be well-established information about where the water sources are located—make note of those and remember if there's a long distance between them at any point. Established campsites are usually near creeks, ponds, or lakes, or at least within short walking distance (300 feet or so) of a nearby water source. If you're striking out on your own on a route that doesn't have a lot of information published about it, the map is going to be your best friend in finding water. Look for lakes, ponds, and tarns along your route, as well as creeks. Just finding any water isn't exactly enough—you still need to be able to get it into your water bottle. If the creek you've found isn't more than a ½ inch deep, you won't be able to get your water bottle deep enough to get any water into it, which means you might be sitting there for quite a while using a spoon to fill your bottle. In the desert, information about water is critical, so research it before your trip. If it's rained recently, you may find potholes full of water in slickrock, but if it hasn't rained in a long time, water sources could be few and far between.

Which water treatment option is right for me?

There are four basic types of water treatment options, and each has its own advantages and disadvantages. Here's a quick rundown:

- **Water filters:** Water filters remove pathogens including protozoa and bacteria but don't remove viruses—this is widely considered to be adequate for wilderness water treatment in the United States and Canada. Filters include pump-style devices as well as gravity filters, filtering water bottles, and filtering straws.

- **Water purifiers:** Water purifiers remove bacteria, protozoa, and viruses. Some purifiers are just pumps with more stringent filter systems that catch viruses, some are pumps with the additional step of a chemical additive, and some are electronic devices that kill microorganisms with UV light.

- **Halogens:** Iodine and chlorine dioxide are chemical additives (usually carried as tablets in the backcountry) that kill bacteria, viruses, and Giardia but not cryptosporidium. Halogens are lightweight but alter the taste of water.

- **Boiling:** Boiling water is the simplest, most effective method of treating water, but it consumes lots of fuel (and time) in the backcountry. Usually the amount of fuel needed to boil all drinking water on a backcountry trip makes it prohibitive.

How do I fish for my dinner?

Types of fish, fishing methods, and equipment used to catch fish all vary widely—as does individual success at catching fish. But a basic and ancient method of fishing, cane pole fishing, can be done with limited equipment: an inexpensive cane pole (made of bamboo, aluminum, or fiberglass), monofilament fishing line, fishing hooks, and bait (or lures, depending on the type of fish you're trying to catch and where you're located). Roll out a length of fishing line a foot or two longer than the pole, tie one end to the top of the pole (there may or may not be an eyelet), and tie your hook or lure to the other end. Bait the hook (if you're using bait), and you're ready to fish. In cane pole fishing, you won't "cast" the line as you would in other types of fishing—you swing the hook/bait out into the water. With the bottom of the pole in one hand, hold the fishing line just above the hook with your other hand, and gently swing the line out into the water. Then remember that this is fishing, so be patient. Wait a few minutes with your line in the water, and if you're not catching anything try a different spot. If a fish bites your line, slowly but firmly pull the line

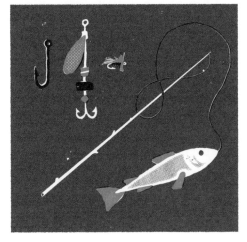

out of the water and bring the fish into shore and your hand. To remove the hook, hold the fish with one hand, thumb on the gills of one side of the fish's head, fingers on the gills on the other side. Work the hook out, making sure to angle the barb correctly so it doesn't catch.

Which stove/fuel should I use?

There are five main types of camping stoves, and all have their pros and cons. There's no one correct stove for all situations, but plenty of them can be used on almost all camping outings.

- **Two-burner propane stoves:** Generally used only for car/campground camping because of their weight and bulk (typically they're the size of a briefcase and weigh around 10 pounds). Although a two-burner stove probably doesn't seem like much compared to most home stoves that have four burners, in the backcountry two burners are a luxury. Two-burner stoves use propane canister fuel, are available at almost all stores that sell camping gear, and are often sold at supermarkets too.

- **Isobutane/canister stoves:** Canister stoves, or single-burner backpacking stoves, are the first choice of most backpackers because they're light-weight, easy to use, and straightforward: you screw a canister of isobutane fuel onto the stove, light it, and adjust the flame to your preference. Many popular models integrate a stove and pot or cup and break down to a small size for packing in a backpack. The isobutane fuel canisters are convenient but are not legal as checked or carry-on baggage on airline flights and are sometimes not available for purchase in all areas. And if you only use half a fuel canister on a trip, it is not refillable, so you'll be starting your next trip with a half-full canister that may or may not contain enough fuel.

- **Liquid fuel stoves:** Liquid fuel, or "white gas," stoves use a fuel bottle that you hand-pressurize with a small pumping mechanism and refill from a larger gas can in between trips. Liquid fuel stoves are single-burner, are used for backpacking and other backcountry activities in which weight and bulk are of concern, and have a reputation for being reliable. They are usually repairable and cleanable in the field, and many people prefer them because they leave less of an environmental footprint—instead of using disposable canister fuel and producing waste, you simply refill the bottle. White gas is generally available in most of the world, and if you're flying, airlines allow empty, cleaned fuel bottles in luggage. One disadvantage to liquid fuel stoves is that they have only two heat settings: high and off.

- **Alcohol stoves:** Alcohol stoves are a favorite of ultralight backpackers; they're tiny, lightweight, and simple, and the fuel—alcohol or often methanol sold as gas-line additives at convenience stores—is readily available. Many long-distance hikers choose to make their own alcohol stove out of an empty beer can. Alcohol stoves aren't a particularly good choice for beginning backcountry travelers because they take a little know-how and practice to use safely and effectively.

- **Solid-fuel stoves:** Solid-fuel stoves run on either special tablets or wood. Tablet stoves are extremely lightweight but are often not as efficient at producing heat as other stoves, and the fuel tablets are expensive compared to other fuels. In dry environments like the desert, solid-fuel stoves (or "twig stoves") can be advantageous because you don't have to carry fuel with you—you pick up dry sticks and twigs and use those to fuel the stove. Obviously twig stoves can be tough to use in places where finding dry firewood is an issue.

How do I forage for food?

Ideally, most of your adventures won't force you to the point of foraging—hopefully they all end with a beer and a cheeseburger back in civilization. But just in case it comes down to survival, here are a few basics of foraging for food.

- The bark of most pine trees and cottonwoods is edible, once you scrape down through the brown/gray outer bark through the green stuff into the white cambium.

- The roots of cattails, roasted over a fire, contain as many carbohydrates as a potato.

- Beechnuts, walnuts, pecans, butternuts, and pine nuts are pickable in the fall and can all be eaten raw. Wild berries are a good source of nutrients. Avoid white berries—they are not edible—but wild red raspberries, blackberries, blueberries, and huckleberries are fair game. Many wild berries are poisonous, but most aggregate berries—berries like raspberries and blackberries, made up of tiny fruits packed together into a single berry—are not.

- Rosehips are great sources of vitamin C and are tasty once you cut them open to remove the seeds.

- The idea of eating insects may be somewhat gross, but they are a good source of protein. Both ants and beetles have 14 grams of protein per 100 grams of weight. Brightly colored insects are usually poisonous. Flies, mosquitoes, and ticks all carry disease and shouldn't be eaten.

What kinds of pots and pans should I take backpacking?

If you're backpacking, you don't want to carry a bunch of extra weight, so your cast-iron skillet is most likely going to have to stay home. Lots of companies make smart cook-sets that include pots, cups, bowls, and even silverware, all nested inside each other in a compact setup that doesn't take up much room in a backpack. A set like this is good to have but is not mandatory—you can assemble a decent cooking setup for a few bucks with a few basic pieces.

- **Cooking pot:** You can use pots with or without a nonstick coating. Nonstick is of course helpful to have but will add a little cost to the pot. Most pots are made of aluminum, but you can also spend a few more dollars and get titanium pots, which are lighter in weight. You'll have to decide if you want one pot or two—lots of cook-sets include two pots, one large one, and a smaller one that nests inside the large one for easy packing. You can cook great meals in the backcountry with only one pot, so buying two isn't 100 percent necessary if you don't mind a one-pot meal. But you can buy the set and leave the second smaller pot at home if you want to go light, bringing it only on trips where you don't mind the extra weight.

- **Cup/mug and bowl:** If you're a true minimalist, you'll learn to eat and drink out of a single cup and not deal with the extra weight of dishes. Backcountry meals tend to be pasta meals eaten out of a bowl anyway, so learning to eat out of a mug isn't such a stretch. A simple aluminum or plastic mug will work great (you don't need a heavy insulated travel mug with a lid). If you're the type of person who absolutely has to have coffee and breakfast at the same time, though, you'll want to bring a bowl in addition to your mug. An inexpensive mug does the job in the backcountry, and a plastic or aluminum bowl won't run you more than ten dollars. Again, titanium bowls and mugs are lighter but more expensive.

- **Spoon and fork or spork:** A good durable plastic spoon will run you about one dollar at most gear stores. If you want, you can also bring a fork. Forks aren't that advantageous in the backcountry—you won't be stabbing salad greens or twirling pasta—but if you want a fork it's not that much extra weight. Or you can split the difference and bring a spork.

Do I need to carry a fork, knife, and spoon?

The backcountry is no place for regular table manners. Actually, the backcountry is usually not the place for a table. You are of course free to take whatever dining utensils you want on a trip, but if you're packing everything in a backpack, you might consider how much weight and bulk you're adding and how much functionality you're getting for that weight. Take, for example, a knife. You should have a pocketknife with you already, or at least one on a multitool, so packing a dining knife is probably redundant. Most backpacking meals tend to be pastas or other spoonable dishes, not steaks or other foods that necessitate a fork. If you limit yourself to a single spoon or a spork, you'll find you can eat pretty much everything with that one piece of cutlery—or at least make do.

Do I have to eat dehydrated meals or MREs?

You absolutely do not have to eat dehydrated meals or military Meals Ready to Eat (MREs). Although plenty of visionary food companies make wonderfully tasty dehydrated meal flavors and you can feast on herbed mushroom risotto and cheese enchilada ranchero, dehydrated meals can be a bit on the expensive side (and can sometimes contain downright dangerous levels of fiber). Instead, bring anything you want to eat on your trip, but keep in mind you'll have limited water and no refrigeration, so you probably won't be bringing a stick of butter along. Macaroni and cheese can be a wonderful one-pot camp meal, and so can lots of other pasta options—check for powdered pasta sauces, and think about tossing in some nuts as a protein source. If you're just camping for one night and you don't want to carry a stove, you can pack leftover pizza, takeout Chinese food, or a burrito and eat it cold.

Three Easy Backpacking Meals

Each of these easy meals should be enough to feed two hungry backpackers.

1. **Pesto Pine Nut Pasta**

   You'll need: 3 cups fusilli pasta, 1 cup pine nuts, 1 package dried pesto, and 2 tablespoons olive oil.

   To cook: Boil water, cook the pasta, and drain. Stir in the dried pesto, olive oil, and pine nuts.

2. **Thai Peanut Noodles**

   You'll need: 2 packages ramen noodles (minus the seasoning packets), ½ cup Thai peanut sauce (repackaged in a plastic container, if necessary), ⅔ cup peanuts, and ⅔ cup dehydrated peppers or dehydrated vegetables.

   To cook: Boil water, cook the ramen noodles and vegetables, and drain. Stir in the Thai peanut sauce and peanuts.

3. **Chili Macaroni and Cheese**

   You'll need: 1 box of macaroni and cheese, 2 tablespoons olive oil, ⅓ cup powdered milk, and 1 can chili.

   To cook: Boil water, cook the pasta, and drain. Stir in the olive oil, powdered milk, and powdered cheese until the sauce is consistent. Pour in the can of chili and reheat the entire mixture over low heat.

How do I wash my dishes in camp?

It's probably your first instinct to take your dishes over to a source of running water to rinse them off, but this is pretty much the worst policy in the back-country—the ecosystem in the nearest creek is much better off without your food scraps floating through it. Since you don't have a nice pair of yellow dishwashing gloves and a sink full of water, make do with what you have: some water from your water bottle and your finger. That's right. Get all the solid food particles out of your pot or cup, and then dump a small amount of water into the dish, scrubbing with your finger to remove food. Scatter the small amount of dishwater in a wide area—preferably far from where you're sleeping (bears!)—or, if you prefer the tough-guy method, drink the dishwa-ter, because come on, it's only food plus a little water. This process won't get your dishes squeaky clean, but this is camping, not glamping. If you've got some stubborn food residue on a pot, such as cheese sauce from your mac and cheese, pour some water in the pot and heat the water on your stove for a minute or two to help loosen it—this is the backcountry version of "soaking" your dishes in the kitchen sink. When you're done washing your dishes, let them air-dry before putting them away.

Can I take perishables like meat and cheese on a backpacking trip?

A good general rule is that if a meat or cheese product can survive at room temperature in a convenience store or grocery store, it will be fine in your backpack for a few days (or sixteen months, depending on the product). Most processed-sausage products are good for several days in the backcountry (salami has long been a staple for outdoorspeople) and are good sources of protein and fat. Jerky is also of course absolutely fine without refrigeration. Cheeses can do surprisingly well on multiday trips, especially semihard cheeses like cheddar and jack, and hard cheeses like Parmesan and Pecorino Romano can last for days in a backpack without spoiling—generally, the harder a cheese, the longer it will keep without refrigeration.

How do I keep from stinking on a long backpacking trip?

On a long backpacking trip, it's a hard truth that you're going to develop some BO. The good thing is that your friends probably don't expect you to smell like the fragrance department at Macy's the entire time—and they will smell as bad as you do. You don't have running water, but a few strategic things can keep you smelling a little better. Carry a couple of wet wipes and take care of the problem areas every couple days (pack out the wet wipes with you), and if you have a chance to do a little washing up, grab a pot of water from a stream or lake and give those same areas a good rinse (don't worry about purifying the water—it's fine as long as you're not drinking it, and the next time you use the pot, bring whatever's in it to a boil first). If you notice the armpits of your synthetic-fabric shirt seem to be smellier than usual, it's not your fault—synthetics have a tendency to develop and hold body odor more than other fabrics. It's just another reality to deal with. You'll get used to it.

Should I bring something to keep me entertained during downtime at camp?

Entertainment is never a bad idea to help pass a rainy day spent in a tent or to give you something to do if you have some extra time in the afternoon before dinner and you aren't the type to, say, just sit next to an alpine lake and contemplate the size of the universe. Keep your source of entertainment light and you won't regret packing it even if you don't end up using it: a deck of cards, a small notebook and pencil or pen, a light paperback book, or, if you're taking your phone on your trip, a book on an e-book phone app. If it's a long trip with a partner who likes the same type of books you do, consider bringing a paperback of short stories (or anything that can be read out of page order), splitting it roughly down the middle at the binding, and carrying half in your pack and half in your friend's pack. You can read your respective halves of the book and trade halves when you're both finished, thus saving a few ounces of weight versus each carrying your own book.

Can I take booze in the backcountry?

When it comes to imbibing around the campfire, you're really only limited by your willingness to carry extra weight in your backpack. Yes, you can take a six-pack of your favorite IPA, but that six-pack weighs just over 4½ pounds—which is a lot of weight. A better solution is to take a flask of bourbon or scotch, which has way more firepower per pound of weight in your backpack. Several companies make lightweight plastic flasks specifically for camping. Whatever you do, don't take glass bottles—a broken bottle inside your backpack will soak everything you need to stay warm (including your sleeping bag), not to mention how broken glass shards will shred the fabrics in your tent, jackets, and sleeping bag. If you think a couple cans of beer are worth it, by all means, stuff them in your pack before you leave, and when you get to camp, bury them in a creek or a snowbank for a few minutes and cool them down (but make sure they don't float downstream). And be sure to take your empties with you when you leave.

What are some easy constellations to see when I go camping?

- **Ursa Major:** Probably everyone who's ever looked up at the night sky outside of a city can identify the Big Dipper. Find that, and you've found the butt and tail of Ursa Major (The Great Bear). Follow the top of the cup toward the bear's head.

- **Ursa Minor/Little Dipper:** Although it's a bit of a stretch to imagine the Little Dipper being a bear, it's easy to find. The tip of the handle of the Little Dipper is Polaris, the North Star.

- **Orion:** Orion is one of the most visible and famous constellations in history. Find it by finding Orion's Belt, the tight row of three stars that connect the shoulders and feet.

- **Cassiopeia:** Cassiopeia is a W-shaped grouping of five bright stars in the northern sky. It's most visible in the fall, but easy to spot year-round.

Should I take an extra pair of "camp shoes" on a backpacking trip?

If you can convince yourself that you can live without your purple dinosaur slippers for a couple nights, a backpacking trip is the time to do that—they're bulky and heavy and will get dirty from walking around camp. Serious answer: Some people prefer to have a second pair of shoes to wear at camp after a long day of hiking or a second pair to wear while wading into lakes or crossing streams. Some people prefer to not pack a second pair of shoes because of the added weight and bulk. If you do pack a second pair, try something lightweight like Crocs or Sanuks or a pair of flip-flops, rather than a second pair of hiking or athletic shoes, which can add up to 2 pounds to your pack weight.

Should I use a bear canister?

Bear canisters, sealed canisters made of hard plastic that have been tested to be bear-proof, are mandatory in some areas, such as Yosemite and Glacier National Park. In others, they're only recommended. Bear canisters are completely bear-proof if used correctly but are bulky and of course heavy (around 2 pounds empty). Fitting one into a pack, and packing all your other gear around it, can get tiresome. On the other hand, when you're tired after making dinner and you're ready to crawl into your sleeping bag for the night, using a bear canister is much easier than stringing up a bear bag—you can just close it, lock it, and walk it a little ways from your camp and leave it for the night. Since they're so sturdy, a bear canister also make a great stool to sit on while cooking. If bear canisters aren't required in the area you're hiking in, it's your call whether to take one. If all your camps are above treeline, the general thinking is that bear canisters are unnecessary because bears spend almost no time above treeline. Another option is the Ursack, a Kevlar sack that closes tight with a Kevlar cord and is lined with a ziplock plastic bag that keeps food odors inside. Ursacks are lighter weight than bear canisters and much easier to pack, but they're not legal substitutes in all areas that require bear canisters.

How do I hang a bear bag?

Bears like food, and they don't care if it's yours. So before you zip yourself into your sleeping bag at night, you need to secure your food from potentially curious bears—and keeping it in your sleeping bag is a bad idea. To secure your food in a "bear bag," you'll need one extra stuff sack that can fit all your

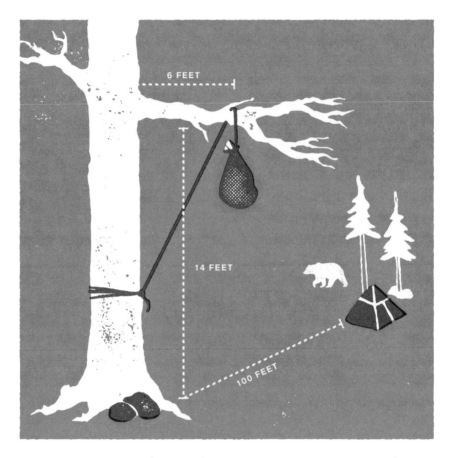

food in it, plus a 60-foot (or longer) length of cord. Grab all your food (and toiletries that have any sort of smell, like your toothpaste), stick them in the stuff sack, and find a tree at least 100 feet from your campsite. Tie one end of your cord to a rock, and toss the rock over a tree branch that's at least 14 feet high. Your cord will trail the rock over the branch. Make sure it loops over the branch at least 6 feet away from the tree trunk (bears can climb up the trunk and reach out). Grab the rock end of the cord, untie the rock, and tie your stuff sack full of food to the cord. Pull on the opposite end of the cord, hauling your bear bag up until it's almost touching the branch—it helps to have a friend pushing the bag from below as you pull on the cord. Tie the non–bear bag end of the cord to something secure (you can wrap it around the tree trunk or other lower branches) to make sure the bag stays in place all night.

How do I keep smaller critters from eating my food?

Bears are a danger because if they've found your food they've pretty much found you, and it's best to not be that close to a bear. Other animals, like mice and squirrels, are much less of a threat to your life but can get into your food and put a huge hitch in your trip, whether it's a weeklong backpacking trip or a day out climbing. If you're leaving your pack somewhere with food in it (such as at the base of a climb, or at camp while you head out for a quick trip to summit a peak), you might consider a little insurance for your food. For small day trips, a screw-top plastic container (like the kind powdered drink mix comes in) can function as a sort of bear canister that protects against aggressive squirrels, who in some areas have learned how to open backpack zippers, or, lacking that skill, might just chew through your pack to get to your PB&J sandwich. For longer trips, an Ursack, a Kevlar bag that cinches tight with a cord at the top, can stop pretty much any critter from getting inside (lots of people carry them instead of bear canisters in areas where they're accepted) and will hold up to about six days' worth of food.

Should I carry a solar panel when I go backpacking?

A small solar panel can give you the capacity to charge electronic devices that charge off a USB port, but to charge anything with an AC plug you have to carry an additional battery and converter that weighs about 1 pound. Decide what your needs are before the trip—if you're recharging only your smartphone and you need to do it only once during the trip, you can probably just take a lipstick-sized USB charger and forgo the solar panel. If you need to charge bigger batteries for, say, a DSLR camera, maybe consider buying one or two extra batteries, which would save lots of weight and bulk over packing a solar panel and battery unit. But if you're going heavy on the electronics for a long trip (and are shooting a lot of video, for example), a small solar panel and battery unit will keep all your gear charged.

Should I take a chair with me?

Rocks are nature's original chairs, but humans have managed to create furniture that offers more back support and a little more cushioning. If you're traveling light and you don't mind sitting on rocks or logs, you'll probably forgo the idea of packing a chair. But if you want a chair, several manufacturers have been making lightweight, nonbulky options for many years—from the classic style that essentially acts as a lightly padded sling holding you by the back and butt as you sit on the ground, to the newer, ultralight miniature-butterfly-style chairs that keep your butt a few inches off the ground. Backpacking-style camp chairs usually pack down to a size smaller than a rolled-up sleeping pad and weigh between one and two pounds.

How do I make a camping trip romantic for my significant other?

As is true in every relationship, romance comes from the little things you do to show someone you care about him or her. A camping trip is no different—just probably smellier than usual. But little things can make a big difference, like blowing up your boyfriend or girlfriend's sleeping pad for them, bringing a string of battery-powered lights to hang up in the tent, or surprising him or her with a small bottle of wine or dessert you secretly packed. Fortunately, when you're roughing it, effort seems to be appreciated more than when you're in the city, so you don't have to 100 percent nail it. Just put in some effort and be creative and it will be appreciated.

How do I dry out damp clothes on a backpacking trip?

If your clothes get wet from sweat, rain, or wading through a creek, sometimes your body is the best dryer—for example, if your pants get soaked up to the knees in the morning and you still have 8 miles to hike that day, they'll be dry by the time you get to camp. But if you got drenched in a rainstorm and the sun comes out, you can treat your backpack as a clothesline, tying some wet layers on the outside of the back of the pack so they can dry in the sun. Just make sure to tie them securely—a shirt falling off your pack behind you doesn't make much noise, so you're unlikely to hear it hit the ground and you might walk miles before you realize it's missing. In camp, hang wet layers on the outside of your tent in the sun (again, hang them securely; the wind can blow them away easily). If you have only a couple damp articles of clothing, such as a pair of socks or a T-shirt, take them off after you've gotten in your sleeping bag for the night and place them near your legs. Your sleeping bag will act like an oven, and in the morning, your once-damp socks and shirt will be dry.

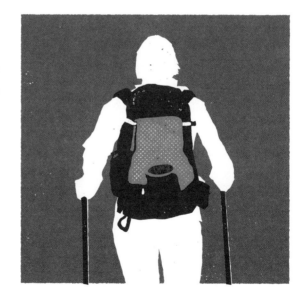

How can I hike the John Muir Trail?

The John Muir Trail has become one of America's most famous long-distance trails: 211 miles through California's iconic Sierra Nevada, from Yosemite National Park to the summit of Mount Whitney. Its fame has, of course, brought popularity: as many as 3,500 people per year apply to hike the trail south to north. If you want to hike it, you'll need a few things (not including the gear).

- **A permit.** Permits to hike the John Muir Trail are distributed by either Yosemite National Park (for hikers going north to south) or the Inyo National Forest (for hikers going south to north). For Yosemite-issued permits, apply exactly 168 days in advance of your desired start date. For Inyo National Forest permits, apply for the lottery starting April 1 for the year of your hike.

- **Fitness.** The hike takes most hikers two to three weeks of walking, carrying up to seven days' worth of food at a time, and it's not a flat walk. It's a good idea to train for your trip (see page 238), and to take a few two- and three-day backpacking trips to get used to carrying your pack.

- **Food.** Two to three weeks' worth of food is heavy, so Muir Trail hikers utilize food drops provided by resorts and ranches along the route, as well as resupply drops arranged in advance with horsepacking services. Research, plan ahead, and figure out how many food drops you'll need for your trip well before your departure date.

Can I hike the Appalachian Trail or the Pacific Crest Trail?

Here's the biggest obstacle to completing a thru-hike of the Appalachian Trail or the Pacific Crest Trail: your job. Yes, the thing you do forty hours a week or more to ensure that you can eat and pay your rent. Here's why: The Appalachian Trail and the Pacific Crest Trail are both journeys of six months or more, the Appalachian Trail being 2,190 miles long and the Pacific Crest Trail being 2,650 miles long. And your employer's vacation policy probably doesn't guarantee you six months of vacation per year, so you have to make arrangements for a sabbatical or make arrangements to quit your job.

So after you quit your job, how tough is it? It's not advisable to take on a 2,000-plus-mile trail as your first backpacking trip (although it has been done), but once you've figured out your systems and you're comfortable with two-, three-, and six-day backpacking trips, there's no reason to think you can't do the Appalachian Trail. The Pacific Crest Trail can, in some years, require a few more mountaineering skills, such as negotiating a snow slope and self-arresting with an ice ax (see page 108), and it's advisable to get a couple of alpine backpacking trips under your belt before taking on the PCT. But the length is the main challenge, both in the time off work required to do it and the day-after-day stick-to-itiveness to finish a six-month walk.

How can I backpack to the bottom of the Grand Canyon?

There are two major challenges to a backpacking trip to the bottom of the Grand Canyon: getting a permit and doing the grueling hike in and out.

The Grand Canyon is a popular backpacking destination, and the best way to see it for the first time is a hike down to the Bright Angel Campground at the bottom, which fills up almost every night during the high season. How do you secure a spot? Fill out a permit request and get it to the National Park Service the first day of the month, four months before the month you want to do your trip (e.g., June 1 for a backpacking trip starting October 15). Weekends are popular (and thus harder to get permits for), so aim for a midweek trip instead and you'll have better odds. Once you've gotten your permit, you need to get in shape.

The tough part of backpacking in the Grand Canyon isn't getting down to the bottom—it's getting back out and up to the South Rim, which is 4,400 vertical feet up a rocky, dusty trail, with all your gear on your back. But if you train for it, there's no reason you can't do it. Prepare by getting as many vertical feet under your belt as possible—if you're at the gym, get on the stair climber instead of the treadmill, and at work take the stairs instead of the elevator. Imagine climbing the stairs to the top of a 440-story building:

that's approximately what you'll do to get from the Colorado River back up to the South Rim of the Grand Canyon. Cardio exercise is obviously good for you, but more important is working and developing those leg, hip, and butt muscles that will help you climb out of the canyon with that heavy pack on your back. So focus on up, up, up when you're training.

Can I take stove fuel, ice axes, and trekking poles on an airline flight?

No type of backpacking stove gas is allowed on any airline flight, even in checked luggage. However, most airlines do allow empty white-gas bottles in checked bags—just make sure you clean the bottle out with soap and water before flying, and leave it unsealed in your bag. Ice axes, not surprisingly, are allowed only in checked bags (make sure you determine whether your ice ax will actually fit in your checked bag a few weeks before you leave—if it's too long, you'll have to buy a shorter one or arrange for another option at your destination). Trekking poles are sometimes okay to take in carry-on luggage, but it's better to be safe than sorry and to pack them in a piece of checked luggage instead of gambling on it.

Can I rent camping gear?

One of the great things about many outdoor sports, like skiing and camping, is that you can often try something out before committing hundreds or thousands of dollars to buying all the appropriate gear. So if you rent a tent and try a couple of nights sleeping in it and find out you totally hate it, you're out only a fraction of the dollars you might have been had you gone on a quick shopping spree before your trip. Many outdoor stores like REI and EMS rent camping gear, including backpacks, tents, sleeping pads, stoves, and sleeping bags. Sleeping bags are typically rented out with a liner (which is washed in between rentals) so you're not spending your nights out under the stars in a dirty sleeping bag. All you have to do is return the gear undamaged and clean.

Rental sleeping bags can also be great for including a friend who doesn't have gear for your weekend camping trip, or for planning a trip where a rented three-person tent would be more ideal than the two-person tent you have at home.

Is it still considered camping if I'm in an RV?

It's funny—people who go camping sometimes have this idea that if they're roughing it more than the people at the next site in a campground—they have a smaller tent, or fewer things to make them more comfortable—they're doing camping correctly. Those in an RV of course have the most comfortable digs at any campground (unless they're sharing it with a world-record-holding snorer/farter), and some people believe that it's not camping. But the number one objective in camping is to have fun, and whether that means sleeping on the hard ground in an ultralight sleeping bag or pulling into a campground in a 44-foot RV, you do you. If you are in an RV, it's good to be courteous and use a generator sparingly (what doesn't sound like much noise when you're inside an RV can be extremely annoying to people camping in tents 50 or 150 feet away from you), and it never hurts on a cold night to invite the neighbors into your rig for some hot chocolate (or wine).

What should I do to make my friend's first camping experience a good one?

If you're an experienced camper and you have friends (or even better, a girl-friend or boyfriend) who you think might like it too, the best thing you can do for them is to make sure they have fun on their first camping trip—because ideally, they'll go with you again, and in the case of romantic relationships won't break up with you. When planning, remember that your friend's experience level is zero, so he or she knows nothing about gear or how to sleep outside or how it's not exactly as clean as, say, a room at the Radisson. Find out if your friend has any gear at all, and if not, do your best to find it for him or her—rent or borrow whatever is needed before the trip. Take care of all the food shopping, cooking, and campsite reservations, and maybe do a little extra to make sure he or she is comfortable. Sleeping outside can be quite a shock to someone who's not used to it, so an extra sleeping pad, a pillow, hand sanitizer, earplugs, or a good camp chair can make a big difference. If your friend has never camped before at all, car camping is probably a better introduction than a backpacking trip, as many campgrounds have restrooms and picnic tables. Start there, and if he or she enjoys the first trip, ease your way into longer trips and the backcountry.

6

ON SNOW

Your relationship with snow should involve more than just knocking it off your shoes, shoveling it off the sidewalk, and building the occasional snowman. Humans have invented plenty of ways to slide down snow, walk across it, climb it, and even build shelters out of it. With so many places on earth covered by snow for several months of the year, learning to enjoy it and to travel on it can make your winter less oppressive and more exciting.

This chapter will help you figure out how to put more fun in your relationship with winter—whether you want to learn to ski, snowboard, get on and off a chairlift without falling, fly through knee-deep powder, navigate moguls, sled, ice-climb, camp on snow, dig a snow cave, build an igloo, or just keep your car from getting stuck in the snow. Because when the snow starts falling, there's more to look forward to than just the possibility of staying home from work because it's a snow day.

How do I get acclimated to cold weather?

Paradoxically, the best way to get acclimated to cold weather is to spend more time in cold temperatures. Nonsense, right? Actually, it's not. The ability to withstand cold temperatures is mostly mental. Your body temperature is not changing that much when you "feel" cold—you're just telling your body that it's cold. To acclimate, you have to change your perception of what is really cold. If you live someplace with distinct seasons, your body will take weeks to understand what's happening when the temperature drops in the late fall or early winter, but there are a few things you can do to help it figure things out. Keeping your house colder in the winter months can help acclimate you to cold weather, as your body won't feel as shocked as it would if you were making a sudden transition from a very warm temperature inside to a very cold temperature outside. Taking regular cold showers in the winter will help your body get used to feeling cold. Additionally, your body will stay warmer if it's properly fed and properly hydrated.

How can I stay active in winter?

Winter is a tough time to stay in shape—it's dark, it's cold, it's generally less comfortable to be outside, and halfway through January you probably think bears might be onto something by choosing to hibernate during the winter. Or you might just find yourself hibernating too, eating lots of rich, fatty foods, having a hard time rousing yourself in the early hours of the morning to get out and exercise, and maybe taking a few more nights off and deciding it might be okay to binge-watch an entire season or four of your favorite TV show.

One of the biggest obstacles to staying active in the wintertime is the notion that it's too cold to exercise outside. People who bicycle on snow-packed roads in Anchorage, Alaska, and in Minneapolis have proven that's a myth, and so have the runners who don't give up just because the temperature drops below freezing. The right equipment and the right clothing can keep you active year-round. If you like running or hiking in the summertime, try snowshoeing or cross-country skiing in winter. If you love riding your bike, look into getting a fatbike or a set of studded tires for riding on snow and ice. You may not be able to do all the activities you do in the summer, but thanks to the right technology you can remain active. And as far as the clothing goes, the saying is, "There's no bad weather—only bad clothing."

How do I dress for cold weather?

Your clothing will differ depending on the activity you choose—obviously you don't want to wear a windproof, insulated ski jacket if you're going for a winter jog in the park—but there are some general principles that will help keep you comfortable.

First of all, you'll want to pay special attention to your extremities, which will often get cold before other parts of your body. Cold fingers and toes can cut a day outside short, so take care to keep them warm. If you're cycling in the cold, invest in a pair of booties or shoe covers that block the freezing wind from blowing into your shoes—a little neoprene on the toes can make a huge difference. Likewise, during a bike ride, your hands will spend a lot of time breaking the wind at the front of your handlebars, so find a good pair of warm, wind-blocking gloves. When running, skiing, snowshoeing, or winter hiking, you won't often find that you've made your hands or fingers "too warm"— actually, it's better to err on the side of too warm instead of too cold. Wear warmer socks than you would in the summer, and be careful to not pack so many layers of socks into your shoes that you can't move your toes—if blood

can't circulate, it can't warm the tissue down there.

Always carry or wear a hat, or wear a hood in the wintertime. If you get too warm, you can always remove your hat and stuff it in a pocket to help regulate your body temperature—a hat is the easiest layer to remove in most cases and can seem to have the greatest effect on your personal thermostat.

When you start to layer clothes on your upper and lower body, remember that you want to minimize the amount of sweat you have on and next to your skin. If you head out for a jog and have too many jackets on, you'll start to sweat, and when the sweat cools on your skin it will drop your core body temperature very quickly. So when you go outside, remember to "start cold." You'll warm up when you start moving, and you want to be warm, but not sweating. You will, of course, sweat some amount, so make sure the layers next to your skin are synthetic (not cotton) so that they'll wick moisture away from the skin and dry quickly.

It may take a little experimentation to figure out the correct layering system, but once you have it dialed in, you'll be much more comfortable exercising in the cold, and more likely to stay active through the winter months.

How do I drive in winter and on snow?

The downside of driving in the winter is that surfaces are slick with snow and ice and it's challenging to control your vehicle. The upside is that when you slide out of control, sometimes your vehicle comes to rest in a snowbank, and damage is minimized—if you're lucky. Lots of times, though, you won't be so lucky, so here's how to drive safely in the snow.

- Make sure your tires have tread on them. No tread, no traction—which means it's hard to get your car moving from a stop on slick surfaces, harder to control it when you're turning, and harder to stop in time.

- Accelerate and decelerate slowly. Yes, you may have antilock brakes and new tires, but that technology won't save you if you misjudge how much distance you need to stop your car at a red light from a speed of 45 mph. Be cautious.

- Give everyone some extra room, and give yourself some extra time. Since stopping takes more distance on slick surfaces, reacting to a car in front of you braking will also require more distance (or you'll end up smashing into its bumper). Give other cars a few extra feet, about double what you would on dry pavement. And give yourself extra time to get to where you're going. If your commute usually takes twenty-five minutes, leave fifteen or twenty minutes early when there are snow conditions.

- Drive in the tracks of other drivers. You'll have more traction if you keep your tires in the lines cleared by the tires of drivers before you.

- Think small movements at the wheel. Don't jerk the wheel to keep the car straight—pay attention (i.e., don't look at your phone), and make constant small adjustments to your path instead of pulling the steering wheel in big movements, which will send you sliding.

What do I do if my vehicle gets stuck in snow?

Spinning the wheels only digs them deeper into the snow—so if you hear your wheels making that whining spinning noise, stop hitting the gas and get out of the car and have a look. When you're stuck in the snow, most of the time it's because (1) your wheels aren't getting enough traction, or (2) your car's body/chassis is hung up on a large amount of snow and the car's weight isn't on the wheels anymore (which circles back to the first problem). This can happen just as often when you're parallel parked on a city street during a snowstorm as it can when you're driving in the mountains. For problem 1, you need to create some traction so your tires grip the snow/ice—it's a good idea to carry kitty litter or sand in your trunk during the wintertime. Sometimes it can be as simple as sprinkling something gritty (e.g., kitty litter or sand) under the wheel that's slipping until the tire grips it and gets enough traction to take off. If you're with friends, get them to get out and push (or rock) the car in the direction you want to move—often it just takes a few pounds of force to get the car onto a spot with some traction. If you're stuck on a snowbank (or the city snowplow flew by overnight and plowed your car in), get to shoveling. The more you clear out underneath the car, the easier it will be when you try to move it. Once you're done shoveling, you may have to sprinkle kitty litter (or pull your floor mats out of the car and use them under the tires) and/or ask your friends to give you a push.

How do I make sure my car starts in cold weather?

Fact: A car refusing to start in the winter almost always has nothing to do with bad luck—even if it feels like it when it happens. It has everything to do with the battery being cold, and if you can mitigate that, you can win the battle against winter. A few different strategies will help you get your car running when the temperature dips below freezing.

- If you park your car inside a garage at night, buy an electric battery blanket, which plugs into an AC outlet and runs to your car to keep your battery from losing its cold-cranking ability as the temperature drops at night.

- Another indoor option: Buy a 3-amp trickle charger to connect to your battery. It slowly charges your battery and in the case of cold temperatures compensates for the power loss as the battery sits in the cold all night.

- If a trickle charger or an electric battery blanket isn't possible for you, you can always take your battery out of the car at night and bring it inside your house or apartment. That way, when you pop it back in the car in the morning, it will be room temperature (or about 40 degrees warmer than freezing) when you try to start the car, which will give it three times more cranking capacity than if it sat outside in below-freezing temps all night.

How do I keep a car weatherized for winter?

Car trouble in the winter is worse than in other seasons because it's unpleasant to stand outside in the cold, let alone open the hood and figure out what's wrong or wait for a tow truck to show up. Here are a handful of things you can do to keep your vehicle running well in the winter.

- **Check your battery.** Without a properly functioning battery your car won't start, and if your car won't start you won't be going anywhere. Clean any corrosion off the terminals with a mix of baking soda and water, and refill the battery fluid if necessary. If your battery is three years old or older, buy a new one.

- **Check the hoses and belts.** Maybe you're not a seasoned mechanic, but you can spot a crack in a hose or a belt. Do a thorough visual inspection, and if you find something cracked take it into a repair shop to have it replaced. Those few bucks spent will help you avoid getting stranded on the side of the road.

- **Check your tires.** Make sure your tires have adequate tread, or you'll have as much traction on snow as a pair of new penny loafers. If you live in a particularly snowy region where snow covers the roads for several months in a row, consider buying a set of dedicated snow tires.

- **Take care of your glass.** Make sure you can see when the roads are snowy and slushy and other cars are flicking brown water onto your windshield. Use windshield washer fluid that includes an antifreeze solution. Get new windshield wipers so they're not leaving frozen streaks across the glass when you hit the mist button.

- **Check your tire pressure.** Tire pressure can drop 1 pound per square inch for every 10-degree drop in temperature.

- **Carry an emergency kit (see page 17).**

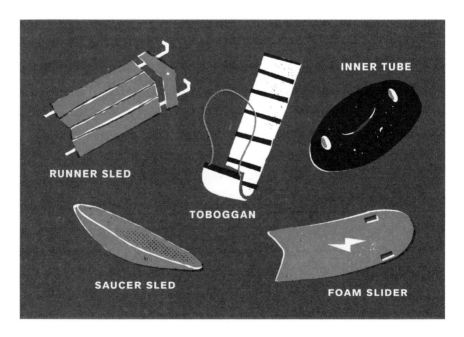

What kind of sled should I buy?

Contemporary sleds (not including dog sleds, bobsleds, and kick sleds, which are not for recreational, slide-down-a-hill-of-snow sledding) break down into five categories.

1. **Runner sled:** A classic but potentially more dangerous sled design. The runner sled is made of wood with two steel runners underneath to glide over the snow. Runner sleds are best (and fastest) on packed snow, not deep powder. As you might imagine, a wood and steel sled can do some damage in the event of a collision with another sledder or someone standing at the bottom of the hill. But this is the only sled type that looks cool hanging over your fireplace.

2. **Toboggan:** Probably the most common sled of the past two decades, toboggans are made of plastic or, less often, wood, and are commonly available at department stores, hardware stores, and even grocery stores. Toboggans offer better steering control than some other types of sleds.

3. **Inner tube:** Inflatable tube-style sleds are the exact same design as an inner tube–style pool float, but with more durable materials and usually plastic handles for carrying and hanging onto while screaming down a hill. Steering an inner tube is pretty much impossible, but if that isn't your thing you'll love the downhill ride on a inner tube.

4. **Saucer sled:** Saucer sleds are made of metal or plastic and are fun if you enjoy having no control over where you're going as you speed down a hill. The saucer sled was made famous by Chevy Chase in the movie *Christmas Vacation*.

5. **Foam slider:** The foam slider sled is the newest sled style. Foam sleds are similar to bodyboards or surfboards in their design and are the most lightweight of sled styles, so they're easy to carry back up the hill for another run. However, depending on the design, these sleds can be the least durable.

Why should I go sledding?

Sledding is the easiest and fastest path to the joy of sliding down snow: all you need is a hill, some snow, and a sled or other object to sit on as you slide down the hill. Sledding requires no specialized equipment, no lift tickets, and really almost no skill (besides knowing when to bail off the sled before it hits something).

What are the different difficulty levels of ski runs?

In North America, ski runs are rated according to a three-color system intended to keep you from tumbling down a 60-degree death sheet of moguls on your first-ever day of skiing. Get to know the system before your day on the slopes.

- **Green circles = easy.** Ski runs with a green circle next to the name are beginner-friendly; they're wide, they're usually groomed, and they have a slope gradient of 25 percent or lower (note that's "slope gradient," not degrees—a 100 percent slope gradient equals a 45-degree angle). If you haven't skied before or aren't very experienced, start your day skiing some green runs.

- **Blue squares = intermediate.** Blue square ski runs have a slope gradient of 25 to 40 percent and are where most skiers at resorts spend the majority of their time. Blue runs are faster and often (but not always) narrower than green runs and are sometimes groomed and sometimes not.

- **Black diamonds = advanced.** Black diamond runs have a slope gradient of 40 percent or higher and are usually not groomed. Note that in Europe advanced runs are indicated with red circles.

- **Double black diamonds = experts only.** Double black diamond runs have slope gradients of 40 percent or higher and often feature narrow chutes between rock walls or trees, and steep drop-offs or cliffs. Note that in Europe, experts-only runs are indicated with black circles.

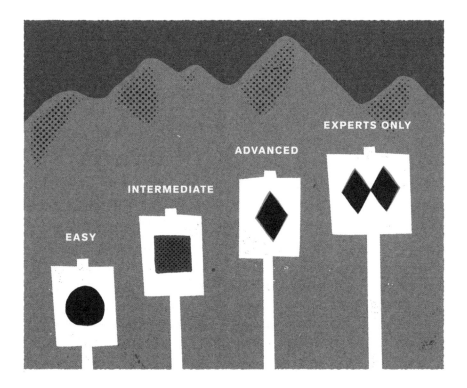

Should I try skiing or snowboarding?

Skiing and snowboarding are both great ways to safely access the mountains in the wintertime—ski resorts provide chairlifts to the top, manage the terrain to minimize avalanches, groom many of the runs so the snowpack is uniform throughout, and provide ski patrollers in case you're injured while skiing. Neither skiing nor snowboarding is inexpensive once you figure in the costs of lift tickets, equipment, and proper apparel, but for thousands of people each year it's worth the money to experience the feeling of sliding and carving turns in the mountains. Both skiing and snowboarding utilize the muscles of your core and upper body, and despite being downhill sports they do require some basic physical fitness and flexibility. A routine of leg-strengthening exercises like squats and lunges can help immensely as you learn to ski or snowboard.

How do I determine if I would like skiing or snowboarding better?

Deciding whether you should try skiing or snowboarding first is a big decision. Thankfully, it isn't like getting your first tattoo, since you're not choosing for life. You can always try skiing if you decide you don't like snowboarding, or vice versa, and you can always do both and love both (although it will probably double your equipment cost).

Snowboarding has a reputation of a steeper learning curve because of a few things: most people feel more natural facing downhill (the way they do on skis) as opposed to the offset stance on a snowboard; the falls on a snowboard, especially at the beginning, tend to be kind of surprising and sometimes abrupt; on a snowboard, you have no poles to help you balance when you're at a standstill; and getting on and off chairlifts seems to be a little bit more tricky at first on a snowboard than with skis.

Skiing has of course been around much longer and has seen many innovations come and go but has withstood the test of time. Ski boots are always going to be somewhat stiff and awkward to walk in (although they've gotten much better) compared to snowboarding boots, which are much softer and more comfortable. Skiing also requires a lot more stuff to carry than just a simple snowboard (two poles and two skis), and a full setup of skis, boots, bindings, and poles can often be almost twice as expensive as a full snowboard setup.

Both skiing and snowboarding are distinct experiences and distinct tastes and have their own pluses and minuses. If you've never tried any sort of snow travel before, you might consider trying skiing first, since it does seem to be a bit more straightforward for beginners—but no matter what you choose, stick with it. It will take some practice and patience, but eventually you'll get the hang of it and you'll have a blast.

What's the proper etiquette for skiing at a ski resort?

Each ski area has its own set of specific rules posted at the bottom of the mountain, but there's also a general set of safety principles called the Responsibility Code, developed by the National Ski Areas Association. The seven points of the Responsibility Code are as follows.

1. **Always stay in control:** Going too fast can put you and others at risk.

2. **People ahead of you have the right of way:** Always give other skiers and snowboarders a wide berth when passing, and pass them carefully.

3. **Stop in a safe place for you and others:** If you stop to wait for someone, avoid the middle of a run and blind corners, and don't stand behind a rise in the run that might obscure you from above.

4. **Whenever starting downhill or merging, look uphill and yield:** Be careful of skiers to your sides and those skiing downhill toward you— they can't read your mind as to what you're planning to do, so let them pass before you start down.

5. **Use devices to prevent runaway equipment:** Your skis should have brakes on the bindings so that when they become detached (in a fall or other situation) they'll stop instead of careening downhill on their own. Snowboards should always attach to snowboard boots with a leash.

6. **Observe signs and warnings, and keep off closed trails:** Skiing on closed terrain not only is dangerous but also can forfeit any liability the ski area has for your safety and/or rescue.

7. **Know how to use the lifts safely:** Not only is crashing while boarding or deboarding a ski lift dangerous, but it stops the ski lift and slows down everyone's ski day.

Can I get altitude sickness at a ski resort?

Here's the thing about altitude sickness: it happens at high altitude. You can get it at seven thousand feet if you normally live at sea level and you don't drink enough water. You can also get it if you live at five thousand feet and ski at ten thousand feet. A lot of ski resorts are located in high elevations, with base areas higher than ten thousand feet and chairlifts that top out just under thirteen thousand feet. If you fly in from somewhere at sea level, like Boston or San Diego, and click into your skis at ten thousand feet only a couple hours after your flight lands, there's a chance you can get altitude sickness. It's an even greater chance if you got so excited about your ski trip you forgot to eat much food, didn't drink much water all day, or had a couple beers on your flight. Just because you're not climbing Everest doesn't mean you're immune to altitude sickness. Drink water, keep tabs on your alcohol consumption, and remember to eat. And think about giving yourself a night to sleep at or near the ski resort before you strap on your skis.

Should I take a ski lesson?

Skiing is not something most of us can just pick up and instantly be good at. Ski lessons are a good idea for just about everyone, no matter what your level of natural athletic ability. If you're new to skiing and wondering if a lesson is worth the money, think of it like this: a day spent in ski lessons will help you not suck way faster. That is, instead of taking five or six days to become proficient enough to go down some easy blue runs, you can learn from a ski lesson the skills to get on those easy blue runs after three or four days (or even two!). Instead of learning from your friend who swears it's the easiest thing in the world to ski (bad idea), or your significant other who's been skiing for years (worst idea), invest a little cash up front for a professional lesson and make your ski season that much better.

What size skis do I need?

There's no exactly right equation for the perfect size ski for everyone—skis don't come in small, medium, and large like jackets—but there are some general guidelines. For a ballpark figure, take your height and convert it to centimeters; that number will give you a starting figure to work with. You'll be looking for skis 15 centimeters lower than your number 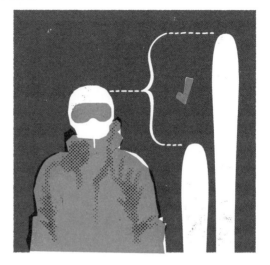 or 15 centimeters higher than your number (on the lower end if you're a beginner, and on the higher end if you're more of an intermediate skier). So if you're 5 foot 11, you're 71 inches tall, or 180 centimeters. You're looking for a ski 165 centimeters to 195 centimeters long. Shorter skis will be easier to turn and maneuver in general when you're first learning to ski, and as you graduate to faster speeds, longer skis will perform better. If you're renting skis for the first time, ski shop employees will help guide you to the right-size skis, so don't sweat it if you don't remember how tall you are in centimeters when you walk into the shop.

How should my ski boots fit?

First things first: Wear thin socks when you're skiing. Yes, it's winter, and you might think that's a good time to wear a pair of thick wool socks, or even two pairs of regular socks, but ski boots are designed to keep your feet warm with minimal sock lining, and thick socks decrease the feel and responsiveness through the ski boot. When you try on ski boots, your longest toes should graze (or come very close to) the end of the boot. If you feel a little pressure on the tips of your toes, try buckling the boot and then leaning forward, putting weight on your shins—this will push your feet back into the proper position. Your feet should not be squished into the boot, but you shouldn't have a ton of room to move around, either—wearing boots that are too big can put a lot of pressure on the front of your tibia and cause a painful condition called "shin bang." When you're wearing the boots, adjust all the buckles so they're snug but not putting pressure on the top of your foot or your ankle or cutting off circulation to your toes, any of which can lead to a miserable day out. Adjust your buckles throughout the day and figure out what works best for you—if you're feeling some pain, you might be one buckle rotation away from being perfect.

Should I rent or buy skis?

If you're going skiing for the first time, buying skis is a big financial commitment—the total cost of new skis, boots, bindings, and poles will be well over $1,000. If you're not sure you'll like to ski, rent skis instead of buying them. If you're going to go skiing only once a year (even if that once a year is for five straight days), you're probably still better off renting skis—by the time you've gotten your money's worth out of those skis, they'll be ten years old (and you'll have been coveting a new pair for the last five of those ten years). If you don't own skis, you don't have to travel with them, which means you don't have to trust baggage handlers with them, pay oversized baggage fees, or drag them through the airport either.

What size snowboard do I need?

Picking a snowboard size is fairly straightforward: stand the snowboard up in front of you, and the nose of the board should touch somewhere between the bridge of your nose and your chin. If you imagine you're going to want to spend a lot of time in the terrain park and concentrate on tricks, lean a little more toward the shorter side. If you think you're going to stay out of the park and just ride the mountain, lean a little more toward the longer side. Also note that snowboards have weight ranges, which of course aren't hard-and-fast weight limits, but know that the board will feel different depending on where you fall in the weight range. If the board you're buying (or renting) has a range of 165 to 185 pounds and you weigh 185 pounds, it's going to feel a little softer. If you weigh 165 pounds, that

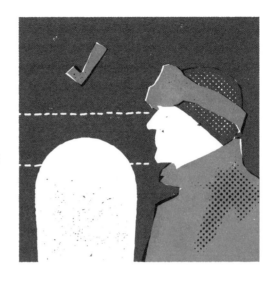

165- to 185-pound weight-range board will feel more stiff.

How do I get on a chairlift if I'm skiing?

Ski up to the front of the line, and remove your ski pole straps from your hands. After the group in front of you loads into their chair, ski up to the loading area and stop. Hold both your poles in your inside hand (if you're on the far left side of the loading area, your right hand; if you're on the far right side of the loading area, your left hand; if you're in the middle, pick a side), turn your torso to the outside, look over your outside shoulder, and wait for the chair to arrive. As the chair arrives, bend your knees slightly, grab the chair with your outside hand, and sit down as the seat bumps the back of your legs. Sit back against the seat, and keep your ski tips up as the chair exits the loading area. When everyone on the chair is comfortable, if there is a safety bar on the chair, ask everyone if they're ready before you pull it down.

How do I get on a chairlift if I'm snowboarding?

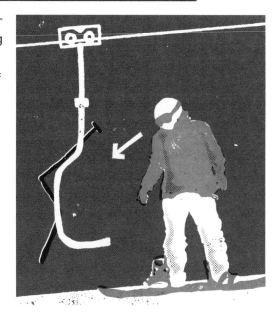

When you arrive at the chairlift line, unbuckle the binding on your back foot so you can "skate," or push yourself through the line using your back foot. After the group in line in front of you loads into their chair, skate up to the loading area and stop, standing with your free foot behind the heel side of the board. Turn your torso, look over your shoulder toward the outside (if you're on the left side of the loading area, over your left shoulder; if you're on the right side of the loading area, over your right shoulder; if you're in the middle, pick a side), and wait for your chair to arrive. Bend your knees slightly, and when the chair arrives and bumps the back of your legs, sit down, and slide back into the seat. Keep the nose of your board up as the chair exits the loading area. When everyone on the chair is comfortable, if there is a safety bar on the chair, ask everyone if they're ready before you pull it down.

How do I get off a chairlift if I'm skiing?

As you start to see signs alerting you that the chairlift is approaching the top station, lift the safety bar (be sure to ask everyone else on the chair first) and as you approach the top, keep the tips of your skis up so they don't get caught in the snow and pull you off the chair. Shift your weight a little bit forward on the seat. The top station should have a flat spot where you'll step off the chair, leading to a downward-sloping ramp that will help you ski forward away from the station. Stand up out of the chair and onto your skis when they touch the flat spot, and be ready to brake a little bit (by slightly snowplowing your skis) as you start down the ramp. It's easy to fit three or four people onto a chair, but it's hard for all of you to offload the chairlift at the same time and ski parallel to each other with the same spacing you had on the chair, so spread out: if you're on the left, try to ski slightly left (and if you're on the right, ski slightly right) as you head down the ramp. Clear the loading area before you come to a complete stop (other skiers are getting off the lift on the next chair, which is right behind you). When you're well out of the way, take the time to put your hands back through your ski pole straps and decide which run you're going to ski down.

How do I get off a chairlift if I'm snowboarding?

As you start to see signs alerting you that the chairlift is approaching the top station, lift the safety bar (be sure to ask everyone else on the chair first), and as you approach the top keep the nose of your board up so it doesn't get caught in the snow and pull you off the chair. Deboarding a chairlift can be anxiety inducing for snowboarders because you have to ride off the chair with only one foot strapped into your board, which makes it hard to steer and edge. Your main goal is to not crash in the unloading area, so relax and do your best to not frantically try to stop by dragging your back foot in the snow (which will likely cause you to crash in the loading area). The top station should have a flat spot where you'll step off the chair, leading to a downward-sloping ramp that will help you skate forward away from the station. As you approach the top station, shift your weight to sit on your back hip (the hip of the foot not strapped into your board), and when your board touches down on the flat spot, stand up with your back foot on the board just in front of the back binding. Use the chair to nudge yourself off, and skate down the slope out of the loading area. If you have to fall, do your best to steer out to the left or right of the loading area so you're out of the way when the next chair empties. Wait until you're out of the loading area before you stop to strap your back foot into your board.

Will I get stuck on a chairlift?

Although there is a horror movie about a group of friends who get stuck on a chairlift after the mountain closes and spend a freezing night out until they finally try to escape and (spoiler alert) all but one are killed by wolves, it is highly unlikely that you will become stuck on a chairlift, especially overnight. (It is also extremely unlikely that you will see a wolf at a ski resort.) Chairlifts will stop operating for a few seconds or a few minutes whenever someone falls while boarding the lift at the bottom or falls while getting off the chairlift at the top. So when you're halfway through the chairlift ride and all of a sudden the lift stops moving, it's perfectly normal. Don't be alarmed; it's just someone who had a hard time at the top or the bottom who is hopefully quickly and efficiently picking him- or herself up off the ground so everyone can get back to skiing.

How do I get on a gondola?

Whether you have skis or a snowboard, loading a gondola is the same process: you'll take off your skis or board and carry them in your hand in line. When you get to the front of the line, you will either hand your skis or board to an attendant to load in the rack on the open doors of the gondola, or you'll load them yourself. If you're loading them yourself, take a second to make sure they're loaded correctly (i.e., the maximum amount of ski or snowboard is in the appropriate slot) so that there's no chance of them falling off the gondola car as you ride up. Once you've secured your skis or board, step inside the gondola car and sit as close to the back as you can so everyone else can load efficiently (and won't have to crawl over you to get to an empty seat).

How do I get off a gondola?

The gondola doors will open when it's time for you to deboard. The people nearest the door will exit first, and the people farthest from the door will exit last. Before the doors open, gather your stuff and take a second to remember near which door your skis/snowboard were loaded so you can grab them in one fluid motion as you step off the gondola and get out of the way and the next person can move quickly as well—it can be anxiety inducing to stand behind people who step off the gondola and block the door while they try to determine the whereabouts of their skis. Be efficient and courteous, and carry your skis or board out the exit door of the gondola station.

Should I chat with other skiers on the chairlift?

A chairlift is one scenic method of public transit most conducive to socializing. It's far more accepted to talk to the stranger next to you on a chairlift than it is on, say, the D train during the Tuesday morning commute. Everyone at a ski area is essentially on vacation, whether it's just for the day or for a week, and should theoretically be in a pretty good mood. So don't be afraid to make small talk with the people next to you on the chairlift about the snowpack, the weather, where they're visiting from, or whatever else. But small talk is not required, so don't feel like you have to chat if you're in a happy zone by yourself.

How do I stop on skis?

There are two ways to stop on skis—well, three, if you include crashing, which eventually ends in a kind of stop. But there are two ways to stop while still standing upright: the wedge and the hockey stop.

- **The wedge:** Also known as the "pizza wedge" and the "snowplow," the wedge is the simplest way to stop, and the first way beginning skiers learn

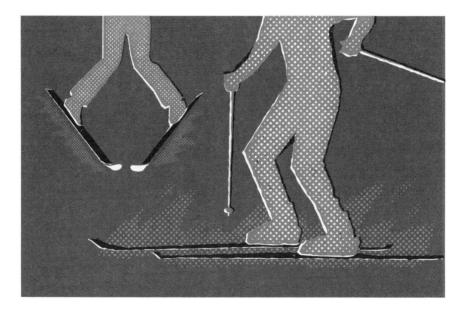

how to control their speed and stop. To do it, gradually point the front tips of your skis together so they're almost touching (but not crossing or touching), and the back ends are pointed out, so that if you saw yourself from above, your skis would form a wedge (or a pizza wedge, if you prefer). Push outward through your feet and experiment with gradually slowing yourself down, and finally use the same outward pressure to come to a complete stop.

- **The hockey stop:** To perform a hockey stop, ski straight downhill (at a slow, controlled speed) with your skis parallel. Transfer all (or most) of your weight to your left ski, and then push your skis into a turn so they end up perpendicular to the slope, turning your lower body with the skis but keeping your upper body facing downhill. To stop, push the uphill edges of both your skis into the snow until you come to a stop.

How do I turn on skis?

Turning on skis is important first and foremost so you can dodge things like trees and people, and also as the best method to slow down without stopping. The best way to learn to turn is at a slow and controlled speed: Simply ski downhill with your skis in the "wedge," and turn yourself left or right, slowly. If you feel yourself getting out of control, use the wedge to stop yourself, or stay in the turn until you're pointing uphill, which will bring you to a stop.

Once you feel comfortable using the wedge turn, try to gradually make your wedge narrower and narrower in preparation for learning the parallel turn. To parallel turn, pick an easy, wide run, and decide which way you'd like to turn (in this case, we'll say you're turning left). Start yourself going downhill, with your skis more or less parallel (a little wedging is okay at first), and transfer your weight to the inside edge of your right ski as you ease yourself into a wide turn to the left. Keep pushing on the inside edge of that right ski, lift up the heel of your left foot slightly so the back of your left ski comes up as you turn, and set it down in the snow parallel to your right ski. Again, if you feel out of control, use the wedge to stop, or keep turning uphill until you come to a stop. Try turning to the right next.

How do I stop on a snowboard?

Let's be honest: You want to snowboard for the going part, not the stopping part. But the stopping part will help you stay alive and avoid making enemies on the slope, so it should be the first thing you learn.

The toe-side stop is probably the most natural, so try that first. Strap yourself into your board and drop down so you're kneeling, with your board behind you and perpendicular to the slope. Use your hands to push yourself into a standing position, and stand so your toe-side edge is the only thing in contact with the snow. Keep the board perpendicular to the slope, and experiment with letting the board slide downhill by dropping your heels slightly and stopping by standing on your toes, which digs the toe-side edge of the board into the snow. Be careful to keep your heel-side edge off the snow, or you'll flip over backwards and downhill (this will eventually happen sometime, but try to avoid it for now). When you're comfortable controlling the board, try to slide with a little more speed and stop more quickly by standing on your toes and digging the toe-side edge in harder. When you're comfortable stopping on the toe-side edge, drop back down onto your knees, flip over and have a seat on your butt, with your board on the downhill side of you, still perpendicular to the slope. Practice stopping with your heel-side edge: let your board slide downhill by tilting your toes slightly down, and stop the board by pulling your toes up and digging in your heels.

Once you're comfortable stopping with both feet strapped in, unstrap your back foot and practice both toe-side stopping and heel-side stopping with your back foot unstrapped but planted on the board's stomp pad.

How do I turn on a snowboard?

The first step in turning a snowboard is subtly changing your direction: pick a wide, easy slope, and slowly practice traversing the slope on your heel edge, very gradually going downhill, zigzagging from one side to the

other (sometimes called "feathering"). Once you're comfortable doing that, try it on your toe-side edge.

Then it's time to learn how to link turns. Stand on your heel-side edge and start a traverse across the slope to the left just as you did before, keeping your upper body facing downhill. Don't wait until you're at the very left edge of the run to

start your turn—try starting it nearer to the middle or three-quarters across the run. Shift your weight to your front foot and point the nose of your board downhill. Now it's time to turn: twist your front foot to turn the board toward the right, and push with your back foot to help the board come around the turn into a toe-side traverse, turning your upper body to face uphill as you transition over to the toe-side edge of your board. Get ready for your heel-side turn, again starting it before you're at the far right edge of the run. Point your board downhill, shifting your weight to the front of the board, and twist your front foot to turn the board back toward the left, pushing with your back foot to bring the board into the heel-side traverse and shift your weight to your heel edge.

If you start into a turn and aren't confident you'll make it, simply back out of it by leaning back onto whichever edge you started on (heel-side or toe-side) and come to a stop before you get to the edge of the run. Linking turns may take a while to learn, and you'll no doubt develop a preference for either heel-side turns or toe-side turns—but you need to learn both.

Can I drink beer in between ski runs?

You can drink beer in between ski runs, and of course everyone around you will appreciate it if you do it in moderation instead of, for example, chugging six IPAs and trying to set a personal speed record while drunkenly straight-lining your last run of the day just as the ski school kids are getting out of their lessons at the base of the mountain. Beer is okay (if a little bit expensive) at ski resorts, but keep a couple of considerations in mind: (1) there's a good chance that the resort is at a higher altitude than where you normally drink beer (especially if you're drinking at the mid-mountain lodge), so the alcohol will have a stronger effect on you, and (2) ski accidents are more likely to occur in the afternoon, when you're tired and less mentally vigilant about not catching an edge. Many vacations have been ruined (and lives ended) when a skier with tired legs was cruising down an "easy" run at the end of the day, made a small misstep, and hit a tree. So be careful with those late afternoon beers if you're up high on the mountain and still have to ski down to get home.

Should I worry about locking up my skis at a ski resort when I go inside for lunch?

Ski thefts are not that common at most ski areas, but they happen, so if you have a brand-new pair of skis that might be coveted (or are worth a few hundred bucks to someone who doesn't mind buying them without knowing where they came from), using a lock is a good idea. Several companies make lightweight $10 to $25 cable locks that can secure your skis to a rack and deter slick would-be thieves from walking off with them. If you're renting skis, theft is pretty much a nonissue—rental skis, while adequate, are not typically high-end models and are usually a little more banged up from their frequent use. You might, however, find that someone mixed up his or her rental skis with yours after lunch and accidentally walked off with yours. Most ski rental shops are now labeling each ski with the renter's name to prevent this from happening.

How do I ski moguls?

Contrary to rumors and conjecture spread widely by ski resort tourists, moguls are not built by ski resorts, nor are they bumps of snow covering rocks. Moguls are simply bumps that form on ungroomed ski runs where multiple skiers turn in generally the same spots. They're challenging to ski, and there are several approaches. For beginner mogul skiing, you should focus on turning on top of the moguls. Your first instinct might be to look at the troughs in between the bumps on a mogul run and try to decipher a line through the run connecting those troughs, but this is actually a more difficult way of skiing moguls, requiring quick reactions and turns to stay upright. An easier way is to plan your turns on top of the moguls themselves—keep your skis together and use the middle of the ski (not the tip or the tail) to turn. Try traversing across the run at first, rather than pointing your skis straight down it. Start your turn on the middle of the mogul as you pass over it, planting your downhill pole on the front side of the mogul at the inside of your turn. By the time you finish the turn, you will have slid off the mogul to the other side

(toward the outside of your turn). Your path down a mogul run should connect the tops of the moguls, rather than the troughs.

How do I ski on powder?

Skiing on powdery snow is just like skiing on groomed slopes, only it's about 400 percent more fun—unless you don't know what you're doing, in which case it can feel like you're skiing on quicksand. If you're lucky enough, one day you'll ski on a 7-inch to 2-foot fresh dump of snow. Here are a few tips to learn to love skiing powder.

- **Make wide turns, not sharp turns.** Think of the letter C as you turn in powder; if you try to turn at sharp angles, you'll just get your outside ski caught and flip over.

- **Bounce.** Imagine yourself lightly bouncing in the snow, like a boxer dancing.

- **Ski with both feet.** As opposed to skiing on groomed terrain, skiing powder requires more even weight distribution. Try to remember to push with both feet when you're turning.

- **Go fast(er).** Yes, even if you're unsure of your abilities, going fast will keep you from getting stuck trying to turn. The deep fluffy snow will sap your energy when you're trying to turn, so go into turns with more speed than you think you need, in order to come out the other side. And if you're worried about crashing because you're going too fast, remember that the landing will be very soft because of all that new snow.

- **Stay off your edges.** You don't need an edge in powder the way you do on regular terrain. Keep your feet close together and push the whole ski in as opposed to concentrating on edging through turns.

- **Build it into a myth.** When you get a powder day, it should become legend. It's like a story about catching a fish in which the reported size of the fish caught becomes larger as the story ages. A story about a day of shin-deep powder will no doubt grow to knee- and then waist-deep powder given enough time.

How do I snowboard in the trees?

Like tree skiing, snowboarding in the trees comes with one golden rule: do not look at the trees. Look at where you want to go: the spaces between the trees. With snowboarding, it's very important to be able to turn quickly, so don't go in the trees until you've mastered turns to the point where you can change directions almost without thinking about it—a glade of stout evergreens is very unforgiving to those who hesitate. Always plan a turn or two ahead, and know when to get out of the trees and where you'll exit (don't shoot out of the trees onto a busy run).

As with tree skiing, be wary of tree wells, which are spots near the trunks of trees that contain less dense snow, forming almost invisible pits.

How do I ski in the trees?

Your number one goal of skiing in the trees, even more than finding untracked snow (that's number two), is to not crash into a tree. Simple, right? Even more simple is the trick that skiers have used for years to avoid hitting a giant ever-green while blissfully flying through a huge stand of them: look where you want to ski, not where you don't want to ski. Or look between the trees, not at the trees. No matter how much you think you're in control of your mind and skis, there's still a cosmic unconscious connection between where your eyes go and where your skis go—if you select one tree out of the whole forest and worry for even a fraction of a second about hitting it, you will very likely hit it. So focus on a path through the trees, always looking one or two turns ahead. Stay in control, keep your hands high (to swat branches out of your face), always ski the trees with a partner, and keep your ski tips up not by leaning back but by subtly pushing through your heels.

One other caution of tree skiing: be wary of tree wells, which are spots near the trunks of trees that contain less dense snow, forming almost invisible pits. Several skiers and snowboarders die every year by losing control and flipping headfirst into tree wells, unable to pull themselves out before they're asphyxiated.

How do I huck a cliff?

As you might remember from your bolder days jumping off objects when you were a kid, any time a human body leaves the ground for more than a few seconds, there can be consequences. Unlike that time you tried to jump off the roof of your parents' house with a bedsheet for a parachute, at least when you jump off a cliff on skis you're landing in snow. But don't think it's foolproof by any means. Here's how to do it (relatively) safely.

- **Check your landing zone.** Just as you wouldn't jump off a cliff into a lake without knowing how deep the water is, you shouldn't drop a cliff while skiing without first inspecting the snow below, where you'll land. Obviously you don't want to stomp the landing only to find you're on 4 inches of snow covering a chunk of granite the size of a car, or a hole with an abrupt edge on its front side. Ski over and make sure there's enough snow and it isn't frozen into a crusty slab, and then make your plan to ski off it.

- **Assess the jump-off.** Ski up to the edge of the cliff, and check out the zone below. You might be surprised to find out that the cliff you thought was vertical actually angles away from the top to the bottom, requiring you to clear 10 feet of rock before you hit snow. Ball up some snow and give it an underhand toss off the cliff and see if it clears. If you have to throw it hard, you'll need significant speed to clear the rocks, or you'll need to find another objective.

- **Fall off the cliff.** Yes, we like to say "huck," but you're really not jumping or doing anything to actively push yourself off the cliff—you're falling. So ski off the edge, keep your speed up (it's easy to freak out at the last second and lose your courage, which usually isn't good), and confidently sail off the cliff. As you leave the ground, it's easy to blow it by doing a couple things: leaning back and windmilling your arms (aka "rolling down the windows"). Don't do those two things. To keep it together, roll yourself into a loose ball and heave your arms forward so they're pointing out from your body at a 90-degree angle. And get ready to land.

- **Keep it together for the landing.** As you approach the ground, straighten your legs (but don't lock your knees, obviously) and prepare them to absorb the impact of your landing. Keep your skis pointed downhill and keep your head forward, and you'll land just fine. When your skis hit the snow, think of your legs as a shock-absorbing spring and let them coil up under you as your quads and hips squeeze to keep your butt from slamming into your skis (and your face from slamming into your knees). If you need to stop or turn to avoid something in your path, don't worry about it until you've landed. Land first, then make an evasive maneuver after your skis are back on snow. When you're in the air, worrying about what happens after the landing will do nothing but throw you off and guarantee a disastrous landing.

How do I snowboard in powder?

Snowboarding on powder is arguably even more fun than skiing on powder because you've got a big, fat board underneath your feet that makes it extremely intuitive to float on top of the fluffy white stuff. The principles of riding powder on a snowboard are very similar to skiing powder: make big wide turns, stay off your edges (visualize yourself surfing on water more than snowboarding on a groomed ski slope), and most of all, lean back: shift your hips toward the back of the board, and put more of your weight on your back foot, to keep the nose of your board out of the snow so you don't catch it and flip over. By the end of a few runs in deep powder, your back leg will have gotten a serious workout, and you'll feel it. Give it a little time to recover between runs—but not too much time, because every skier or snowboarder with any sense will be on the powder putting tracks down all the runs.

The Six Best North American Ski Resorts

1. **Whistler-Blackcomb, British Columbia:** The continent's biggest in terrain (8,000-plus acres) and the second biggest in vertical drop (more than 5,300 vertical feet) gets 400-plus inches of snow per year.

2. **Stowe, Vermont:** Maybe the most famous (and most challenging) resort skiing on the east coast of North America, Stowe is rich in history and in fine dining too.

3. **Big Sky, Montana:** One of the biggest resorts in the United States, with easy and expert terrain, minus the crowds, lift lines, and flashiness of other well-known American destinations.

4. **Jackson Hole, Wyoming:** The birthplace of extreme skiing and ski mountaineering in North America, Jackson Hole is famous for its steep in-bounds terrain as well as the rewards to be had by those who don't mind a bit of hiking too.

5. **Alta, Utah:** This ski town offers 500-plus inches of Utah's famous deep, light, and plentiful "greatest snow on earth" and enough terrain to ditch the crowds.

6. **Silverton, Colorado:** One ski lift serves Silverton's experts-only, guide-mandatory terrain, where skiers pay $140 a day for hiking-accessed couloirs and steeps, carrying avalanche beacons and shovels.

Do I need to wear sunscreen while skiing or snowboarding?

If you want to go back to your office after your ski vacation and show off a ski-goggle-shaped sunburn, do not wear sunscreen. If you're interested in avoiding a sunburn, then wearing sunscreen is a good idea, for a couple reasons: altitude and snow. If you're skiing, especially in some of the ski areas in the western United States, you'll be at a higher altitude than normal (often around or above 10,000 feet), and the sun is more intense at high altitudes—even on a cloudy day up high, you're getting sun exposure. The snow, although it might make you think, "Snow equals winter, and who gets a sunburn in winter?," can actually act as a reflector on sunny days in the mountains, so you're getting a sort of double exposure to sunlight. Be sure to cover your entire face thoroughly and don't forget the bottom of your nose. Plenty of people can attest to a very surprising sunburn on the bottom of their nostrils after a long spring day out skiing under bluebird skies.

Do I need to wear ski goggles or are sunglasses okay?

Goggles are generally more prevalent and preferred among experienced skiers and snowboarders for a few reasons: they work better if you're skiing in falling snow (i.e., they keep snow out of your eyes), don't ice up like sunglasses do, and are far less of a risk for breaking and/or injuring your face or eyes if you happen to fall and hit your head. Modern helmets have a clip or snap that secures goggle straps, so they integrate seamlessly. Of course, just because everyone's using them doesn't mean you have to. If you can't find a pair of goggles that doesn't fog up, or goggles hurt your nose, or you just flat out don't want to buy one more piece of equipment, rock your sunglasses.

Do I need to wear a helmet?

No ski resort requires helmets, but they've become way more fashionable and accepted over the past twenty years. People die at ski resorts, and although helmets prevent head injuries (and deaths from blunt-force head trauma), lots of those people die from hitting trees, which causes trauma to their internal organs, something a helmet wouldn't have helped anyway. But helmets are warmer than hats, offer much more protection than hats, and can save you a headache or concussion from a nasty fall on hard-packed snow or even a tree branch you thought you could clear before you accidentally glanced it with your head. The other—possibly most important—thing helmets can protect against is other skiers who are out of control and slam into you with no warning. Yes, you might be a great skier, but that guy zipping down the run behind you (who may or may not have had four beers for lunch) might not be a good skier, and he might think he is. All that said, it's up to you whether you want to wear a helmet on the slopes.

What's a "gaper"?

Gaper is a pejorative term for a person who doesn't know, or doesn't seem to know, what he or she is doing at a ski resort. Gapers are named after the "gaper gap," or the large gap between the top of their ski goggles and the front brim of their helmet, but not all gapers sport a gaper gap, and there are many other gaper symptoms: tucking your pants into your ski boots, going into a tuck to go fast but pointing your ski poles upward toward the sky instead of backward, and skiing with your jacket unzipped all the way to the hem. If you want to avoid looking like a gaper, just keep yourself from looking sloppy and you should be okay. Or don't worry about what other people think and just ski.

The Six Best European Ski Resorts

1. **La Grave, France:** With a 7,000-foot vertical drop, miles of expert terrain complete with cliffs and couloirs, only one ski lift, and no ski patrol, La Grave is Europe's most adventurous ski resort.

2. **Verbier, Switzerland:** Just as famous for its nightlife, Verbier's skiing is top-notch, with nearly one hundred ski lifts accessing all levels of terrain, including some of the best off-piste runs in the country.

3. **Zermatt, Switzerland:** Although it sits in the shadow of the famous Matterhorn, Zermatt's skiing is anything but overshadowed by the mountain: four interconnected resorts sport 200-plus miles of ski runs and a towering vertical drop of over 7,500 feet.

4. **Kitzbuhel, Austria:** Despite boasting one of the steepest ski race courses in the world, Kitzbuhel is actually quite friendly, with fifty-plus lifts accessing more than 100 miles of runs for all skill levels.

5. **Chamonix–Mont Blanc, France:** One of Chamonix's most famous runs, the Vallée Blanche descent, is 12 miles long and drops almost 9,000—but it's just one attraction of the town's four ski resorts, all accessible with one pass.

6. **Cortina d'Ampezzo, Italy:** This charming town perched in northern Italy's limestone Dolomites boasts 70 miles of runs on its own, not to mention the nearly 700 miles of terrain in the neighboring twelve valleys included in the Dolomite Superski pass.

What's a ski-in, ski-out property?

Booking lodging for a ski vacation is a lot like buying a house or renting an apartment—there's a lot of language intended to sell you the place. Remember how that one apartment was advertised as "five minutes from downtown" but you could never manage to get from there to downtown in less than twenty minutes? Just take "ski-in, ski-out" with the same grain of salt. Ideally, it means the back door is a fifteen-second downhill ski trail from the resort, but sometimes it can mean it's a five-minute walk down the street, then a five-minute ski (including one point where you have to traverse slightly uphill) to a green run that eventually leads to the base of the mountain. When you're shopping for a condo to spend your ski week in, just be aware that "ski-in, ski-out" covers a pretty wide spectrum and adjust your expectations accordingly—or call and verify with the booking agency or owner before renting.

How do I get back on my feet after I fall down on my skis?

Unless you are among the most preternaturally talented skiers on the planet, you will fall at least a few times. So you need to know how to get back on your skis. First of all, you'll need to make sure your skis are downhill from you. If you crash and end up with your feet above you, twist yourself around until your skis are on your downhill side, perpendicular to the slope. It can help to remove your pole straps from your wrists as you do this—that's one

more thing that you don't have to manage and keep from tangling as you wrangle your limbs around. Once you have your skis downhill and perpendicular, get your upper body in front of your feet. Put the tips of your poles in the snow above your uphill knee, and push yourself up onto your poles, keeping your skis in place so you're not sliding across the slope as you try to stand up. If getting up on your own is too difficult, a friend can lend a hand, or, as a last (and time-consuming) resort, you can just click out of your skis, stand up, and put your skis back on.

How do I get back on my feet after I fall down on my snowboard?

One of the side effects of falling on a snowboard is the great abdominal/core workout you can get trying to get yourself in position to stand up again. If, after a crash, you magically end up with your feet downhill, you're in luck. If not, you need to get yourself in that position, and there's often no graceful way to do it—don't get self-conscious that you're not using the correct technique, because there really isn't one. Simply wriggle and crawl around until you can get your board downhill of your body, and once you do, dig in the appropriate edge. If you're facing the hill, dig your toe-side edge into the snow and push yourself up using your hands, and get ready to do a heel-side turn as you start going again. If you're facing away from the hill, dig in your

heel-side edge and push yourself up with both hands (or push up with one hand while grabbing the toe-side edge of your board with your other hand), stand up and get ready to do a toe-side turn as soon as you start downhill. Learn to get up on both sides of your board—toe-side and heel-side—so you don't have to waste time rolling over to one side when you crash.

How do I find a ski patroller?

If your ski partner crashes and needs medical attention or help getting off the mountain, you will need ski patrol's assistance. Move your friend to a safe place if possible (but not if you think there is a neck or spinal injury), remove the skis, and plant them in the ground tail end first above him or her, crossing the skis. Make a mental note of your friend's location (halfway down Run X, near the intersection of Run X and Run Y, etc.), then ski to the nearest emergency phone, which should be marked on the resort map. If you don't have a map or don't see a phone near you on the map, ski to the nearest chairlift—both the top lift station and the bottom lift station have emergency phones and will be able to contact ski patrol.

Can I duck ropes at ski resorts to access more terrain?

It's tempting: there's all that untracked terrain just outside the rope. But if you do duck under the rope and decide to see what's beyond it, you'll venture into terrain that isn't managed for avalanches (which means it could avalanche and bury you), you'll be difficult to rescue if you do crash, get hurt, or get lost, and if you get caught the resort will very likely confiscate your lift ticket or season pass. If you're looking at the ski area map and thinking, "It's just on the other side of the rope, there's no way I'll get lost," remember that ski area maps are not topographical, so a terrain feature that looks as if it funnels right back to the resort's base area might lead down into a drainage that takes you a mile away from your car. Untracked powder is one reason you might think about venturing off the marked trails, but there are plenty of reasons not to.

Can I get caught in an avalanche at a ski resort?

Avalanches are extremely rare at ski resorts. Terrain inside ski area boundaries is carefully managed by resorts with daily monitoring and frequent avalanche blasting. In addition, the low angle of most beginner- to intermediate-level runs (greens and less-steep blues) makes them unlikely to slide. In-bounds avalanches have happened, but the National Ski Area Association has reported that only one in-bounds avalanche fatality happens per hundred million skier visits. Step outside boundary ropes at a ski area, or poach closed terrain in bounds, and you're definitely rolling the dice, as those areas are not managed for avalanches or patrolled.

What should I wear skiing?

Fashion on the mountain comes and goes, and function always comes first, because you won't have much fun skiing if you're freezing. There are some key pieces you'll need to wear.

- **Base layer top and bottom:** Go with noncotton pants and a long-sleeve shirt for under your jacket and pants.

- **Ski jacket:** Your jacket should be insulated with a waterproof or water-resistant shell layer (you can also just wear a waterproof shell jacket/rain jacket with a fleece or other warm layer underneath).

- **Ski pants:** These should also be insulated with a waterproof shell (or fleece pants with rain pants layered on top). Don't wear cotton or denim, as cotton will soak up water and freeze.

- **Beanie:** Wear a thin knit hat under a helmet, or wear a thicker knit hat if you're not wearing a helmet.

- **Gloves:** You'll want warm insulated gloves with a waterproof outer shell and a leather palm durable enough to handle ski edges. If your hands get cold easily, consider adding a liner glove underneath.

- **Ski or snowboard socks:** Find thin wool (or wool-blend) full-calf-length socks that won't bunch up under your boots.

- **Neck gaiter:** A neck/face covering will block the wind chill you'll create while skiing fast downhill.

What's backcountry skiing?

Backcountry skiing is skiing outside of resort boundaries—usually in an entirely different area, as opposed to just outside ski area ropes. Backcountry skiing is great because of the adventure and the lack of crowds, but the price you pay for those things is the total assumption of risk: backcountry ski areas are not patrolled, and they are not managed for avalanche mitigation. So by skiing in a backcountry area, you are taking on the responsibility for determining whether is safe to ski—and in the event of an avalanche, locating and digging out ski partners who are buried and evacuating them to medical help. Hundreds of people ski in backcountry areas around the world every year without incident, and most have been properly trained in avalanche safety and carry proper equipment. Still, several people (trained and untrained) are killed every year in backcountry avalanches, so it's not an activity to take on lightly. Backcountry ski areas also do not have ski lifts, of course, so you climb up every foot you ski down, and backcountry runs are not groomed, so they can vary from deep powder to ice to breakable crust, sometimes within just a few feet.

What do I need to ski in the backcountry?

If you want to ski in the backcountry, at the very minimum you need this equipment.

- **Skis, bindings, and boots capable of going uphill and downhill:** Alpine touring, or AT, bindings release the heel of the boot for climbing up and clip it back in for descents. Telemark bindings are free-heel all the time and require the mastery of a turning technique far different from that of a regular ski turn. A splitboard is a snowboard that splits apart lengthwise for backcountry ski ascents, then clips back together for descents.

- **Climbing skins:** This fabric attaches to the bottom of your skis (or splitboard) for climbing up snow slopes.

- **An avalanche beacon, probe, and shovel:** A beacon is an electronic device that helps you find partners if they become buried in an avalanche. The probe helps you find your partner under several feet of snow and to determine where you should start digging. An avalanche shovel is, of course, for digging your partner out.

- **Avalanche education:** At minimum, backcountry travelers should have what's known as level 1 certification, a basic level of knowledge about snowpack, avalanches, and rescue. Level 1 certification requires a three-day class totaling twenty-four hours of instruction.

- **Partner:** Someone who has all the above mentioned equipment and education and is competent and trustworthy—this is the person who'll be digging you out if you get buried in a slide.

Should I try cross-country skiing?

Cross-country skiing has many advantages over downhill skiing: it's free (once you have the equipment), it's easy to learn, it's great cardiovascular exercise, and there are no lift lines. The downside is that it lacks the exhilaration of speeding downhill on a carpet of snow—so if that's your favorite wintertime feeling, cross-country skiing might not be your thing. But if you're looking for an activity that burns as many calories as running (minus the impact, plus the joy of gliding over snow) and is smoother than snowshoeing, you'll love cross-country skiing.

Should I try snowshoeing?

If you like hiking and you like winter, you'll probably love snowshoeing. When winter comes and snow covers trails in the mountains and forests, you can either try to hike through the snow (which means a lot of exhausting postholing, or your feet punching through the top crust of the snow and sinking in up to your mid-shin or knee, turning every step into a high step) or get a flotation method (snowshoes or skis) to distribute your weight so you're walking on top of the snow. Snowshoeing is a very simple skill—it's literally just walking with snowshoes strapped to your feet. Snowshoeing is relatively inexpensive to try (compared to other winter sports like skiing and snowboarding)—most snowshoes cost between $100 and $250, will last for years, and are usually available to rent for $5 to $10 per day. Since snowshoeing is a very low-speed, low-impact activity, it's also relatively safe with regard to injuries (compared to skiing and snowboarding).

How do I snowshoe?

Snowshoeing might be the easiest form of winter travel to master: you simply strap on your snowshoes and walk. The only guideline is that you should

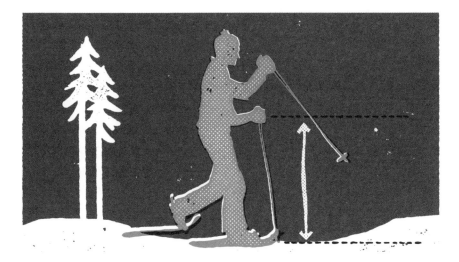

avoid trying to walk backwards, as lots of snowshoe tails will drop when you pick up your foot and stick in the snow just as you try to put your weight down. Make sure you buy or rent a pair of snowshoes appropriate to your body weight (and remember you might be wearing a backpack that will add 10 to 15 pounds to your weight), and start on a popular or well-marked trail—it's very easy to get lost in the winter, when dirt paths are buried under snow and a space between two trees can look an awful lot like a trail.

Should I use poles with my snowshoes?

Snowshoeing with poles is a matter of personal taste—of course they will help you balance as you're walking, and if the trail isn't well packed the extra points of contact can be nice to have. On long snowshoe outings, poles can also be nice to lean on when you're resting. If you don't want to spend the cash on snowshoe poles, try to find a decent pair of used ski poles at a thrift store. To find the right-size pole, flip it upside down and grab the pole just below the basket—your forearm should be parallel to the ground. Baskets on ski poles come in a lot of sizes—the bigger the better if you're snowshoeing in powder. If you have a pair of trekking poles, you can use those for snowshoeing, and the manufacturer likely makes a snow-specific basket you can order and put on the pole.

What should I wear snowshoeing?

Snowshoe apparel falls somewhere between what you'd wear skiing and what you might wear going for a jog in the winter—it's cold out, but you'll be moving. You want to avoid sweating, so layering is usually a better option than wearing a single, heavy jacket. Ski pants and ski jackets can work great, especially if they have zipper vents you can open when you start to warm up while snowshoeing uphill. Wear synthetic base layers and, as in all other back-country pursuits, avoid cotton. Footwear is an important consideration: winter boots with insulation, or, at the very least, waterproof hiking boots (you'll probably kick up a fair amount of snow onto your shoes). Gaiters (see page 89) are a good idea if you're tromping through any fresh snow or powder, as it will probably end up on your lower legs. Thicker socks are okay for snowshoeing (again, no cotton), but don't put so many layers on your feet that you can't move your toes—constricting blood flow will make your feet go numb.

Should I worry about falling in a crevasse?

The only way you will fall in a crevasse is if you are on a glacier, something that will be very obvious to you. Most crevassed glaciers in the lower forty-eight US states would be difficult to reach on a one-day snowshoe outing, and the vast majority of snowshoe trails of any popularity will not cross a glacier. It's safe to assume that you'll probably be snowshoeing in a wooded area somewhere, and if you are next to a tree, you are not on a glacier—so you don't have to worry about falling in a crevasse. You're more likely to fall in what's called a "tree well," the area of unconsolidated snow next to a tree trunk (the tree warms the snow immediately next to it so it melts faster than snow farther away), so take care when walking, snowshoeing, or skiing right next to trees in wilderness areas.

How do I keep my water from freezing on a snowshoe outing?

When you're thirsty on a snowshoe outing, nothing is worse than realizing your water has frozen into a block. Well, realizing you forgot to screw the lid on a water bottle properly and finding that it's completely emptied itself inside your backpack is a little worse, but freezing is pretty bad too.

If you're carrying a water bottle in cold weather, keep it inside your backpack. Your instinct might be to keep it in an external water bottle pocket on your pack, but on the outside it's exposed to wind chill and also is out of contact with your body heat. If it's inside your pack it's protected from the wind, and if it's against the back of your pack it can benefit at least a little from the heat of your back. If you can't bear to stash your water bottles out of reach inside your pack, several companies do make insulated water bottle carriers, which are basically foam-lined cylinders that attach to the waist belt of your backpack, keeping your water warm enough to stay in liquid form.

If it's really cold outside, fill your bottles with warm or hot water before the start of your outing—with a few degrees' head start, they won't freeze nearly as quickly.

Hydration reservoirs are hard to rely on in cold weather. The hose that leads from your pack to your mouth holds a very small volume of water, is very exposed to wind chill and cold temperatures, and can freeze solid much more quickly. It's best to avoid reservoirs in the winter months.

Can I camp in the winter?

The good news about winter camping is it's never crowded. The bad news is it's really cold. There are some basic differences between camping during the warm weather and camping in the cold. Keep these in mind.

- **More fuel:** To get water to drink and to cook with, you'll need to melt snow, which requires a lot more stove fuel than a summer camping trip.

- **Snow:** Camping on snow requires some different equipment, including something to put under your stove to make sure it doesn't melt a hole in the snow you're cooking on and sink down a foot while you're not looking. You can use an old license plate or cut out a section of the bottom of an aluminum pan.

- **Staking your tent:** Regular tent stakes are almost useless for staking out a tent in snow. They can, however, be used as deadmen—buried parallel to the ground with your guyline tied to them. You'll need to bury them, then compact the snow on top of them. You'll also need to stomp out a flat tent platform in the snow before you set it up.

- **It's cold:** Your 15°F sleeping bag probably won't cut it. Buy or rent a cold-temperature sleeping bag (rated to 0°F or lower), or line a 15°F sleeping bag with a lighter down or synthetic sleeping bag (32°F or 40°F rating).

How do I dig a snow cave?

To dig a snow cave, you need five things: consolidated (not powder) snow, subfreezing temps, a short but steep slope (30 to 40 degrees), a shovel, and enough dedication to finish the job, which is not a quick process. Find a slope or a snowdrift that will allow for a 2-foot-high ceiling and a roof thickness of at least 2 feet and is deep enough to allow for a small room (i.e., you don't want to hit the ground after a few feet of shoveling). Once you've done that, start digging. You're going to dig a door-shaped entryway 5 feet tall by 2 feet wide, and once you've dug that 4 feet deep, make it into a "T" shape by digging out a shelf about 2 feet tall and 2 feet deep. The T shape will allow you to shovel snow out the sides as you dig the sleeping room. The floor of your sleeping room should be at about waist height to keep cold air from blowing into the cave all night. Dig your main sleeping room, remembering that your front wall and ceiling both need to be 2 feet thick. You can dig any shape you want (circle, square, rectangle), but you'll need a rectangle of about 7 by 5 feet for two people to lie down next to each other, and more room for your backpacks. The ceiling should be at least 3½ feet high so you can sit up comfortably. While you're digging, imagine the dimensions of a two-person backpacking tent, because that's exactly what you're making. Once you've got a solid room dug, dig out the ceiling to make it dome shaped and smooth it out so water will run down the sides of the cave instead of dripping (your body heat and breath will warm the inside of the cave considerably throughout the night). Dig a small trench lining the wall for all the moisture to run into, and once you've done that, you've got your snow cave. Use a trekking pole to carefully punch two ventilation holes in the ceiling. Fill in the arms of your "T" with packed snow or blocks of snow, and bring your stuff inside, using a tarp to keep your sleeping pads and bags dry. Don't cook inside the cave, and when you leave in the morning, make sure to collapse the cave and smooth out the site so an unsuspecting skier or snowshoer doesn't crash through the roof later.

How do I build an igloo?

Building an igloo is one part manual labor (digging and sawing snow blocks) and one part engineering. It's not exactly a quick process, so leave yourself plenty of daylight to do it. You need, in addition to your winter camping gear and snowshoes or skis, a shovel and a snow saw.

The first thing you'll need to find is an area for your "quarry," where you'll cut the blocks that will form the walls and roof of your igloo. You'll need consolidated snow, so find an area with some hard, wind-packed snow, or find deep snow (at least 3 feet deep) and consolidate it by stamping out a long trench (4 feet wide by 25 feet long) in a place where you can cut and dig out blocks. If you're stamping out snow, you'll need to wait a half hour after you've finished for the snow to totally consolidate. Then get to work cutting: cut blocks 8 to 12 inches thick, 2½ feet long, and 18 inches wide—you'll be trimming some of these blocks into smaller sizes later. Cut forty-five to fifty blocks.

Stamp out a circle 8 feet in diameter, and arrange the blocks in a circle to form the bottom of your igloo wall. The ends of the blocks will not exactly fit together because you've cut the ends at 90-degree angles, so you'll need to trim them so they're snug against each other. Pick out three or four blocks and saw a continuous, gradually sloping ramp into them—you'll be placing all the subsequent blocks in a spiral formation, and this is the start of that spiral. For the second tier, you'll start to make the walls lean inward, so bevel the bottom edge of each block with your saw before you place it. You will also have to trim the sides to angle inward toward the top of the igloo to fit against the edges of the other blocks.

After your second tier, bring the remaining blocks you've cut into the inside of the igloo, because you'll be building from the inside and won't be able to get out to fetch more blocks. Continue spiraling up and building the inward-leaning walls, cutting blocks to fit tightly against one another and eliminate gaps. Your final block will be oval shaped—cut it bigger than the hole in the roof and carefully lift it through the hole and slide it into place. Cut two ventilation holes in the roof at 45-degree angles. Cut an arched-shape doorway out of a block on the bottom tier that you can crawl through and crawl outside. From the outside, hand-pack snow into the gaps between your blocks, and then move all your gear inside your igloo.

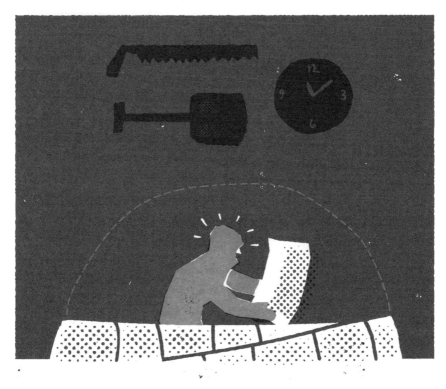

How do I stay warm during a strenuous winter hike?

You can put on layer after layer until you look like the Michelin Man, but that's not a good plan—especially when you're going to be moving. Here's a detailed plan for warmth.

Starting in the car on the way to the trailhead: if you're not already wearing your boots, keep them near a heat vent so they're not ice cold when you put your feet in them at the start of your hike (it takes a long time for your feet to warm the boots up).

Once at the trailhead, start cold. If you're comfortable standing outside the car, you're going to be too warm once you hike up the trail a few hundred feet, and either you'll have to stop to take off a layer or you'll sweat, which is worse. Of course your goal is to stay warm while hiking in the cold, but if you're warm enough that you start sweating enough to make your base layer of clothing wet, you'll find it nearly impossible to warm up again. If you are sweating, stop and take off a layer—don't just tell yourself you'll adjust, or that it'll be fine in a few minutes. When you do stop for breaks, have a warm layer (like a down jacket) ready at the top of your pack, and put it on immediately before you start digging around for snacks or water. Better yet, when you're packing, put your snacks in the pockets of your down jacket, and then when you stop and put on the jacket, your food will be right there.

How do I know if it's safe to cross a frozen lake?

A solid rule that will keep you alive (and dry) is that it's never actually safe to cross a frozen lake, because it's impossible to know what conditions are like all the way across the lake. The ice could be much thicker on one side of a lake than the other or in the middle. Generally, 4 inches of thickness should be enough to support the weight of a human being (though again, it's tough to know if the ice is 4 inches thick all the way across). If you have no choice but to cross the frozen lake, it's good to take small steps and walk across slowly. If you're wearing a backpack, unstrap it and carry it in your hands in case you punch through the ice—it'll be hard enough to crawl out of a hole in the ice with just your body weight, let alone the weight of a backpack that will begin taking on water weight immediately. If there's visible water on the surface anywhere on the lake, or melted-out sections, don't risk it.

What if I fall through ice?

If you fall through ice and you're carrying your backpack in your hands, you can heave the pack on to the ice and use it as a sort of anchor to pull yourself out. Hang on to the ice around your hole with your hands as best you can, and get your body horizontal—arms on the ice and legs in the water.

Kick your legs just like you're swimming to propel yourself out of the water. Ice is of course hard to grip with bare hands, so dig a knife out of your pocket and use it as a sort of claw. If you have car keys, you can use them as another sort of claw for your other hand.

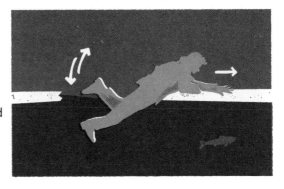

Heave yourself up onto the ice in a belly flop motion and stay horizontal as you pull your legs out. Roll yourself to the edge of the lake and get out of your wet clothes as soon as you can.

When do I need crampons?

Crampons, in addition being a great tool to accidentally rip your pants, are designed to climb ice. More accurately, they're used to help you keep footing on ice you might otherwise slide off—so when walking across a frozen pond you probably don't need them, but when climbing a steep gully of hard-packed snow that has thawed and refrozen, you do. The old method of climbing ice was to chop steps in it with an ice ax, essentially building handholds and footholds as you went. Crampons with points on the toes changed that, and now we can climb up ice and frozen snow at very steep angles. If you're climbing a mountain with a steep, snowy section, you'll need crampons (and an ice ax). If you're hiking a trail that might have some remnants of winter snow on it, or has a section that stays iced over long into the winter, you might want to take crampons—but probably

hiking crampons as opposed to ice-climbing crampons. Hiking crampons, or trail crampons, are lighter, more packable, and much less expensive than climbing crampons. They're made of stretchy rubber, have shorter points, and often aren't sharpened—and they usually provide just enough grip to walk across icy sections of trail. They weigh only about a pound and pack down small, so they're easy to throw in the bottom of your backpack just in case you run into snow or ice up high.

Should I try ice climbing?

Ice climbing is appealing because it feels and looks exotic: you're hacking away at a frozen waterfall, driving a pair of sharp axes into the ice, standing on sharpened crampon points, ice shards falling all around you. If you like climbing (or the idea of climbing) and you don't mind cold, you will probably like ice climbing. It's a very visceral experience, with ice chunks sometimes bouncing off your knees (ouch), water sometimes running into your sleeves (brr), and a very specific kind of muscle fatigue from hanging all your weight on two ice axes and the very tips of your feet.

Where can I try ice climbing?

Unlike rock climbing, ice climbing has yet to be replicated in a climbing gym, so the best place to try it is outside. A handful of ice-climbing festivals in Colorado, New Hampshire, and Michigan, among others, offer the opportunity to check it out. Guides offer how-to clinics in safe environments, and gear companies provide demo gear like crampons, ice axes, and climbing boots that you can try during a beginner clinic. If you can't make it to an ice-climbing festival, your best bet is to find a climbing guide who offers beginning ice-climbing lessons—but be prepared to travel, because ice climbing isn't available everywhere in the United States. Guide services offer ice climbing mostly in the Northeast (New York, New Hampshire, and Vermont) and the Mountain West (Colorado, Wyoming, Montana, Utah, California, and Washington) and Minnesota.

What are the "screaming barfies"?

The screaming barfies are a phenomenon specific to ice climbing, and one of its somewhat sick charms. The term *screaming barfies* comes from pain in the hands that makes an ice climber want to both scream and vomit at the same time. Typically, the screaming barfies happen after you have climbed a pitch, and after you've had your hands above your shoulders for several minutes while climbing it; you lower your hands back to your sides, and your hands are flooded with excruciating—but temporary—pain. This happens to ice climbers because of a combination of factors: cold, which constricts blood vessels especially in the extremities; holding ice tools above the heart for long periods, which reduces blood flow to the hands; and tight gloves and/or leashes that constrict blood flow as well. While you're climbing, your hands go numb, and when the blood rushes back in after the climb, waking up the previously numb nerve endings, voilà, screaming barfies. Thankfully, they last for only a few seconds or a couple of minutes before subsiding.

How do I keep my fingers and hands warm?

Keeping your hands warm is simple if all you're doing is going for a walk—unfortunately, in the outdoors you often have to use your hands and fingers for things like buckling and unbuckling backpack straps, eating, drinking water, navigating, and fastening and tightening ski boot straps. So you can't exactly keep them stuffed inside your jacket against your belly where they'd stay nice and cozy. So you do your best to keep them warm, as in literally helping them retain warmth, as opposed to letting them get cold and then desperately trying to rewarm them. Since you'll have to do all these tasks requiring dexterity, the best thing you can do is get a pair of liner gloves to wear under a pair of warm outer gloves. When you need to tie your shoe or cinch down a snowshoe strap, pop off your outer glove and tie your shoe or

cinch the strap, and your liner glove will keep your fingers way happier than if they were out completely exposed in the chilly air and/or breeze. When buying gloves, make sure your liner glove isn't so bulky it constricts your hands inside your gloves; if your blood can't freely flow in and out of your fingers, they'll get cold much faster.

Keep your hands dry, too: if you're going to be handling snow (melting snow while winter camping by scooping it with your hands into a cooking pot, making snowballs for a snowball fight, repeatedly picking yourself up from falls while skiing), get waterproof outer gloves. Soaked glove insulation can sap the heat out of your hands and the fun out of your day outside.

If you continually have problems with cold fingers or hands no matter what gloves you wear, consider picking up some chemical hand warmers for really cold days. They're inexpensive, and a little artificial warmth inside your gloves can extend the time you can handle being outside in the cold.

Mittens or gloves?

The debate will never be settled. Gloves have better dexterity, and mittens are warmer because they keep all your fingers together. It's that simple. Pick one.

How do I rewarm my fingers or toes after they go numb?

If your fingers or toes go numb (or just become really cold), there are a number of methods to rewarm them.

- **Get them near your core:** Pull your hands into the sleeves of your jacket, cross your arms inside your jacket, and place your fingers in your armpits. Leave them there until they're warm.

- **Centrifugal force:** With your elbows straight, windmill your hands around in big circles. The centrifugal force will push blood back into your fingertips.

- **The Penguin:** Hang your arms down at your sides, and turn your palms to face forward. Move your shoulders up and down in exaggerated shrugs, trying to touch them to your ears at the top each time.

- **Go home:** Just get in your car, turn on the engine, and turn the heat up as high as it will go.

How do I keep my toes and feet warm?

Two mantras can keep your feet happy in cold weather: Insulate and circulate.

- **Insulate:** Buy boots that are actually made for wintertime activities. It can be tempting to save money by skipping the winter boots and instead wearing waterproof hiking boots in the winter (and it can work for some people), but a good pair of winter boots will keep your feet warm and dry and will last for several years—when you look at the price tag, remember you're probably not going to use them nearly as much as your summer hiking boots or shoes, and the outsoles will seem to last forever because they're walking mostly on snow instead of abrasive rocks and trails. So find a good pair of warm, waterproof winter boots, and convince yourself that the cost will be spread out over five or more years. Second, get a good pair of thick socks, or layer one pair of socks over another one, to retain the heat next to your skin. Don't wear cotton socks—they'll get wet with sweat and stay damp, sapping the warmth from your feet. Get wool or wool-blend socks, which will wick moisture away, stay drier, and keep your feet warmer.

- **Circulate:** Remember when you're on the trail that if blood can't flow it can't warm your extremities, especially your toes. If your socks add so much volume to your feet that when you put them in boots you can't even wiggle your toes, you're going to have problems. If you tie your boots so tight that they restrict blood flow on any spot on your foot, you might find yourself with cold, or even numb, toes. Tie your boots snugly, but pay attention how they feel. If you notice a tight spot when you start hiking, stop sooner rather than later and loosen the laces in the appropriate spot.

ACKNOWLEDGMENTS

Thanks to all the policy makers who work hard to keep public lands like our national parks, national forests, and other areas open to all, and thanks to all the government employees at all levels who manage those lands every day.

Thanks to the folks at REI, who hired me for my first outdoor industry job, selling backpacks and sleeping bags on the sales floor at the Paradise Valley store.

Thanks to Outdoor Research, Vasque, and REI, who financially support my adventures and the stories I tell about them at Semi-Rad.com.

Thanks to Tim McCall, who took me on most of my early forays into the mountains.

Thanks to Dustin Ewald, who first taught me how to rock climb, and to Lee Smith, who taught me traditional climbing, ice climbing, and mountaineering.

Thanks to my parents, for showing me the mountains when I was eight years old, and to my dad, for pointing me west.

Thanks to Forest Woodward, Sinuhe Xavier, Graham Zimmerman, and Adam George, for contributing their specific knowledge to this book.

Thanks to Judy Pray at Artisan Books, for reaching out to me with the idea that became this book.

Thanks to Seth Neilson, for his artistic vision, which has given this and a number of other projects wonderful visual style.

And finally, thanks to Hilary Oliver for putting up with the long days in the mountains and the long days at the keyboard that make books like this possible.

INDEX

© Forest Woodward

BRENDAN LEONARD is a writer and filmmaker whose work focuses on travel and adventure and the human experience with both. He's a contributing editor at *Climbing*, *Adventure Journal*, and *The Dirtbag Diaries*. His stories have appeared in *National Geographic Adventure*, *Outside*, *Men's Journal*, and *Sierra*, among others. He lives in Denver, Colorado. Find him on Instagram @semi_rad.